The Fairfax Co

Asian American History Project

A Contemporary History Honoring
143 Years of Asian Residents in Fairfax County
(1867-2010)

Special Edition with Color Photos

Corazon Sandoval Foley

The Fairfax County Asian American History Project

©Copyright 2010 Corazon Sandoval Foley
ISBN-10: 145153762X
ISBN-13: 978-1451537628
Printed in the United States of America
Publisher: CreateSpace

Book Design and Editing by Corazon Sandoval Foley, Burke, Virginia
Book Layout and Pre-press by Allen Wayne Ltd., Chantilly, Virginia
Manufactured by Allen Wayne, Ltd., Chantilly, Virginia

Disclaimer: The Fairfax County Asian American History Project (FCAAHP) is an all-volunteer organization of Fairfax County residents who worked together to develop this book, contributed their own funds and other resources for the associated website and other products, as well as raise funds from community donors to print the book and cover related project costs. The author – Corazon Sandoval Foley – bears sole responsibility for the material contained within this 2010 FCAAHP book. The County of Fairfax cannot be held responsible for omissions or errors, and therefore disclaims all liability in connection with the book on the Fairfax County Asian American History Project.

Cataloging-in-Publication Data available from the Library of Congress
ISBN-13: 978-1-4515376-2-8

The Fairfax County Asian American History Project
A Contemporary History
Honoring 143 Years of Asian Residents in Fairfax County (1867-2010)

Corazon Sandoval Foley

What Contributions Have Asian Americans Made in Fairfax County?

How have Asian Americans shared their Heritage with County Neighbors?

Appendices

FOREWORD

By The Honorable Sharon S. Bulova
Chairman, Fairfax County Board of Supervisors

During World War II my dad, Larry Schuster, served in the Pacific Theatre. It's a miracle that I even exist because as a young Marine, Dad survived the deadly engagements of Okinawa, Saipan and Iwo Jima. Unlike some veterans, Dad liked to recount stories about his years as a Marine. My siblings and I loved to hear about the rugged training he underwent, the camaraderie he experienced as a member of an elite force, and some light moments in the midst of punishing battle. Left unsaid were the harder stories of tremendous and tragic loss of life on both sides of these heated engagements.

It wasn't until I was an adult that I learned I was named after a town on the Island of Saipan called "Charon" or "Charon Konoa." Dad thought the name was beautiful and vowed that if he "ever got out of this alive and had a daughter", he would name her (me) Charon – or, as it turned out "Sharon".

Perhaps the name instilled in me a fascination for things Asian. In high school I became pen pals with a Japanese girl. Her name was Lize Araki. She was fifteen and lived in Chigasaki City, Kanagawa Prefecture, famous for its "Southern Beach." For several years Lize and I exchanged letters, cards and gifts. I still have a pretty little doll she sent me, along with all of her letters. Sometimes I wonder whatever became of my little friend, and if she ever thinks of me.

Tech Sergeant Larry Schuster, 1943. He served with the Marines in WWII in Okinawa, Saipan, and Iwo Jima. (Courtesy of Sharon Bulova)

That long ago friendship might have influenced me when I said "yes" to Cora Foley's request to sponsor a book capturing the stories of Asian Americans who have made Fairfax County their home. It might also have been the enjoyment I had experienced working with volunteers on another history book project, "A Look Back at Braddock" (ALBB), which collected oral history interviews of people who remembered how the central part of the county (the Braddock District area that I represented at the time) had evolved during the 20th Century from a farming community into our present day neighborhoods and retail areas.

During that project, I learned that the capturing and telling of history was enjoyable most of all for the process, the journey our little group took toward publication of a wonderful book. This has definitely been the case with our Asian American History Project.

Our core group coalesced beginning with a town meeting I hosted in Braddock Hall on January 23, 2008. At the meeting Anne Cahill, Fairfax County's Chief Demographer, provided interested volunteers with statistics regarding the immigration of Asian Americans who had arrived in the U.S. and settled in Fairfax County. Mary Lipsey and John Browne, veterans from the earlier ALBB project, participated in the town meeting and stayed on to provide help and support throughout the Asian American History project. Christina Fullmer in my office provided staff support to members of the group.

Hank Chao and Ted Gong, both Chinese Americans, assumed leadership roles early in the process, beginning with their organization of a tour of the Immigration Library in Washington D.C., which was followed by lunch at Hank Chao's restaurant in Chinatown. Terry Sam, who shared with us his father's heritage as a "Paper Son", became the group's official photographer. His photos soon graced a new website created by Cora, which also cataloged oral history interviews and other project activities. Jaya Kori and Swati Damle joined the group as the Asian-Indian group leaders, while father-daughter team Dzung and Vy Nguyen headed up efforts for the Vietnamese community. Vy, still in high school, created a Vietnamese American History Website as part of our project. Linda and Joe Yao assisted with publicity and Soo Yee engaged Korean American high school students in a discussion of their heritage.

Thanks to Cora and our Asian American History Project volunteers, a first-time-ever Naturalization Ceremony was organized and hosted in the Fairfax County Government Center. Task Force members Yearn Hong Choi and Viyaya Ligade wrote beautiful poems for the program. Seventy-five new Americans were welcomed as citizens at the ceremony that took place on May 29, 2009. Members of the AAHP group who helped with activities and our frequent potluck dinners were Carolyn Sam, Nathan Wang, Heisung Lee and Jackie Bong Wright.

Another activity (Ted Gong's suggestion) was a display at the Fairfax County's Pohick Regional Library, "Remembering 1882 Exhibit"(The Chinese Exclusion Act), which depicted the difficulty Chinese Americans encountered as they attempted to become American citizens. Fairfax County staff who worked with our group included Suzanne Levy of the Virginia Room, Jean Johnston of Pohick Library, and Mike Gatti, Director of Document Services who assisted with publication of this book.

Our project has spanned an interesting period of time for me personally. When first agreeing to the project in 2006, I was serving my fifth term as Braddock District Supervisor on the Fairfax County Board. In the fall of 2008, Chairman of the Board, Gerry Connolly, won election to serve in the U.S. Congress. Throughout an intense special election during the winter of 2008/2009 to fill the Chairman's seat, I was warmed and buoyed by the friendship and support of the many new friends I had come to know through our AAHP activities. And so, as the project draws to an end, I am serving my first term as Chairman of the Board of Supervisors

As Chairman, it has been my pleasure to sign Sister Partnership Agreements with Songpa-gu in Seoul, Korea and with Harbin, in China. I am sure that these collaborations will enhance and build upon the celebration of the Asian American presence in Fairfax County. It has been an honor to have played a role in making sure their stories are told.

Photo Gallery of Chairman Sharon Bulova with Fairfax Conty Asian Americans

From Top Left to Right: Chairman Bulova and Corazon Sandoval Foley, Lady Fairfax 2009; August 2008 Recognition of FCAAHP -Vy Nguyen; with Jaime Chang; 2008 Asian Pacific American Heritage Month Proclamation; with Goto family; Recognition of Fairfax County Asian American History Project (FCAAHP) Task Force for first-ever naturalization ceremony in Fairfax County Government Center on May 29, 2009; 2009 Asian Pacific American Heritage Month Proclamation program. (Fairfax County Government photos)

A Filipino American Odyssey in Fairfax County and the Formation of the Fairfax County Asian American History Project

By Corazon Sandoval Foley

In January 1980 my husband Mike, our son Joshua, our daughter Melinda, and I joined the rapidly accelerating movement of people who have decided to choose as their home this special corner of the world – Fairfax County, Virginia. Since then, we have watched the dramatic changes in the county's landscape and demographic composition.

Our county had grown to a megalopolis of a very diverse population of over a million residents by 2009 from a semi-rural community with many dairy farms totaling 40,929 residents in 1940. Many more Asian Americans moved to the county after World War II, the Korean War, the 1965 Immigration Reform Act, and the Vietnam War. By 1990 the county's Asian residents had become the largest minority group – and growing even more to 16% or 162,000 by 2007. And since our move in 1980, I watched with some regret the loss of farms and old country roads near our home in West Springfield in order to make way for shopping centers, new housing and expanded roads. All these have resulted in a more cosmopolitan hometown, albeit with rising concerns about infrastructure requirements among county residents.

Home is Fairfax County. In 1996, my family created our own marker in the county's transition when we had a home built by Stanley Martin in the then-new Edgewater development in Burke, Virginia (some 3 miles away from our first home in West Springfield, Fairfax County). The neighborhood was carved out of a large old farm that had a small cemetery reportedly for freed slaves who lived and worked in the area. Edgewater is located about a mile from the house built around 1824 on a hill then overlooking the valley of Pohick Creek by Silas Burke (1796 -1854), a 19th century farmer, merchant, and local politician after whom was named our area of Burke in Fairfax County. The Burke area has eight separate sites, especially along Pohick Creek, where examples of artifacts have been found of Necostin (Algonquin) Indians – stone-age people who had settled down to an agricultural life.

1980-1996   From 1996   Foley Homes, Fairfax County

The county provided a wonderful nest from where Mike and I rode off every morning to work for the federal government. And I had long been fascinated by the idea of learning more about our dynamic hometown but had to defer my desire for local history research because of the demands of raising a

Top to bottom Left to Right: Cora Foley with Rosa Parks; with former Secretary of State Condoleezza Rice; Foleys and Hannas at 2007 wedding of Joshua and Clare; Melinda in 1980 preschool; Cub Scout Joshua; College Graduate Melinda with Philippine flag vest over toga.
(All photos in this chapter from Cora Foley)

family and pursuing my professional career in diplomacy and intelligence with the US Department of State.

We chose Fairfax County as our home because of the excellent education for our children who started in a private preschool Springfield Academy in Edsall Road, Springfield. They then attended Hunt Valley Elementary School, Irving Middle School, and West Springfield High School. Fairfax County's George Mason University provided my son with an excellent college education in information technology while my daughter decided to go to California, my husband's birthplace, and study in the University of California in Santa Cruz. My son chose public service with the federal government like his parents while my daughter followed her own drummer to become a playwright in Los Angeles.

Civil Rights and State Department Career. Burke's history of community activism – American democracy in action – has also been very inspirational for me as a longtime county resident. In 1951 the US Civil Aeronautics Administration announced plans to condemn 4,520 acres (18 km²) of land in Burke to construct a second airport to serve the Washington metropolitan area. After a lengthy and effective lobbying campaign by Burke area residents, the government in 1958 selected a site near Chantilly that is now Washington Dulles International Airport instead of Burke. Thanks to the success of the Burke citizenry, I am able to enjoy a beautiful home in what would have been the center of the proposed Burke International Airport.

My own civic activism has long involved working on diversity and civil rights issues, particularly those affecting the Asian American community of federal employees. I was a 1984 founding member and 1989 President of the interagency group FAPAC -- the Federal Asian Pacific American Council.

I also founded and led the Asian Pacific American Federal Foreign Affairs Council for many years. As a Congressional Fellow with then-Congressman Norman Mineta, I was privileged to play a lead congressional role in the successful passage of the law establishing the National Memorial to Japanese American Patriotism in Washington, DC. As chairman of the Asian Pacific American Federal Foreign Affairs Council, I managed numerous seminars on the Asian American experience, as well as several exhibits in the State Department about Filipino American and other Asian American history and contributions, often in collaboration with the Smithsonian and museums, particularly Hawaii's Bishop Museum.

My most memorable experience with my American civil rights activities was my participation in the 1989 White House ceremony honoring 25 years of the historic 1964 Civil Rights Act. It was a moving ceremony presided by President George H. W. Bush in which my civil rights hero, Rosa Parks, was one of the honored guests. My experience with diversity and civil rights issues during my 30-year State Department career thus gave me the confidence to continue working on Asian American projects in my own hometown of Fairfax County -- when retirement blessed me with time and some energy for personal passions without worrying about bureaucracies and job requirements.

Asian Pacific American Federal Foreign Affairs Council Board

Honoring our Family Heritages. My family has honored both my Filipino American heritage and my husband's Irish American heritage. During her college graduation, my daughter Melinda decided to honor her Filipino American heritage by wearing a long vest with the Philippine flag over her toga while she delivered the student response. And when my son was married in St. Raymond's Church (the newest Catholic Church in the Springfield area that opened in December 2006), the ceremony included the Philippine traditional veil, cord, coin ceremony – as well as an Irish bagpiper. In fact, the veil was the same one that I used when Mike and I were married in St. Rita's Church in Alexandria, Virginia in March 1973.

Both our children had left the nest when at long last my husband and I retired on the same day – April Fools' Day 2007. And after some 30 years of public service with the State Department, I finally received the wonderful gift of time and opportunity to learn more about my hometown and neighbors and to continue my engagement in diversity issues.

In 2007, I had been an American citizen for some 34 years and a resident of Fairfax County for 27 years; my American odyssey had become a much larger part of my life than my first 19 years growing up in Manila. I came to live in Washington, DC in 1970 to study for my Masters Degree in Business

Administration in George Washington University -- moved to Northern Virginia in 1972, served with my husband overseas with the US State Department – and finally settling down in Fairfax County in 1980.

The Fairfax County Jamestown Legacy Project and the Filipino American Story. Serendipity occurred in 2007 when I answered the call for volunteers for the Fairfax County Jamestown 400 Committee – tasked with developing programs to commemorate the four hundred years since the settlement of Jamestown on May 13, 1607. I joined enthusiastically and participated in meetings to decide on public messages and other outreach programs for the anniversary celebration.

A major committee project was to develop a Jamestown 400 Legacy Book entitled *"Fairfax County Stories 1607 – 2007."* I asked how such a project could be developed without a story about the Asian American community that has become the largest minority group in the county. The response, of course, was that it was a great idea and that I should be the one to write such a story. As my husband teases me frequently, I always end up flunking an important life lesson well known in the military – "Never Volunteer." I remember when my son wanted to join the Cub Scouts and was told that there was no space available -- I called and asked how I could help my son and the response: "Congratulations, you are now a den mother." So, for a couple of years, I ended up taking a day off from work every other week to work as one of two den mothers to my son's group of Cub Scouts, but my son was very happy, so it turned out fine.

My father on right side with my grandfather in photo dated 1920 in Manila (Courtesy of Cora Foley)

Graciniano and Virginia Sandoval seated in the center with the Sandoval and Foley families at the first Foley home in Fairfax County in Springfield celebrating Christmas 1991.
(Courtesy of Cora Foley)

Since I am a Filipino American, I decided to write a story entitled *"It Began with the 1898 Spanish-American War"* and described how that war marked the start of America's imperialist role – with the Philippines becoming an American colony. This triggered migration of Filipinos to the US to work on plantations and other business operations. I narrated how Filipino Americans joined other Asian Americans in moving to Fairfax County – and how they grew to become the largest minority group in the county by 2007.

In writing the story, I thought of my Sandoval family, particularly my father, Graciniano Angeles Sandoval (born 1913) and my mother, Virginia Diy Sandoval (born 1919) who started life as American nationals in Manila, the capital city of the American colony of the Philippines. My father's father Manuel Manlave Sandoval served as a Congressman from 1909 – 1919 in the first free legislative body in Asia established during the American colonial period; he later served as Governor of Palawan. As for my parents, the hardships of World War II marked their life very deeply and they often shared with us the hard lessons from that era.

My parents both moved to the US in the early 1970s along with their six children – and spent most of their American years in Fairfax County that three of their children chose to call home. My father died when he was 90 years old on February 28, 2004 and was buried in Fairfax Memorial Park on Braddock Road – his last home in Fairfax County. We purchased several adjoining gravesites for the Sandoval and Foley families in that beautiful memorial park. And in part to honor the memory of my father, I had agreed at my retirement to organize the Filipino American National Historical Society of Northern Virginia (FANHS-NoVA) that became the keystone of the Fairfax County Asian American History Project (FCAAHP).

Meeting Supervisor Sharon Bulova. After the Jamestown Legacy Book *"Fairfax County Stories 1607 – 2007"* was published in 2007, I started inquiring as to why no historical research has ever been done on the Asian American community in a county that has a rich tradition of historical research (after all, George Washington called Fairfax County his home). I was advised by then-Chairman Gerry Connolly of the Fairfax County Board of Supervisors to seek support from Braddock District

Supervisor Sharon Bulova who, as a recognized history buff and a pre-eminent local historian, had just finished in 2007 a local history book entitled *"Braddock's True Gold."*

I would like to think that my father introduced me to Supervisor Sharon Bulova. For serendipity struck again when on the 50th anniversary of the Fairfax Memorial Park while visiting my father's grave, I met Supervisor Bulova who was the keynote speaker for the anniversary program. I explained to her my interest in doing historical research on Fairfax County Asian Americans – and much to my delight, Supervisor Bulova expressed interest and support for the idea. She invited me to meet at her office and we decided to develop a team effort modeled on the *"Braddock's True Gold"* oral history project.

My father's last home in Fairfax County with adjoining gravesites for our family in Fairfax Memorial Park where FCAAHP began when I met Supervisor Sharon Bulova in Memorial Day 2007.
(Photo by Cora Foley)

The FCAAHP Evolution. On January 23, 2008, we held a kickoff meeting for the project – Terry Sam, our official photographer, and Ted Gong, leader of the Chinese American team, joined us then.

Vy Nguyen, a student at Flint Hill High School, and her father, Dzung Nguyen, attended a later meeting and became leaders of the Vietnamese American team that was later joined by Amy Trang. Soo Yee, a Fairfax County expert on pandemic flu, became the head of the Korean American team. Jaya Kori, a Fairfax County information technology official, and Swati Damle, an NIH official, teamed up to head the Indian American team. Masako Huibregtse later agreed to head the Japanese American team. The leadership of the Fairfax County Asian American History Project (FCAAHP) was completed with the participation of Hank Chao as our video team leader and Linda Yao, Fairfax County human rights official, as our publicity team leader.

The FCAAHP team developed three websites in which interviews were posted, including videos on youtube. This approach facilitated information gathering and documentation for the project. Vy Nguyen, the youngest team leader, created, on her own initiative, the Fairfax County Vietnamese American website and was honored with a recognition by the Fairfax County Board of Supervisors when she graduated from high school. Jaya Kori also created a website focusing on the Indian American community in Fairfax County. I created and managed the main website for the Fairfax County Asian American History Project at: http://fairfaxasianamericans. community.officelive.com.

The Fairfax County Public Library System was a major resource for the project – with Suzanne Levy of the Virginia Room assisting me in researching census records of Asian residents. Her help was instrumental in our tracing 1870 as the first year in which an Asian resident was recorded in Fairfax County by the US Census. Moreover, Pohick Library with its wonderful and extremely helpful manager Jean Johnson, became a major project venue where we held oral history interviews, seminars, cultural performances, and a display of the exhibit *"Remembering 1882"* (Fighting for Civil Rights in the Shadow of the Chinese Exclusion Act of 1882).

We also received support from other groups, like the Filipino American National Historical Society of Hampton Roads that sent Veronica Salcedo to provide us a briefing on how historical research was conducted for their book on Filipino Americans in the military. We received helpful publicity from the *Pacific Citizen,* a newspaper of the Japanese American Citizens League, as well as the *Washington Post* and other local newspapers. In addition, longtime Fairfax County residents, who are not Asian Americans, provided us with vital information about their Asian American neighbors who moved to the county in the late 1940s and 1950s.

By 2009 our project has gained so much strength and vitality that we decided to initiate the first-ever naturalization ceremony in the Fairfax County Government Center. FCAAHP facilitated the ceremony for 75 new Americans (of various races and ethnicities) on May 29, 2009 as part of the county's Asian American Heritage Month events – as our way of commemorating the very long struggle for naturalization rights of the Asian American community even as we celebrate the great progress in civil rights in the US. The program was jointly sponsored by FCAAHP; the Fairfax County Government; the US Citizenship and Immigration Services; and Cox Communications, the sole corporate sponsor of the event. Members of the Daughters of the American Revolution supported the program while the Vietnamese American Voters Association helped in the voter registration of the 75 new Americans.

FCAAHP has expanded its operations beyond just oral history interviews – we have organized a Literary Club to pursue historical research with poetry, songs and stories, as well as a Genealogy Club to pursue more in-depth library research on the history of Asian Americans who live in Fairfax County. We have also organized programs to assist citizenship education and naturalization of new Americans (of all races and ethnicities) in Fairfax County as part of the leadership role that the largest minority group should be playing in the county.

FCAAHP even made history by initiating and organizing the first-ever naturalization ceremony in the Fairfax County Government Center for new American citizens of all races and ethnicities. On June 22, 2009, the Fairfax County Board of Supervisors headed by Chairman Bulova recognized the FCAAHP team for the May 29, 2009 first-ever naturalization ceremony in Fairfax County. And on August 3, 2009, FCAAHP was selected to be a participating organization in the critical Fairfax County Census 2010 Complete Count Committee. The Fairfax County Board of Supervisors has recognized FCAAHP work during the 2008 and 2009 Asian American Heritage Month proclamations. The Board also honored FCAAHP with several recognition awards for FCAAHP members, including one for Vy Nguyen on August 4, 2008 for creating the Fairfax County Vietnamese American website and one on June 22, 2009 for Terry Sam for his excellent work as the FCAAHP official photographer.

2009 Lady Fairfax (At-Large) Award from Supervisor Sharon Bulova beside a photo of our 1973 wedding in Alexandria with Philippine traditional customs/rites.
(Courtesy of Cora Foley)

Chairman Sharon Bulova on June 1, 2009 kindly bestowed on me the wonderful title of 2009 Lady Fairfax (At-Large) for my work on FCAAHP and other local history projects, as well as the creation of the Burke/Springfield District Senior Center Without Walls to provide innovative wellness programs for Fairfax County seniors.

You will meet many of the participants in the Fairfax County Asian American History Project in this book. We hope to assist the Fairfax County History Commission by providing you with a better understanding of the largest minority group in Fairfax County – by learning more about the history and heritage that we brought to the county, about the contributions that we have made as Fairfax County residents, and how we share with all our neighbors our Asian American heritage. For after all, we do not want a blank page in the Fairfax County history books when it comes to the heritage and contributions of over 16% of the county population. We hope you will appreciate the good things that we have done to improve the quality of life in Fairfax County – our home. ##

What Stories Did Asian Americans Bring to Fairfax County?

Overview of Asian American History in Fairfax County

By Corazon Sandoval Foley

The Fairfax County History Commission has expressed interest in developing a more accurate and a more balanced historical research that reflects the county's diverse ethnic reality since 1990 – which coincidentally, was the year that Asian residents became the largest minority group in Fairfax County. This is the first in-depth attempt to assist the History Commission by developing a research project based on oral history interviews with members of the Fairfax County Asian American community – and this project has become a reality because of the leadership of Fairfax County Chairman Sharon Bulova.

The US Census Bureau defines Asian Americans as those persons having origins in any of the original peoples of the Far East, Southeast Asia, and the Indian subcontinent. The first census record of an Asian resident in Fairfax County occurred in 1870 with a Chinese student Suvoong residing in Falls Church, then part of Fairfax County. By 2007, Asian residents in Fairfax County totaled over 160,000 or 16% of the population – the largest minority group in the county of over a million people, as shown in table below.

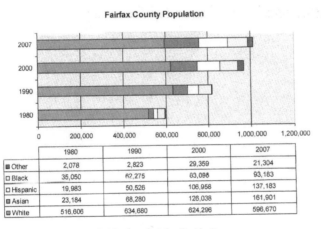

Fairfax County Population

In 1990, Asians became the largest minority group in Fairfax County at 8.3% of population – rising to 16% in 2007.

	1980	1990	2000	2007
▪ Other	2,078	2,823	29,359	21,304
▫ Black	35,050	62,275	83,098	93,183
▫ Hispanic	19,983	50,526	106,958	137,183
▪ Asian	23,184	68,280	126,038	161,901
▪ White	516,606	634,680	624,296	596,670

Year	Population
1870	12,952
1900	18,580
1910	20,536
1920	21,943
1930	25,264
1940	40,929
1950	98,557
1960	275,002
1970	455,021
1980	596,901
1990	818,584
2000	969,749
2007	1,010,241

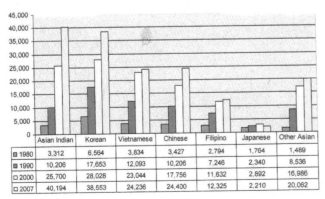

Fairfax County Asian Residents

	Asian Indian	Korean	Vietnamese	Chinese	Filipino	Japanese	Other Asian
▪ 1980	3,312	6,564	3,834	3,427	2,794	1,764	1,489
▪ 1990	10,206	17,653	12,093	10,206	7,246	2,340	8,536
▫ 2000	25,700	28,028	23,044	17,756	11,632	2,892	16,986
▫ 2007	40,194	38,553	24,236	24,400	12,325	2,210	20,062

Graphs from US Census data created by Corazon Sandoval Foley for Fairfax County Asian American History Project (3/13/2009).

From 1870 to 1930, three Asian groups were recorded in the census as residing in Fairfax County: Chinese, Filipino and Japanese. By 2007 the largest Asian groups were Asian Indians, Koreans, Chinese, Vietnamese, Filipinos and Japanese. Meanwhile, the numbers of Asians from other groups (including Pakistanis, Cambodians, Bangladeshi, Tibetan, and others) have continued to rise.

In developing this history project, teams were developed based on the six largest groups described by the US Census. A similar project in the future may well develop different teams based on the evolving census figures. We in FCAAHP hope that this book would be the first of what could be many more books/publications about the history, the heritage, and the contributions of the Asian American community.

This book includes some descriptions of the Fairfax County historical context in the stories of Asian residents. Before World War II, Fairfax County was still largely rural. Farms and fields surrounded the intersections at Seven Corners (now the bustling area for the huge Vietnamese American Eden Center). The public schools were segregated; medical, educational, transportation facilities were lacking -- no Beltway (many roads were either unpaved or in poor condition), no shopping malls, no Dulles airport.

Gradually, emphasis shifted from farming towards service-oriented businesses. This was spurred on by the tremendous growth of the Federal Government associated with WWII, the Korean War, the Vietnam War, and the Cold War. The second half of the 20th century became a period of suburbanization. Large land holdings have been broken up and replaced by developments of apartments, single-family dwellings and townhouses. And with the development of Dulles Airport, subways, highways and parkways, Fairfax County became an attractive location for regional and multinational firms – and in time, the county emerged as a high-tech haven and internet capital.

Fairfax County in 2010 has truly become a multicultural megalopolis with over a million residents among whom the Asian residents form the largest minority group – highly visible with remarkable educational achievements, successful large and small business enterprises, and actively engaging county residents in cultural festivals and traditional celebrations in the many centers of faith ceremonies. Asian food has become quite popular with numerous restaurants offering high quality cuisine from East, Southeast and South Asia. While many newer Asian immigrants still struggle to learn English and adjust to the American culture, many more Asian Americans have become an integral part of their Fairfax County home – volunteering for numerous community activities, participating in political campaigns, and improving the overall quality of life and the cosmopolitan atmosphere of Fairfax County.

We in FCAAHP sometimes wonder what those early residents, like Suvoong who lived in Fairfax County in 1867 - 1870, would say if we were able to bring them back in some time travel arrangement. However, that would be for a fascinating fantasy book and not a history project – so we move forward with sharing this book's stories created without a magic wand but with dedicated FCAAHP team effort in library/internet research, oral history interviews, photography sessions, website creations, and video productions.

From 1867 -- Chinese American History in Fairfax County
By Corazon Sandoval Foley

Starting from a small handful of Chinese residents, the Chinese population of Fairfax County totaled 24,400 in 2007 – making them the county's fourth largest Asian group. Census records indicate that Chinese residents were the first Asians to reside in Fairfax County.

- In 1870, Suvoong, a 26- year old male Chinese student resided in Falls Church Township in Fairfax County, according to the US Census. He was one of several seminary students under the supervision of Charlotte Fuller, a 30-year old white female from South Carolina who was the matron of the Virginia Theological seminary. Suvoong was in a class of seminarians with Thomas Boone, a 20-year old white male and son of an American missionary then living in China.
- In 1900, Wing Moy, a laundryman, was recorded as living in Falls Church Township. Wing Moy was a 40- year old male, listed as a head of household, born in March 1860. His father and mother were both born in China and Wing Moy immigrated to the US in 1897. He was able to read, write, speak English and he was renting a home.
- In 1920, Ying Jung, born in California and thus a Chinese American by birth, was recorded as serving time in the DC Workhouse in Lorton,
- In 1930, three Chinese Lee Hing, George Lee, and Chin Wing were serving time in the DC Work House (Lorton Prison) in Fairfax County.

1870 and a Fairfax County Recovering from Civil War. The young Chinese seminary student Suvoong would have found a Fairfax County in 1870 with a population just under 13,000 and its society recovering from the devastation caused by the Civil War. On January 26, 1870, by a close vote in both the House and the Senate, the State of Virginia (including Fairfax County) was finally readmitted to the Union. On Monday, July 25, 1870, the Fairfax County Board of Supervisors held its first official meeting. On Sunday, September 18, 1870, Thomas Moore was named the first Superintendent of Fairfax County Public Schools. Schools and churches were being built or restored, and a new railroad from Alexandria south to Fredericksburg was started. Telegraph lines, post offices, and post roads were being extended. Postal villages (Falls Church, Vienna, Herndon) were growing and new ones were coming into being at Accotink, Chantilly, Merrifield, Lewinsville, and Thornton Station (near present Reston). In 1870, the list of businesses in Fairfax County included carriage and cabinetmakers, grist and flour mills, and others associated with serving an agricultural economy.

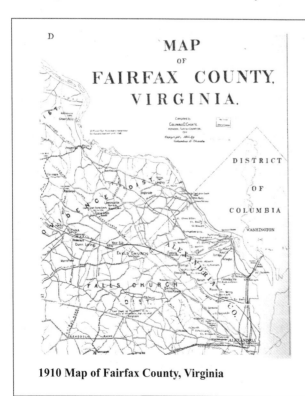

1910 Map of Fairfax County, Virginia

Who was Suvoong? By engaging in intensive web research and following advice from Virginia Room's Suzanne Levy, I was able to find enough information to flesh out details about Suvoong, the first recorded Asian resident in Fairfax County in the 1870 census.

His name was Vung Piau (also written in other documents as Pian or Piang) Suvoong and he was a very intelligent and accomplished medical missionary. An American missionary report described him as a Dr. Suvoong who comes on Sundays to treat any difficult cases that might occur, " a Chinaman who has spent 15 years in the US pursuing his studies and was a pupil of Dr. Agnew in New York. He has made diseases of the eye and ear a specialty, and is very skillful in this department." (May 1875 annual report of the Presbyterian Church Mission in China page 68)

1870 Census report of Fairfax resident Suvoong from China

My research indicated that Suvoong probably arrived in the US in 1864. I found him listed in the 1900 Phi Beta Kappa handbook as an 1867 Phi Beta Kappa graduate of Kenyon College in Gambier, Ohio – the oldest private college in Ohio founded in 1824. The small, all-male college originally graduated clergymen for frontier America but soon became a highly regarded seat of classical education with graduates including statesmen such as US President Rutherford B. Hayes.

From 1867 to 1870, Suvoong lived in the Falls Church Township of Fairfax County, Virginia as a student of the Virginia Theological Seminary in Alexandria. The seminary's faculty and students attended services in the Falls Church Episcopalian Church that was built in 1732 on the road to the falls of the Potomac River.

Suvoong was in Alexandria, Virginia on May 15, 1868 when he was recommended as a candidate for deacon's orders. The historical record of the Virginia Technological Seminary indicated that Suvoong graduated in 1870.

Virginia Theological Seminary during the Civil War –a scene from Suvoong's daily life as a student from 1867 – 1870. (Courtesy of Virginia Theological Seminary)

The Virginia Theological Seminary was founded in 1823 and among its founders were Bishop William Meade, the third Bishop of Virginia, and Francis Scott Key whose 1814 poem *"The Defence of Fort McHenry"* became the text for the National Anthem in 1931. In 1818, Francis Scott Key formed "An Education Society" and five years later opened the "School of Prophets," that then became the Protestant Episcopal Theological Seminary in Virginia. When the school opened in Alexandria with two instructors, 14 students were enrolled.

During the Civil War, the Virginia Theological Seminary was used to house 1,700 wounded Federal troops and to bury 500 of their comrades. After the war, two professors and 11 battle-weary veterans reopened the Seminary. By 1923, the year of its Centennial, the Seminary had regained the resources, the certainty of full enrollment, and the invested funds that had characterized the institution in 1860. Suvoong appears to have been one of the early (if not the earliest) Chinese students in the Virginia Theological Seminary; but his educational experience was repeated by many more Chinese seminary students as shown in the photo of the class of 1927.

Virginia Theological Seminary (VTS) class of 1927 with Kimber H.K. Den and Graham Yu Ling Lieo (front row, left) from China.
(Courtesy of VTS)

Fairfax County and the China Missionary Connection. The Census record indicates that Suvoong's story in Fairfax County was related to the Protestant missionary work in China that began in 1807 with Robert Morrison of the London Missionary Society and ended in 1953. His classmate in the Virginia Theological Seminary Thomas Boone appears to be related to the Reverend William James Boone who in 1843 was appointed to the Protestant Episcopal Mission in Shanghai and served as the first Episcopalian missionary bishop of China from 1844 until his death on July 17, 1884. His son William James Boone Jr. graduated in 1868 from the Virginia Theological Seminary in Fairfax County and became the fourth Episcopalian bishop of China from 1884 – 1893.

The first Bishop Boone presided over establishment of boarding and day schools, as well as a medical hospital. In 1879, a successor-bishop Samuel Isaac Joseph Schereschewsky founded St. John's College (later University). Before the Chinese civil war, it was regarded as one of the most prestigious universities in Shanghai and China. In 1952, the university was broken up and its faculties were joined with similar faculties from other universities to create several specialist universities.

Another related historical footnote is the Fairfax County connection with the family of noted author and Nobel Prize winner Pearl Sydenstricker Buck. In 1909, Reverend Christopher Sydenstricker, an uncle of Pearl S. Buck, started using a picnic grove for an evangelistic camp meeting and the site later became Sydenstricker Methodist Episcopal Church located in Gambrill road (later renamed Sydenstricker Road). The church known in 2010 as Sydenstricker United Methodist Church is located about three miles from our first Foley home in West Springfield.

Later in this book we will pick up a piece of the thread in the tale of the connection between American missionary work in Shanghai and Fairfax County residents. In particular, one of the most active members of the Fairfax County Asian American History Project has been Dr. Nathan Yining Wang who was a graduate of the prestigious St. John's University in Shanghai. Dr. Nathan Wang's story is in the section on Senior Centers for he has been a leader in developing the Chinese American Silver Light Senior Association of Fairfax County.

St. John's University, Shanghai, China

What happened to Suvoong after Fairfax County?
The next record in my search for Suvoong was the Alpha Delta Phi report that in 1873, Vung Pian Suvoong, received his medical degree from Columbia College in New York. So, after graduating in 1870 from the Virginia Theological Seminary in Fairfax County, Suvoong moved to New York City.

Then Suvoong went back to China and became very active in medical missionary work in Shanghai. The 1875 report of the Shanghai Presbyterian Church noted that difficult cases were referred to Dr. Suvoong. And in 1880, a Mr. Farnham of the American Presbyterian Board noted that " Dr. Suvoong subsequently studied medicine, and in the special departments of the eye and ear is supposed to have no equal in the East. "

In 1881, the Department for the Translation of Foreign Books at the Kiangnan Arsenal, Shanghai, (established in 1869) reported that Suvoong took over a translator job, adding that he was "a Chinese graduate of the United States who has begun to enrich the collection of books by translations of medical and other works for which task his long residence and studies in America have well qualified him." Suvoong was also reported as teaching English. And in 1893, Suvoong joined the Freemason at the Masonic Hall in Shanghai.

Suvoong's medical expertise was invoked during a 1904 hearing in the US State Department about intervention with England to relieve China from compulsory treaty obligations to tolerate the opium traffic. The remarks of Frank D. Gamewell, 20-year missionary in China and officially representing the Methodist Episcopal Missionary Board included the following statement: "One of the best known medical men of New York City, knowing that I had been in China, spoke to me some years ago of a Doctor Suvoong, a Chinese who had received his medical education in the US and whom he regarded as one of the most remarkable men he had met. This Dr. Suvoong says: 'Opium is a moral poison and is largely responsible for the decay of the Empire'."

Suvoong wrote many articles in Chinese medical journals and maintained his respect and affection for his American education. He named his son after his medical professor – Cornelius Agnew Suvoong was born in China on the 12th of December 1877. He graduated from the University of Aberdeen in Scotland in 1900 and received his diplomate in Tropical Medicine in 1904.

We will leave the completion of Suvoong's family history to future researchers for we must now return to Fairfax County and more stories of its Chinese residents.

Back in America – 1870 and Rising Anti-Chinese Sentiment Suvoong's apparently smooth life in Fairfax County and America was not representative of what was going on with many Chinese residents in the US.

1870 marked rising anti-Chinese fears and anxieties with the publication in the *Overland Monthly* of Bret Harte's poem *"The Heathen Chinese."* In that same year, Henry George published his analysis of the "Chinese problem" in the *New York Tribune,* warning that the Chinese immigrants were peculiar aliens in America – unlike the European peasant, the Chinese immigrant could not be transformed into an American, that they were "unassimilable."

By 1870, there were 63,000 Chinese in the US – most of them (77%) were in California but they were also elsewhere in the West as well as in the Southwest, New England, and the South. From 1865 to 1869, 12,000 Chinese were employed by the Central Pacific Railroad, representing 90% of the entire workforce that laid the tracks for the transcontinental line leading east from Sacramento. In 1870, the Chinese constituted 18% of all farm laborers in California.

The 1882 Chinese Exclusion Act. Hostility towards the Chinese was underscored by the Exclusion Act of 1882 when Congress voted to make it unlawful for Chinese laborers to enter the US for the next ten years and denied naturalized citizenship to the Chinese already in the US. Support for the law was overwhelming. The House vote was 201 yes, 37 nays, and 51 absent. Congressmen from the South and West gave it unanimous support. Support for the anti-Chinese legislation was national, coming not only from the western states but also from states where there were few or no Chinese. Although very few, there were critics of the 1882 Chinese Exclusion Act, including the anti-slavery/anti-imperialist Republican Senator George Frisbie Hoar of Massachusetts who described the exclusion act as "nothing less than the legalization of racial discrimination."

Aimed initially at Chinese "laborers," the prohibition was broadened in 1888 to include "all persons of the Chinese race"; exemptions were provided for Chinese officials, teachers, students, tourists, and merchants. Renewed in 1892, the Chinese Exclusion Act was extended indefinitely in 1902. For Congress, one way to solve the "Chinese problem" was to legislate the disappearance of the Chinese presence in America.

By the end of the 19th century, the Chinese had spread geographically: only 51% resided in California and 14,693 or 16% lived in the North Atlantic region, representing the beginnings of Chinatowns in Boston and New York City.

In the mainland, the Chinese had been forced to retreat into ethnic islands – their own separate economic and cultural colonies. During the early decades of the 20th century, the Chinese became increasingly urban and employed in restaurants, laundries and garment factories.

1900 – A Chinese Laundryman in Fairfax County. The second record of an Asian resident in Fairfax County was that of Wing Moy, a Chinese laundryman in Falls Church Township.

Wing Moy immigrated in 1897 and we do not have any information as to how he evaded the restrictions of the 1882 Chinese Exclusion Act – but he, like many Chinese, was forced to go into laundry work, a retreat from a narrowly restricted labor market that was growing very hostile toward Chinese workers. Crowded into laundry work, one out of four employed Chinese males in the US in 1900 was a laundryman.

The Chinese laundryman personified the forced withdrawal of the Chinese into a segregated ethnic labor market. They had not always been laundrymen; in 1870, of the 46,274 Chinese in all occupations, only 3,653 or 8% were laundry workers. By 1920, of the 45,614 gainfully employed workers, 12,559 or 28% (nearly one out of three) were laundry workers.

The Paper Son Phenomenon. This FCAAHP book includes a personal story about another phenomenon resulting from the hostility against the Chinese in America -- the subterfuge called "paper sons." Terry Sam, FCAAHP official photographer, will discuss his family's experience for his father was a "paper son."

The US Naturalization Law of March 26, 1790 limited naturalization to aliens who were "free white persons," thus excluding Asians. In 1898 the Supreme Court ruled 6-2 in a case brought by Wong Kim Ark, a Chinese born in the US, that under the Fourteenth Amendment, a child born in the United States to foreign parents who are subject to US jurisdiction automatically becomes a US citizen. Children fathered by Chinese Americans visiting China were American citizens by birth and eligible for entry to their country.

Others came as impostors: known as "paper sons" who adopted a lineage on paper so as to gain entry to the USA. They had purchased the birth certificates of American citizens born in China and they claimed that they were citizens in order to enter the US.

The "paper son" phenomenon was energized by a natural disaster that changed the course of Chinese American history. On April 18, 1906, an earthquake shook San Francisco. The fires destroyed almost all of the municipal records and opened the way for a new Chinese immigration. Chinese men were able to claim that they had been born in San Francisco and, as citizens, they could bring their wives and children to the US. Exactly how many Chinese men falsely claimed citizenship as "paper sons" will never be known. Some calculations indicate an average of 800 children per Chinese woman living in San Francisco before 1906 for every claim to natural-born citizenship to be valid.

But purchase of a birth certificate did not mean entry, for the "paper sons" were detained at the immigration station on Angel Island in San Francisco -- where they had to pass an examination and prove their American identity. Immigration officials would query each passenger at the port of entry: how many siblings and children did he have; in-laws; the numbers of rooms in his house; the streets and landmarks in his claimed home village?

The dreaded interviews led to the creation of elaborate "crib sheets." The immigrant purchased study guides in China and on the trip to America; they memorized information about the families of their "fathers." Few of these crib sheets survived for immigrants were supposed to throw them overboard. FCAAHP team leader Ted Gong donated to the Smithsonian one of the few extant "crib sheets" shown in the photo.

The presence of "paper sons" often led to confusing situations in families. A father named Wong could have two sons, each with a "paper name," having entered as "sons" of other men. A Mr. Lee could come here as "Mr. Wong," his wife would use the name "Mrs. Wong" and his children would register for school and selective service as Wongs. But to their family and in the Chinese community, they would be Lees.

Chinese Crib Sheet donated to Smithsonian by FCAAHP-Ted Gong

Note on Lorton Prison in 1920 and 1930. The DC Workhouse (Lorton Prison) was the recorded residence in 1920 for one Chinese American Ying Jung born in California. By 1930, three Chinese and one Filipino were reported by the Census as residing in the Lorton prison. We do not have much more information than the census records for the Asian prisoners but we do have some information about life in the Lorton prison that started in 1910 and was officially closed in 2001.

The lives of the handful of Asian prisoners in 1920s and 1930s would have been complicated by segregated arrangements in Lorton Prison. According to the memoirs of William Cooke, a federal prison guard in Lorton in the early 1930s, "the gangs of prisoners were made up of about 20 men each and were either all black or all white." (The memoirs were written by Cooke's son William Apperson Cooke and were included in page 38 of the book *"Franconia Remembers"* published in October 2003 by the Franconia Museum.)

Lorton proper was established in 1875 by an Englishman, Joseph Plaskett; he named the area after his house in Cumberland County, England. In 1910 under the direction of President Theodore Roosevelt, 1,155 acres were acquired for building a new prison facility. An attempt to incorporate progressive ideals into the prison included features such as an open-air design. Prisoners built the arcades out of bricks made at the on-site kiln complex along the Occoquan River. President Teddy Roosevelt envisioned a place where prisoners could be rehabilitated. The prison reformatory, designated for serious offenders, opened in 1916.

According to the Cooke memoirs, in the early 1930s the DC Workhouse was in Occoquan, Virginia and part of the DC Penal Institution. The Workhouse was minimum security and for prisoners with minor sentences of which most were 100 days or less. The maximum sentence was a year and a day. Prisoners with more than a year were sentenced to the Lorton Reformatory, part of the same complex. A brickyard, a sawmill, and a large produce farm existed, along with a dairy farm and hog farm in the Occoquan complex. The Workhouse was practically self-sufficient, providing materials and produce for government institutions in DC, such as the city jail and St. Elizabeth's Hospital. It had regular runs to large institutions, such as hotels and hospitals in the District to collect their garbage for the hog farm.

The prison complex closed on December 31, 2001. Various parts of the prison complex have undergone changes and face-lifts. As part of the reuse plan, the grounds of the prison have been renamed Laurel Hill and opened for recreational sports. New housing developments, shopping centers, schools, and a new water plant have become the landmarks of Lorton. In 2008, the Lorton Arts center displayed works of Asian artist residents of Fairfax County – slightly different arrangements than those experienced by early Asian prisoners in Lorton.

More information may turn up on the Asian prisoners in Lorton but we now pick up the thread of Chinese immigration to the US – and to Fairfax County – till recent times.

Chinese Immigration After WWII. Once the US and China became allies in World War II, President Franklin D. Roosevelt sought to bring the Chinese Exclusion Act era to a close by signing the 1943 Magnuson Act. Congress in 1943 repealed the Chinese exclusion acts and provided an annual quota for Chinese immigration. Only 105 Chinese would be allowed to enter annually and only an average of 59 Chinese came to the US during the first ten years (1943 – 1953).

Among longtime Fairfax County Chinese American residents who participated in our history project were Sam and Ruth Wong who immigrated to the US in 1948. Sam met his wife Ruth in 1955 and later learned that they came to the United States on the same ship. Sam Wong shared his book *"Stories Not to be Forgotten"* written to teach his four children of their family history; he achieved more than that by detailing the history of the Chinese Diaspora of the 20th century. I will only focus on the Fairfax County portion of his story.

1963 with Sam and Ruth Wang as Fairfax Residents. In 1963 Sam and Ruth Wong (with Angela, Arnold, Alex, and Andrew) moved to Kings Park in the Springfield area of Fairfax County. Sam Wong continued to work in "Electrical R/D Laboratory" of the US Army Department in Fort Belvoir in Fairfax County. They had a home built in 1963 and cultivated a wonderful garden blooming with lovely huge hibiscus amid a charming landscape. Kings Park was begun in 1960 by the Richmar Construction Company on 200 acres of land on Braddock Road. 265 additional acres were added in 1961. By 2009 there were over a thousand homes in the community.

Sam recalled: "After working at Fort Belvoir for one year, we bought our own piece of the American dream. We put a down payment on a new house in Springfield, Virginia. This is our home today and we plan to remain here. As a new homeowner, I knew little about maintenance and home improvement. We chose our one-story L-shaped rambler for its location and solid construction. Covering the minimal down payment left little in our savings account. Our sturdy rambler has proved to be an excellent investment as real estate prices in Northern Virginia have risen steadily. And I've become the Harry Homeowner, able to handle most routine home repairs, sometimes with help from my three sons. Even today, I can still climb up on the roof and clean the gutters."

Sam and Ruth Wong's home built & bought in 1963 in Kings Park, Fairfax County.
(Photo by Cora Foley)

Sam wrote of working in Fort Belvoir: "My job as a project engineer at Fort Belvoir required true engineering discipline and knowledge. Reports were due at the completion of a task or project. The technical work was within my capabilities, but I struggled with writing. It had been several years since my college English classes. My supervisor, Ted Cooper, diligently reviewed and corrected my first report. My performance evaluation at the end of my second year read: "Strength – Mr. Wong is conscientious and hardworking; he exerts every effort to accomplish his assigned tasks within assigned schedules. Weakness—although by no means inadequate in this respect, improvement in written communications would work to increase Mr. Wong's effectiveness in his position." Ted and I discussed my writing skills. He advised, "Sam, I realize you have problems writing in English. Don't feel badly about it. Keep working to improve it. My father had the same struggles when he came here from Europe. In fact, all the immigrants struggled when they came from Europe." I thanked him for his encouragement and candor. It has taken years to improve my ability to communicate in English, both written and oral. My vocabulary is still limited. I still think in Chinese and translate my thoughts into English. I calculate and solve math problems in Chinese, just as when I first learned my basic math principles in elementary school."

Ruth and Sam Wong in front of the Four-bank warehouse behind Suzhou River in 1980 during their first visit to China since they left in 1948.
(Courtesy of Sam Wong)

Sam very proudly shared his children's accomplishments in Fairfax County:

- 1964 – Angela Wong started her first grade at Little Run Elementary School.
- 1974 – Arnold Wong set a PVAAU (Potomac Valley Amateur Athletic Union) 1650-yard freestyle swimming record in the 13/14-year old group.
- 1974 – Alex and Andrew Wong, members of the Royal Swimming Team, set a NVSL (Northern Virginia Swimming League) 100-meter Medley Relay record in the 11/12-year old group.
- 1976 – Alex and Andrew Wong, members of the Royal Swimming Team, set two NVSL relay records in the 13/14 year-old group. These two records lasted more than ten years.
- 1978 – Arnold Wong was accepted to ODU (Old Dominion University) under a 4-year swimming scholarship. He set a Virginia State 200 butterfly record.
- 1979 – Arnold Wong set six individual ODU school swimming records.

Daryl and Betty Kan with Phyllis Walker Ford, a descendant of a founder of the Laurel Grove Colored School, during the school's historical marker dedication on June 13, 2009
(Photo by Cora Foley)

Ruth and Sam Wong count among their friends Betty and Daryl Kan, also longtime Fairfax County residents, whom I met during the June 13, 2009 unveiling of the historical marker for the Laurel Grove Colored School. The school's story began in 1881 when William Jasper, a former slave, and his wife Georgianna deeded one-half acre of land from their thirteen-acre farm to the local Franconia school district to address the urgent need for education of their children.

Since 1965, the reform of the immigration law triggered a tide of new immigrants from China – radically transforming that community from 61% American born to 63% foreign-born, becoming again mainly an immigrant community with the family-unification provisions opening the way for demographic change.

Representing this new trend for Fairfax County Asian Americans is FCAAHP member Sarita James – shown in photo wearing a traditional Chinese costume.

Shaomin (Sarita) James

1999 with Joe and Linda Yao moving to Fairfax from West Virginia. FCAAHP members Joe and Linda Yao shared their story of moving from Taiwan to West Virginia, where their daughter Gwendolyn was born, and then in 1999 to Fairfax County. Joe and Linda Yao met each other in Taipei, Taiwan when Joe returned from the US to visit his parents in Taipei. During Joe's 3- week visit, Joe and Linda met, through a matchmaker (which is a traditional way to meet a future spouse). They became engaged and married, all within Joe's 3-week vacation time. At the conclusion of the vacation, Joe brought his bride to the US and settled in Charleston, West Virginia, where Joe was working for the City government as a computer engineer. Linda, with a law degree and international trade business work experiences from Taiwan, quickly found a job and worked for the State Attorney General's Office. Ever since that time, Linda has been working as an employee for the state, county, and in 2009, federal government.

Gwendolyn Yao was born and raised in a very beautiful city – Charleston, in the "almost heaven" state of West Virginia. At the age of 9, Gwendolyn moved to Fairfax County with her Taiwanese-native parents, Wei-Chiu Yao (Joe) and Tsong-Fen Ho (Linda). Gwendolyn has often returned to West Virginia to visit her childhood friends who owned a farm where she played with deer and horses. Despite being laughed at and teased by her Fairfax county friends that she is one of the "rednecks" or "bared-foot" mountain people, Gwendolyn loves West Virginians and enjoys visiting her "Hillbilly" friends, who once called her "Chinese" and told her to "go back to China, your country."

Sharon Bulova with Linda and Joe Yao.

In 1999 Joe started his career at AARP and relocated his family to the Fairfax County because of its excellent school system. Joe is an active member of the AARP Asian Employees Group that has promoted diversity and multicultural programs in that agency. The Yao family loves Fairfax County where they learn, grow, and enjoy their lives. Linda had worked until 2009 for the Fairfax County government. Having been a long-term member of the Fairfax County Diversity Committee, a bilingual educator, and a government Equal Opportunity officer, Linda Yao has devoted herself to promoting the cultural diversity awareness among various ethnic groups. In her profession and volunteer work, Linda plays the role of a mediator, a communicator, and a bridge among western, eastern, and other ethnic populations in developing multicultural appreciations.

Gwendolyn Yao, their daughter, was selected as the 2006 representative from Woodson High School into the Fairfax County Youth Leadership program. Gwendolyn is also the first Asian American student who received a 2004 Army's Web-based Science Competition beta test winning award. Gwendolyn in October 2009 is a student at the University of Virginia and her goal is to become a medical physician.

In Fairfax County: Chinese American Stories of Four Generations and Paper Sons. As part of the Fairfax County Asian American History Project, we are sharing with you stories from two Chinese Americans. Ted Gong of Mason District in Fairfax County, and a former diplomat with the US State Department, is a fourth generation Chinese American. Terry Sam of Springfield District and a former official with the Internal Revenue Service, is a second generation Chinese American and child of a "paper son."

Stories about Sugar Men, Ears and Me
By Ted Gong

I first came to Fairfax County to work for the U.S. Department of State in 1980. I was one of the newly hired Foreign Service Officers being inducted and trained at Washington DC. It was the first time I had ever been east of the Mississippi.

My entire life up to then had been in the Pacific West Coast. Part of that time was in Washington state and Hawaii (interspersed with time spent even further west to where it became the "Far East" in Taiwan and Hong Kong for a couple of years), but mostly in California. This is the state where historical circumstances had concentrated Chinese Americans. My great grandfather, for example, settled in San Francisco when immigration from China to the United States was unrestricted. He worked on the wharfs "sorting potatoes," according to my father, saving enough money to retire in China and to send his son (my grandfather whose English name was "Harry") to the United States as a "merchant." By then, U.S. immigration law restricted Chinese laborers from coming to the United States. Harry Gong created a livelihood in grocery and meat markets, and in clan associations.

Gong Family 1957 (Courtesy of Ted Gong)

Importantly, the clan -- mostly Gong's and Young's -- did not concentrate in San Francisco Chinatown. They ventured into the areas where California's agriculture industry was growing. This was not done necessarily by choice. I remember my father saying the Gong's in San Francisco were not many, nor powerful. Unlike the tai-shan speaking Lee's or Chang's who dominated restaurants and retail businesses within the city by virtue of having come earlier and in larger numbers. My father frequently pointed out at Colma near San Bruno during Chinese Memorial Day (when we "walked the mountain" to pay annual respects to our forebears) that our clan was relegated to a corner of the Chinese cemetery. The so-called "Six Companies" dominated the larger, nicer locations.

As it was at the cemetery, so it was in the business district. The consequence was that Gong's tended to reach beyond Chinatown in search of their economic niche. New networks were made in the rural parts of California in the Salinas Valley, Lodi and into the Central California towns of Fresno and Hanford. Today, many of the Gong's have supermarkets. Several of these markets have grown into large chains.

The movement into the rural areas also meant that our family members tended to be more integrated into the local communities than were our Chinatown cousins because, for us, there were fewer Chinese with whom to socialize. Where we grew up in the rural community of Cutler Orosi near Fresno, there was initially one other Chinese family. And, it was through that family's grocery business that my father Jack Gong arrived to Cutler-Orosi as its butcher and its PR guy. I recall seeing a glossy publicity photograph of him, at the store with Howdy Doody promoting Rainbow Bread or something. He later found his own market called the Midway Market (because it was midway between Cutler and Orosi). Later still, he started an insurance business, became a county supervisor (appointed by the first Governor Brown) and committed himself to ensuring all his children (seven brothers and sisters) would complete high school and study at least two years at community college.

He saw that commitment fulfilled. All my brothers and sisters finished college, and several have advanced degrees, not bad for my father who had completed formally only the fourth grade. Revealingly, he was almost refused enlistment into the U.S. Army in WWII as an "imbecile" because he did not know enough English at that time to pass the Army's standard IQ test.

Aside from English, the language most spoken in Cutler-Orosi was Spanish. This reflected the nature of the agriculture community that relied on migrant Mexican farm workers to pick crops. The population of Cutler-Orosi often tripled during the picking season. Another part of our community, Japanese-American *(nisei* and *sansei)* generally owned and operated family farms and trucking firms. There was also a significant Filipino *(pinoy)* population. But, the dominant language and culture was English and white, with a mix of Spanish and brown. Sharing tamales during Christmas was as much a part of my growing up as sharing moon cakes during Chinese New Year and having turkey for Thanksgiving.

When my brothers started school, they were placed in the school district's "deaf and dumb" class because the teachers had no idea about what to make of the Cantonese my family spoke. Guided by "melting pot" theories, well-intended teachers admonished my parents to speak only English in our household for the sake of integrating us children quickly into the American school system by what I assume to be tactics to purge cultural and linguistic impediments to success. In that respect, the school system was successful. None of my sisters had to attend the special remedial classes that their older brothers had to attend. We all graduated with distinctions and awards. None of us retained any of our Cantonese either, other than a few comfort words –such as "time to eat," or fan for "rice," or chasui bow for a type of barbeque pork bun.

Gong Family 1966 (Courtesy of Ted Gong)

This shaky knowledge of Chinese tradition and language made us (along with our generation of American born and educated cousins) more gullible to stories about our Chinese heritage, family relationships and customs. My parents could have said all Chinese got straight A's and ate chicken feet, and we would have believed them. The TV images of Hop Sing and of Charlie Chan and his Number One Son were true to us. Fortune cookies and chop suey were indeed essential Chinese food.   Moreover, our confusion was compounded by paper concoctions of identities and false names.   Many of them were designed deliberately to outwit immigration authorities (called "green shirts" by my mother's generation for the color of their uniforms or *la migra* today) trying to deport friends and relatives under provisions of racist immigration laws.

Who was a Young?   Who was a Gong?   Who was really related to whom?   How did the family get here from China?   And, by the way, what was grandma's name actually…   All seemingly simple stories, they had stories within them.

My mother would spin stories about Harry Gong being a "hit man" for criminal organizations called Tongs.   He was an opium addict and great grandmother killed him as his final cure.   My mother told us how her ear prevented her from immigrating to the United States as our Aunt Lola after spending a year in a detention facility on Angel Island in San Francisco Bay.   My father told us that Chinese people were called tong jen, or "sugar men," in Cantonese because of their work in the villages planting and harvesting sugar beets.

Of course, many of the stories were outright wrong.   The Cantonese word for "sugar" does sound like *tong* in the Cantonese word *tong jen* in reference to themselves as *jen* (men or people) of China, but *tong* here actually refers to the Tang Dynasty.   This was the great dynasty that incorporated into China the southern coastal provinces that included the Canton (Guangzhou) and Hong Kong region. Many scholars believe the Chinese dialect now called Cantonese is closer to the Chinese language spoken throughout China during the Tang Dynasty than is Mandarin which is now considered China's national language.   My family roots are in the Hong Kong and Guangzhou region.   They are the same roots of almost all the Chinese in America before Mandarin speakers from Taiwan and North China began immigrating significantly to the United States decades later in the sixties and seventies, and well before the later wave of migrants coming from Fukien who spoke yet another Chinese dialect.

But many of the stories they told were right -- fantastic as they seemed.   The story about my mother's ear, the story about roosters substituting for my father at a village wedding, the stories about opium, and about a heart-broken sister left in China because of poverty and war…they were all true.

During my first assignment for the State Department as a visa officer sent to Guangzhou, the stories began to sort themselves out.   Impressions began to solidify.   Stories found realities.   I never did find a single sugar beet growing in the ground but the assignment provided opportunities to meet time-lost relatives.   They filled details into my parents' stories and added new ones about my father and mother, their generation and my forebears.   I visited the village where my father lived briefly after grandmother had brought him, two brothers and a sister to China from the United States.   My grandfather had abandoned the family and, depending on the version of the family story, grandmother either took the children to China to force her errant husband to reform or went to China in an ill-considered effort to repair a poverty broken and fatherless family during the Great Depression.

Other assignments over thirty years provided more insights. They yielded additional stories about the immigrant experience. My career allowed (even required) me to understand trends and patterns of migration and their impact on individuals and families. An integral part of that career was to apply regulations and to develop policies affecting American Citizens, their protection overseas, legal and illegal immigration, human trafficking, students and academic exchanges, refugees and border controls. My last assignment before retiring from the State Department on May 1, 2009 involved studying and advising on comprehensive immigration reform.

These issues relate to who can come to the United States and who can become a member of the American community. The history of this experience has not been pretty. The first comprehensive immigration law by Congress in 1882 was one of exclusion. It deprived my grandmother and grandfather American citizenship just because they were Chinese. My mother was held at the age of 16 on an island in San Francisco Bay for a year before being deported because she was Chinese. Thousands of individuals were driven out of their homes and shops or killed. Fundamental civil rights were trampled upon by state governments, municipalities and mobs, whose countless acts of violence were given legitimacy by the 1882 federal law. That law was extended 10 years later as "An Act to Prohibit the Coming of Chinese Persons into the United States." The exclusion concepts it articulated for Chinese were expanded in later laws to apply to all peoples from an Asiatic Zone,

Ted Gong and "Remembering 1882" Exhibit by FCAAHP in Pohick Library in June 2009
(Photo by Cora Foley)

from India to Japan. It was not until 1965 that race, ethnicity and national origins were eliminated as a basis for immigrating to the United States. In signing the Hart Cellar Act, President Johnson characterized previous laws as "un-American in the highest sense."

While President Johnson marked a watershed in U.S. immigration policy, one legacy of the 1882 law was to establish exclusion as a principle fundamental to all subsequent laws and to embed the ethos of exclusion throughout the bureaucracy that administers them. Even if specific statutory reasons for exclusion have changed over the years, the laws essentially seek to keep people out whether they are Chinese, lunatics, prostitutes, criminals or Communists. The sentiments expressed at the base of the Statue of Liberty notwithstanding, U.S. immigration laws have never been for purposes of welcoming huddled masses to the United States nor are they for the purposes of attracting people into the country because of their position, talents or skills. To the extent that there are laws for employment and family reunification, it is because government tolerates them. The entire immigration bureaucracy from when it was organized within the Departments of Treasury and Labor to its current manifestation in the Departments of Homeland Security and State is designed to uncover why a person seeking to live in the United States should be excluded.

However, I believe that America's national strength comes from inclusion. It is not just the right thing to do as President Johnson recognized in a civil rights sense. It is also in the nation's self interest to welcome anyone energetic and bold enough to seek to become a member of a community that accepts as self-evident the right to pursue happiness. Thus, the first Fairfax County naturalization ceremony in May 2009 was an important event to see organized. It took as its basic principle the idea that individuals and their families should not only be welcomed into our community they should also be encouraged to participate at its most basic level –at the county and neighborhoods where governments by the people most directly manifest.

Indeed, if we expect the ideal community to be preserved, there is both a responsibility to participate in its governance on the part of its members and a responsibility to protect the right to participate by its newest members on the part of government. When government (and the people behind it) fails to protect the right of any member to participate in the community, the nation suffers.

This is seen in the legacy and consequences of the Chinese Exclusion Laws. These laws were passed through democratic processes in 1882. They were enacted in response to demands by dozens of state and local bodies of democratically empowered leaders to exclude Chinese from "our" communities and to expel or eliminate them altogether. Four years after 1882, an Oregon political cartoon of a Yosemite Sam-type character summarized the anti-immigrant story: "You can go, or you can stay." Those who went were driven out or left because political entities made life difficult purposely to force the Chinese out of their jurisdictions. Those who stayed were dead bodies under a smoking gun.

What is encouraging to note, however, is that despite the failings, the concept of America is still so strong that government, driven by the same democratic process that might elect demigods at times, eventually gets it right. In the meantime, we see throughout our history that people from different countries choose to undertake extraordinary measures to come to the United States.

Once here, they build the nation by constructing its railroads and harnessing atoms and electronics. (My uncle was at Los Alamos as a scientist and his life's research into low-dose radiation was potential Nobel Prize material.) They have defended America's homes and founding principles in wars from the Civil War to Afghanistan. (My father and uncle fought in the Asia-Pacific and European theaters. My other uncle served in Korea and Vietnam, as did my brother.) Everyday, they make America by being its factory workers, field hands, shopkeepers, insurance salesmen, teachers, guardsmen, craftsmen, civil servants and moms and dads driving kids to community theater or coaching soccer and softball.

The energy and commitments of new members strengthen the community for everyone, including for its oldest members. The nation as a whole gains from the talents and confidence of individuals seeking a better life because they have judged that it is more possible in America than it is in the country they left. And, it is the promise of that possibility to all people regardless of their nationality and culture that drives the continuous process of invigoration to ensure the future of the United States.

As for our different traditions from past countries, I would close by adding my own story to the family collection of stories:

During my father's first trip to China after I was assigned to the U.S. Consulate in Guangzhou, we visited his father's and grandfather's graves. China had just opened formal relations with the United States. The commune system was still in place. The consequences of the Cultural Revolution were still apparent. Ancestral temples, tombs and gravesites were particularly targeted during the struggles that sought to obliterate the past at the cost of hundreds of thousands of lives. Stories abound about relatives committing suicides, attempted escapes and horrifying destruction.

The concepts and consequences of the Cultural Revolution discredited, local cadres were eager to welcome a native son (my father who was raising funds to rebuild the village school). When he expressed a desire to visit our ancestors' gravesites, they eagerly searched for them and soon accompanied us to a picturesque hillside near the village where my father worked the fields briefly as a boy, where he had married my mother after WWII and where my grandfather was killed according to our family stories.

We trudged up the hill, my father and me, "walking the mountain" as we had done so many times at Colma for my grandmother during Chinese memorial days. The chatty cadres led the way. They directed us to recently cleared mounds of dirt that, in the absence of stone markers, indicated where my forebears were interred. Local villagers who were our distant relatives, they said, had maintained them throughout foreign occupation, civil war and political strife. Father burnt incense before the mounds. He served tea and bowed three times as I had seen him do annually at his mother's grave near views of San Francisco Bay. The cadres stood respectfully behind, satisfied that they had reconnected another native son to China.

As we returned to the official cars waiting at the foot of the hill, there was a moment when my sugar man dad and I were alone. I asked him if he really believed those mounds of dirt marked our ancestors' gravesites. "Nay," I recall him matter-of-factly replying. "They probably just made them up for our visit. But, it doesn't matter. I've waited thirty years to return to China to pay my respects to my father. At least, we now have a place to go. It's the idea that counts."

I have gone back to that hill several times -- a couple of times by myself. Again, shortly after I was married to Mohkeed and once more when Alison was a few months old. The weather alternated between overcast and humid; but, at the top of hill, there was always a soft breeze and a sense of wholeness.

Allison, Ted, Russel, Mohkeed Gong at Reston Asian Festival, Fairfax County on August 9, 2008
(Photo by Terry Sam)

I never did find the gravesites again. They were difficult to locate originally and the tall grass and undergrowth perennially removed distinctions in the cemetery of haphazardly placed markers and burial mounds. Although I understand a cousin has since placed stone markers where the dirt mounds were, it doesn't really matter. I will tell my son Russell when we visit there, as his grandfather had said to me, it's the idea that counts. Knowing our heritage from China provides us deep roots and a sturdy trunk that shows its strength by its many hardened scars; but, for us, my son and me, it is the growing limbs, unfolding leaves and new fruit in the United States that count even more. ##

Songs of a Chinese Family:

A Personal History of the Gong Family's Journey to America that began in 1880

Baba: A Tribute to Working Chinese Fathers

By Kathy Gong Greene (Ted Gong's sister)

Father built the railroads
Slaves of coolie labor
From scorching heat in desert sand
To carving High Sierras

Father was a farmer
Farmed on delta land

Kathy Gong Greene (Photo by Terry Sam)

A miner's spirit deep inside
Less golden in your hand

Fly away on dragon wings
Graceful wings unfold
Pilot through the ancient sky
For now you're in control

Sailing through the clouds above
Through wind and rain and snow
Free to rid your soul at last
Of all that you did hold

Father was a soldier
Fought in World War II
A veteran of the foreign wars
A mason free and true

Father was a butcher
A traveler and a storekeeper

Insuring minds with security
Raising children in the valley
Descendants of the dragon
Has come for you at last
Time to release your weary mind
From a strange and haunting past

Father died in ninety-four
With no mention of regrets
Traditions of his long hard word
Will finally come to rest

Kathy Gong Greene and her husband William Greene performed the song "Baba" at the June 27, 2009 meeting of the Fairfax County Asian American History Project in Pohick Library. She allowed FCAAHP to reprint the song for which she holds the copyright.

Note from Russell Eliot Gong, 5th generation Chinese American son of Ted Gong who was 18 years old when he gave this interview on May 31, 2008 for FCAAHP:

"Before I enrolled at the University of Richmond, I really did not feel a distinct identity as an Asian American. In Fairfax County, you feel very blended. In Woodson High School, you're noticed as an Asian American but you do not feel such a structured identity that separates yourself from other peers.

"When I went down to Richmond, something was far different. The way that I was perceived by other people, other races, that made me feel very much that I was an Asian American. No, I did not feel that way in Fairfax County where I felt just like anybody, just an American. I did not feel a special identity here in Fairfax but in Richmond, it was different.

"In Richmond, it is not as cosmopolitan in the sense of different races, different ethnicities. In the beginning, it was negative. I felt some prejudice in some sense. And I never felt that in Fairfax. I did not grow up in Fairfax but I went for four years in Woodson High School. I never felt differences – felt we all shared the same culture as Fairfax County classmates or in sports teams.

"I don't know why it felt so different in the University of Richmond. There are fewer Asian Americans there while there were many Asian Americans, particularly Korean Americans, in Woodson High School. I did feel more welcomed because there were many more Asian Americans." ##

Paper Sons – Joe and Mabel Sam Immigrating to Detroit
By Terry J. Sam

I am an American of Chinese heritage. I was born in Detroit, Michigan in 1937. My parents were born and raised in China and immigrated to the United States. My father came in 1921, my mother in 1933. (See figures 1 and 2) Their immigration was dominated by the 1882 Chinese Exclusion Act, the first US immigration law. It barred most Chinese immigration for ten years and was renewed and extended to other Asians through the decades by later laws until its repeal in 1943. By definition Chinese were the first illegal aliens.

How did tens of thousands of Chinese immigrate during the life of the Act? They came as illegal aliens, but they did it with finesse in a very Asian way to meet the requirements for allowed immigration in the Act. It was not, "How can I go to the USA"? But, "How can my son go to the USA"? Also, "How can we get around the Exclusion Act?" The Chinese created paper sons. They learned how to exploit false identities 100 years before stolen identities became an artifact of the Internet. Here is one scenario of how it worked.

In the year after a visit home to China, a Chinese legal US resident receives a letter from China about a new son born in China and often about his wife dying in childbirth. The new son is not real. He is a son only on paper. Fifteen to twenty years later, the family in China sells the paper son identity to a family with a son ready to immigrate to the US. My father immigrated with the identity of Joe Sam, a student and the son of Joe Wing, a merchant. As a student, he was permitted by the Chinese Exclusion Act to enter the US. Merchants also were permitted US entry by the Act.

My mother's immigration identity was created differently from my father's. A consequence of the 1882 Chinese Exclusion Act and the Immigration Act of 1924 was greatly restricted immigration of Chinese women. There were no paper daughters created for identity sale. However, Chinese women could immigrate with another form of identity sale. My mother immigrated with the identity of Mabel Woo. In 2008 I realized that while I know my father's true name and his paper name, I only knew my mother's paper name, Woo. We had many Woo relatives, but were they true relatives? If they were not true relatives, then what was Mom's true family name?

I talked with a Woo uncle for answers to my questions. The woman whose identity Mom used to immigrate was born in Madison, Wisconsin and was an American citizen by birthright. She returned to China with her parents and siblings and later married and had children in China. The original Mabel Woo did not want to return to the US. I assume that Mom's or Dad's family bought Mabel Woo's identity enabling Mom to enter the US as an American citizen. Mom's family and the real Mabel Woo's family lived in a village where most of the families were Woo's. Mom's true family name is also Woo. All of our Woo uncles were not true relatives as we define them in America. One of our Woo uncles was the brother of the real Mabel Woo. I remember another Woo uncle referring to my mother as his sister. I believe he was acting out the charade of paper identities to avoid detection of the use of paper identities.

The US Immigration and Naturalization Service noticed all of the Chinese families with sons but not daughters and established the Angel Island and Seattle interrogation centers. Chinese immigrants were interrogated at length to assure that the immigrants' identities were true. We learned in our visit to the Immigration Library that transcripts of the interrogations are archived. I intend to obtain the interrogation transcripts of my parents from the US Citizenship and Immigration Service to learn what they had to endure on their entry to the USA.

Employing paper son identities had consequences on my family's life well beyond my parent's immigration. It affected our family name, confused me about family relationships, created an obligation of my parents to support the extended family back in China, and put us in constant fear of discovery by immigration officers.

My father's true name is Lin Tau Wong. (Family name of Wong is last by the custom in the US.) His paper son identity is Joe Sam. (Family name of Joe is first by the custom in China.) The immigration official in Seattle recorded his name as Joe Sam, and he became known officially as Mr. Sam. My father did not care what part of his paper name became his official family name. Thus, the Sam family name was created. Among Chinese our family name is still Wong.

Iris Chang wrote in *The Chinese in America* about how families in China exploited their sons in America by demanding money for decades. My parents corresponded with their families in China, but I do not have knowledge of them sending remittances to their families. I do have evidence of my father creating paper son identities that his family could sell to help meet his obligation to them for purchasing his paper son identity. In my father's Petition for Naturalization he lists five children, not the three that I know, Joann, Donnie, and me. I derived the following timeline from information on the petition. (See figure 3) The paper son birth events are italicized and underlined. Notice that each paper son birth is preceded by a trip to China by Joe Sam in the preceding year.

1921 Lin T. Wong arrives at the port of Seattle as Joe Sam on June 10
1921 - 1924 Joe Sam resided in Chicago, Illinois
1924 Joe Sam moved to Detroit, Michigan
1927 Joe Sam visited family in China returning to the US in 1928
1928 Joe Len born in Canton China on August 20
1932 Joe Sam visited family in China returning to the US in 1933
1933 Joe Hoy born in Canton China on Oct. 21
1933 Mabel Woo arrives at the port of Seattle on August 10
1933 - 1942 Joe and Mabel Sam operate Fair Star Inn on Mack Ave.
1934 Joe Sam and Mabel Woo married on June 3 (Probably married in China in 1933)
1934 Joann Sam born in Detroit Michigan on October 16
1937 Terry Sam born in Detroit Michigan on August 3
1939 Donnie Sam born in Detroit Michigan on January 10
1942 Joe and Mabel Sam move Fair Star Inn to Warren Ave.
The Joe Len and Joe Hoy identities would have been marketable during and shortly after World War II, so they were probably not sold and used.

My siblings and I enjoyed citizenship by virtue of our birth in Detroit, Michigan. We owe our citizenship birthright to Wong Kim Ark. In 1895 he was denied reentry into the US after a trip to China to visit his parents. He filed a writ of habeas corpus asserting that his birth in San Francisco entitled him to American citizenship. In 1898 the US Supreme Court ruled for Wong Kim Ark, declaring that all children born in the US are American citizens, even if their parents are ineligible for naturalization.

While growing up in Detroit in the 1940s and 1950s it seemed to me that every Chinese family I knew had a real name and a paper name. Families lived in fear of discovery by the INS. Family relationships were confusing to me. Who were real relatives? Who were paper relatives? I caused fear one time with a telephone call. My cousin and his father lived in Kansas. I called and awkwardly asked in English for Leon's father, because I was not confident of my pronunciation of my uncle's name. The man who came to the phone was not my uncle. Later I learned that my cousin and uncle were at the same restaurant as the paper father of my cousin's paper son identity. The paper father responded to my call in case I was a Government official. We also heard rumors of the deportation of Chinese families including children born in America. ##

(Photos and documents in this chapter are courtesy of Terry Sam.)

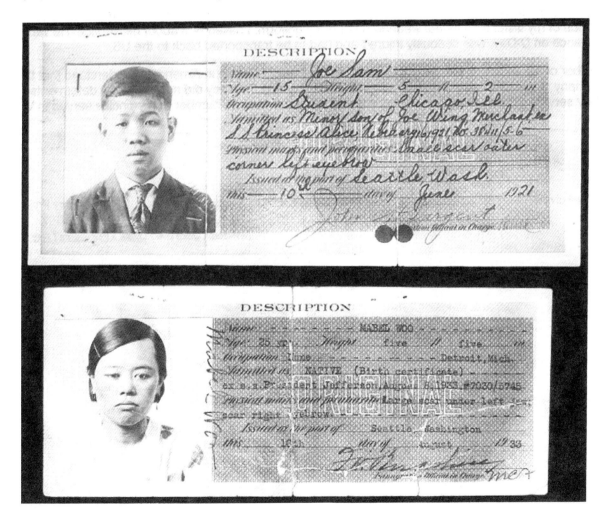

Statement of Facts To Be Used in Making and Filing My Petition for Naturalization

3

(1) My full, true, and correct name is JOE SAM _____

(2) My present place of residence is 16321 E. WARREN Detroit, Wayne Mich (4) I am 7 2 years old

(3) My occupation is OPERATES RESTAURANT

(5) I was born on NOV. 14 1906 in CANTON CHINA

(6) My personal description is as follows: Sex MALE, color BROWN, complexion BROWN, color of eyes BROWN, color of hair BLACK height 5 feet 7 ½ inches; weight 140 pounds; visible distinctive marks SMALL SCAR outer CORNER LEFT EYE BROW race CHINESE DESCRIBED CHINESE

(7) I am married; the name of my wife is WOO SHEE DIETER ? MAGIE WOO ON we were married on JAN. 1934 at DETROIT, WAYNE MICH. she was born at Madison, Dane Co. Wis. U.S.A. on DEC 12 1907 for permanent residence in the United States at _____ and now resides at _____ or became a citizen by _____

(8) I have _____ children; and the name, sex, date and place of birth, and present place of residence of each of said children who is living are as follows:
JOE LEX. MALE AUG 20, 1928 CANTON, CHINA
JOE HON MALE Oct. 21, 1933 CANTON CHINA
JOANN SAM FEMALE Oct. 16, 1934 Detroit Mich U.S.A.
JERRY JOE SAM, MALE, AUG 3, 1937 Detroit, WAYNE, Mich, U.S.A.
BONNIE JOE SAM, MALE, JAN. 10, 1939 Detroit, Wayne, Mich.

(9) My last place of foreign residence was CANTON CHINA (10) I emigrated to the United States from HONG KONG CHINA

(11) My lawful entry for permanent residence in the United States was at SEATTLE WASH under the name of JOE SAM JUNE 10 19 on the M.S. PRINCESS ALICE

(12) Since my lawful entry for permanent residence I have _____ been absent from the United States, for a period or periods of 6 months or longer, as follows:

DEPARTED FROM THE UNITED STATES			RETURNED TO THE UNITED STATES		
Port	Date (Month, day, year)	Vessel or Other Means of Conveyance	Port	Date (Month, day, year)	Vessel or Other Means of Conveyance
SEATTLE	JUNE 1928	PRES. LINER	SEATTLE	MAY 1928	PRES. LINER
SEATTLE	NOV 1932	PRES. LINER	SEATTLE	AUG 1933	PRES. LINER

(13) I declared my intention to become a citizen of the United States on 1947 in the _____ Court of _____ at DETROIT WAYNE MICH

(14) I have resided continuously in the United States of America since JUNE 1921 and continuously in the State of MICHIGAN where I now live since SEP 19 1933

(15) I have _____ heretofore made petition for naturalization No. _____ at _____ in the _____ and such petition was _____ and the cause of denied by that court for the following reasons and causes, to wit: _____ and such dismissal or denial has since been cured or removed.

(16) I wish the naturalization court to change my name to JOE SIM

(17) (1st witness) TOM WAY JUM residing at _____ I first met this witness in the United States on _____

(18) (2d witness) _____ residing at _____ I first met this witness in the United States on _____

I CERTIFY that the above statement of facts has been read by or to me and that the statement is true to the best of my knowledge and belief.

DO NOT FILL IN BLANKS BELOW	DO NOT FILL IN BLANKS BELOW
Affidavit of witnesses to show residence of petitioner as follows:	Corrections numbered _____ to _____ in this Preliminary Form for Petition for Naturalization, N-400, were made by me or at my request.
United States _____	
State _____	Applicant _____
Examiner _____	Date _____

69410

2

(18) In what places in the United States have you resided during the past five years?

CHICAGO	ILL	From	JUNE	1921	to JULY	1924
Detroit	Mich	From	JULY	1924	to AUG	1930
Detroit	Mich	From	AUG	1930	to JUNE	1932

(19) What were the names, occupations, and addresses of your employers during the last 5 years?
FAIR STAR RESTAURANT 16422 MACK, Detroit Mich 1933-1942
FAIR STAR RESTAURANT (OWNER) 16321 E. WAREN, Detroit, Mich, 1942-1947

(20) Have you read the following oath of allegiance? YES

I HEREBY declare, on oath, that I absolutely and entirely renounce and abjure all allegiance and fidelity to any foreign prince, potentate, state, or sovereignty of whom or which I have heretofore been a subject or citizen; that I will support and defend the Constitution and the laws of the United States of America against all enemies, foreign and domestic; that I will bear true faith and allegiance to the same; and that I take this obligation freely without any mental reservation or purpose of evasion: So Help Me God.

Are you willing to take this oath in becoming a citizen? YES
Of what country are you now a citizen or subject? CHINA

(21) If necessary, are you willing to take up arms in defense of the United States? YES
Have you ever, during the time this country was at war, deserted the military or naval forces of the United States, or departed the jurisdiction of the enrollment district or the United States to avoid draft into the military or naval forces of the United States? NO

(22) How many times have you ever been married? TWO TIMES

(23) Have you ever been an inmate of an insane asylum? NO

(24) Have you ever been arrested or charged with violation of any law of the United States or State or any city ordinance or traffic regulation? NO
If so, give date, place and cause of arrest and disposition of each case _____

(25) Have you ever been deported from the United States, or are deportation proceedings now pending against you? NO
If so, state all facts _____

(26) During the last ten (10) years I have been a member of the following organizations and no other OPERATES FAIR STAR RESTAURANT

(27) Was your father or mother ever a citizen of the United States? NO If so, give full particulars _____

(28) Did you register under the Alien Registration Act of 1940? YES
If so, state the number of your Alien Registration Receipt Card 2699417

(29) If male, did you register under the Selective Service (Draft) Law of 1940 as amended? YES
If so state your Draft Board No. 21 Located at MACK AVE DETROIT, WAYNE MICH.
Classified in class 3A/H, 3D Reason for such classification _____

(30) Did you yourself fill out this form? YES If not, give the name and address of the person who did _____

(31) It is my intention in good faith to become a citizen of the United States and to renounce absolutely and forever all allegiance and fidelity to any foreign prince, potentate, state, or sovereignty of whom or which at this time I am a subject or citizen, and it is my intention to reside permanently in the United States. I am not, and have not been for the period of at least 10 years immediately preceding the date of this statement, an anarchist; nor a believer in the unlawful damage, injury, or destruction of property, or sabotage; nor a disbeliever in or opposed to organized government, nor a member of or affiliated with any organization or body of persons teaching disbelief in or opposition to organized government. I am able to speak the English language, unless physically unable to do so. I am, and have been during all of the periods required by law, attached to the principles of the Constitution of the United States and well disposed to the good order and happiness of the United States.

I CERTIFY that all the statements made by me in this application and form are true to the best of my knowledge and belief.

_____

34781

Acceptance of Asian Americans in Detroit and Fairfax County
By Terry Sam

Living in Detroit

Growing up in Detroit, Michigan, I was keenly aware of being Chinese American. It was not just seeing my physical differences in the mirror. I was born in 1937. Chinese had been demonized and belittled in public media and general communications well before I was born. It was routine to be the target of epithets, crude puns, and mockery with sing song gibberish. In Detroit there were good people too who spoke up for us and told the bigots where to go. Even so I was very sensitive to the taunts, more sensitive than my sister and brother were. My self-image was affected.

Our parents owned and operated the Fair Star Inn, a Chinese restaurant. Our waiters and cooks worked 10 to 12 hours a day, six or seven days a week. You could call our place a sweatshop, but our family worked those same hours too. It was a hard life. In about 1936 my mother needed help to tend to her daughter while she worked in the restaurant. My sister, Joann was a toddler then. Lydia Hensel took the job to release Jo from being belted into her high chair. No one knew then that this would become a lifelong association. The Hensels often cared for Jo at their home two blocks from the restaurant, so she was the first child in their home. I was next. The Hensels adopted a baby girl, Linda, in 1938. Then my brother, Don, was born in 1939. My parents lived in an apartment behind the restaurant and the Hensels in the nearby house. We had bedrooms in the Hensel home and stayed there as often as we did with our parents. The Hensels treated the three of us like we were their own children and like siblings to Linda. To this day we call Linda our sister and she calls us her brothers and sister. We called Lydia, Moo. One of my Woo uncles said it means aunt in Chinese. (See Sam Family photo gallery page 43.)

Joe and Mabel Sam with children in 1940.
(Courtesy of Terry Sam)

We in effect had four parents. Being a second generation Sam (See the Paper Son essay) meant more than having the Wong and Woo DNA and nurturing from our parents. It also meant the character, integrity, and American tradition the Hensels brought with them from Western Pennsylvania. Murhl Hensel worked at the Chrysler factory. Lydia's maiden name was Pyle. She was a member of the Ernie Pyle clan. He was the famous World War II journalist. My father and Moo gave us unconditional love. Dad led us by example. My mother was very demanding and, like Chinese mothers do, pushed us to excel in school. Murhl was disciplined and expected us to be disciplined. He often read newspaper articles to us of how bad things happen to good people. I do not know if we fully understand the qualities we acquired from our four parents. We truly are Chinese American.

The Fair Star Inn was on the far-east side of Detroit about a mile from the exclusive Grosse Pointe communities. In the 1940s and 1950s our location was in a middle class white neighborhood in a city of racially segregated neighborhoods. The dwellings were nearly all detached houses. We were about ten miles from Chinatown, so outside of our home and restaurant we would rarely see other Chinese or other minorities. In my elementary school, Stellwagen, we were one of two Chinese families enrolled. With such a low percentage of Chinese in the area little children would stare at us, much to my discomfort. In the outer suburbs of Detroit even adults would stare at us. My ideal was San Francisco Chinatown where I would not stand out.

As a teenager I wanted to fit in with my American friends and be with it. I was not interested in Chinese culture or the rare Chinese teenager fresh off the boat.

The worst decade of my life started in 1953. My sister eloped with a Caucasian man she met as a freshman at Wayne State University. They married after a tumultuous period when my parents tried to dissuade her from marrying this man. To the 1953 Chinese American community, this marriage was a disgrace and a family embarrassment. Within a week, my father died during a heart attack. I was 15 then.

In the following year Mom sent Donnie and me to Chinese school in Chinatown on weekends. Her intent was for us to meet Chinese American girls. It worked; Don met his future wife at Chinese school. We met several other Chinese American teenagers and developed friendships that lasted many years after we left Detroit.

In 1956 I was 18 and a freshman at the University of Michigan when my mother died due to a scarred heart valve from childhood scarlet fever. Within days, Moo had a stroke and went into a coma that lasted for weeks before she died. She and Joann had a special relationship. When Jo entered her hospital room Moo reacted while in her comatose state. I suspended my education and went home to operate the restaurant. Joann returned to Detroit and helped in the restaurant while she raised her family. Linda married and raised a family with four children. Don graduated high school and attended U of M. Later he started a family, earned a PhD in chemistry at the University of Wisconsin, and joined DuPont. After a career in chemistry research he retired as the highest-ranking Asian American executive in the DuPont Corporation.

Resolution of my mother's estate lasted until 1963. She had mortgaged our commercial properties just before her death. We never found out what she did with the money. The mortgages created a Catch-22 like scenario trapping the assets in the estate. Operating the restaurant as a family obligation became a seven-year ordeal. I am only including key events in this description of my worst decade. The details are too painful and I do not have enough space in this essay for them. The overarching issue is that my worst decade put me in the restaurant and in Detroit in 1962. That is where and when I met my wife, Carolyn, the best thing that ever happened to me.

In the many years I was at the restaurant and earlier, I became an observer of the civil rights struggle of the 1950s and 1960s. Detroit has a tradition of racial animosity. With that as a backdrop, I saw the school integration conflicts unfold across the country. African Americans fought to open many doors that Asian Americans could then walk through. As much as I felt the sting of anti-Chinese sentiment, I observed that Chinese are not all without sin. I saw many Chinese in the postwar era who were prejudiced and even bigoted against African Americans. That includes my mother. I do not know about my father. I never heard him say a bigoted statement against African Americans or act in a bigoted way. (Another conversation I wish I had had with him.)

My mother was such a woman of contrasts. She lived at least 60 years before her time. In today's world with the right cultural background, she would be an executive, maybe a CEO. She was so savvy. She knew how to stroke people whether they were customers, employees including African Americans, suppliers, or government officials. She could leave them all with a warm feeling. She had some primitive beliefs. That type of misinformation may have been the source of her prejudice against African Americans. One time when she had a respiratory infection, I saw her rub the edge of a spoon on her chest until it was almost raw. She was hastening the departure of the infection from her body.

In an example of her awareness, Mom challenged the doneness of breaded pork cutlets a cook placed on a plate for serving. My father cut it open and found it was bloody. He said, "So, you knew it was not done." She had observed that when the breaded pork is done it floats on the hot fat of the deep fryer, and this one did not float. Then she said, "If we were still in China, I could not say a word, but we are in America now." At that time all of our cooks were men. She was referring to the subjugated role of women in China.

Living in Fairfax County

When I was a teenager my father worried about the inability of me and my siblings to speak Chinese. He foresaw us needing to rely on the Chinese American community someday, but being unable to talk with it. He could not foresee how our education in America would help us obviate the need for reliance on the Chinese American community. Likewise I saw my children growing up in Fairfax and not learning the lessons of racial prejudice I learned growing up in Detroit. I could not foresee that they would not need those lessons in current day Fairfax County.

I joined the Federal Government in 1974 with JFK's Inaugural Address ringing in my ears. In 1975 we moved to Fairfax County due to a transfer from a job at the IRS Data Center in Detroit to a job at the IRS National Office in Washington, DC. We bought a townhouse in Burke, Virginia where our daughter Mika was born. Although I did not take note of it at the time, the Asian American experience was immediately and vastly different from our Detroit experience. The realtor that helped us find our new home was a Japanese American who had been interned in his boyhood. Our townhouse block consisted of eight contiguous homes with three Asian American families. Next to our home was a Korean construction worker with his family. A US Army officer from Guam with his large family was down the block. This was the highest density of Asian American neighbors we had ever had. In Burke we did not encounter any anti-Asian incidents. Our son, Kenneth, was born in 1977 while we lived there.

We bought a detached single house two miles east of Centreville, Virginia in1979. Our family was the first racial minority homeowner in the community of 26 homes. We were well received, as was an African American family that moved in later. Our children began their education at Centreville

Elementary School. The Centreville student body then straddled a seam between the DC suburbs and rural Virginia to the west. In the early 1980s during President Reagan's first term in office we experienced at least three anti-Asian incidents of angry words directed at us. It was shocking because they were like flashbacks to post World War II Detroit and the time before the civil rights struggles. It is hard to say why those bigots expressed their anti-Asian anger. In each case they were young adult white males. Does each new generation have to learn the lessons of racial equality? Were these youngsters inflamed about the influx of Southeast Asian refugees after the Viet Nam War? Were they rural Virginians who were less worldly than our immediate neighbors?

Our children's school experience was populated with Asian Americans. Although most of their friends were non-Asian, they had some Asian American friends in Fairfax schools, more than I had in Detroit schools. Mika attended the Thomas Jefferson High School for Science and Technology where more than a quarter of the students are Asian American. In my schools I could not dream of having a date with an Asian American girl; there were none. Kenneth invited a Korean American girl to a school dance. The concept of their daughter being out on a date at night was too much for her first generation parents, and they said no. For his senior prom, he coupled with a platonic Caucasian friend. They doubled with a large African American friend who dated a tall willowy blond girl. That did not happen in my Detroit when I was in high school.

After joining the Fairfax County Asian American Project I am aware of the high percentage of Asian Americans in the Fairfax County population, 16%. One in six people in Fairfax County is Asian American. Non-Asians are accustomed to seeing Asian Americans here. They do not stare at us. This is very comforting. I feel more like I am a part of the community. It is not San Francisco Chinatown, but given how good life is here, Fairfax County is the best place for Asian Americans on the East Coast. ##

Terry Sam with Fairfax County Board of Supervisors Certificate of Recognition of June 22, 2009 at Fairfax County Government Center. (Photo by Cora Foley)

Terry Sam, FCAHP Official Photographer, working hard during the April 19, 2008 briefing on Asian immigration history at the Department of Homeland Security Library. (Photo by Cora Foley)

Photo Gallery of Terry and Carolyn Sam
Team Leaders of the Fairfax County Asian American History Project

Top three and left center photos, and recognition certificate – see Terry Sam Chapter. Fish carving by Daisuke Yenari in Rohwer Internment Camp and five bottom photos, including one of Carolyn's parents in the 1930s – see Carolyn Sam Chapter. (Hajime Yenari photo, below fish carving, by Carl Iwasaki; other photos courtesy of the Sam Family)

From 1930 - Filipino American History in Fairfax County
By Corazon Sandoval Foley

Filipino American History Month in Fairfax County. On October 20, 2008, in response to the active historical research work done by FCAAHP, then-Chairman Gerry Connolly proclaimed that for the first time ever, Fairfax County officially recognized the month of October as Filipino American History Month.

The Filipino American National Historical Society (FANHS) had proclaimed October as Filipino American History Month in the year 1988. In California and Hawaii where large numbers of Filipino Americans reside, Filipino American History Month is widely celebrated. This commemoration is also officially recognized by the California Department of Education.

The FANHS resolution reads in part: "Whereas, the Filipino American National Historical Society had declared the year 1988 to be the 225th Anniversary of the Permanent Settlement of Filipinos in the Continental United States and had set into motion its year-long national observance in order to focus on the story of our nation's past from a new perspective by concentrating on the critically economic, cultural, social, and other notable contributions Filipino Americans had made in countless ways toward the development of United States History…and whereas the earliest documented proof of Filipino presence in the Continental United States falls on October 1587…annotating H. R. Wagner's Unamuno's Voyage to California in 1587…"

It took a long time from 1587 in California through 1793 with Filipino settlement in Louisiana; then 1898 with the American acquisition of the Philippines as colonial territory; followed by 1906 immigration of Filipino laborers to Hawaii – before Filipino residents were recorded in 1930 in Fairfax County.

1930 and the first Filipino Residents of Fairfax County. Filipino residents in Fairfax County were first recorded in 1930 and have since grown to total 12,325 in 2007, making them the fifth largest group in the county's Asian population.

The 1930 census report included three Filipino residents in Fairfax County:
- Ramon Rojo, a Filipino soldier and WWI veteran, was stationed in Camp Humphreys (now Fort Belvoir);
- Benjamin Trillanes, a Filipino servant, was working for a private family in Camp Humphreys (now Fort Belvoir);
- Roscoe Manats was serving time in the DC Workhouse or Lorton Prison in Fairfax County.

1898 and Filipino Americans. Research has indicated that Filipinos were in mainland North America since the 1500s as forced labor in Spanish galleons plying the Manila-Acapulco trade. In 1763 Filipinos reportedly established settlements in Louisiana after jumping ship and escaping their Spanish colonial masters.

But significant migrations of Filipinos to the US did not occur until after the 1898 Spanish-American War that resulted in the Philippines becoming a territory of the United States. Large numbers of Filipino workers migrated from the Philippines first to Hawaii in 1906 and later to mainland US, including Fairfax County and the rest of Virginia.

By 1930 some 150,000 Filipinos had migrated to the US, mainly in Hawaii. Some of them – several hundred, possibly a few thousand – were *pensionados* or government sponsored students. The vast majority of the migrants were laborers from poor and uneducated farming families. In the mainland US there were approximately 45,208 Filipinos – with over a hundred in Virginia in 1930 (with three in Fairfax County).

Filipino Residents in Camp Humphreys (now Fort Belvoir) in the 1930s.

Fort Belvoir brick barracks and classroom building built in the late 1920s -- a scene that the 1930 Filipino residents (Ramon Rojo and Benjamin Trillanes) would have seen frequently.

As World War I approached, the army moved its school for the Corps of Engineers from the Washington Barracks (now Fort McNair) to a small site on the peninsula in the Potomac known as Belvoir Neck. The site had been used as a summer training camp by the school since 1915; it later expanded and was named Camp A. A. Humphreys, after a Civil War Engineer officer. In 1917, it was renamed Fort Humphreys and its size was enlarged to cover the entire peninsula (10,000 acres). In 1935, at the request or President Franklin D. Roosevelt, the name was changed to Fort Belvoir, in honor of the manor of Lord Fairfax.

Benjamin Trillanes, Filipino resident of Fort Belvoir in 1930. Many new immigrants, including Irish and other Europeans, started life in the US as domestic servants – and so did many Filipino immigrants. The census recorded a Benjamin Trillanes, a Filipino in Fort Belvoir in 1930 working as a servant for a private family.

Benjamin Trillanes was a 23-year old, male, and single. He was able to read and write English. He was born in the Philippines and both his father and mother were born in the Philippines.

Based on the census record, it appears that Benjamin Trillanes was a servant in the family of Frank Staples who has a wife, Mildred, and a daughter, Helen. Frank Staples was 48 years old in 1930, a veteran and a clerk in the War Department living in Fort Belvoir. His daughter Helen was 20 years old in 1930 and was born in the Philippines. Therefore, Frank Staples and his wife were living in the Philippines in 1910 and he was probably involved in organizing the US military and government structure for America's first colonial experience in the Philippines. It is likely that the Staples family had employed Trillanes in the Philippines as a servant and then took him along with them when Frank Staples was assigned to Fort Belvoir.

Ramon Rojo, Fairfax Filipino American Soldier. Camp Humphreys (now Fort Belvoir) was not the only destination for Filipino soldiers coming to America during the colonial period – as evidenced by the 1904 photo of Filipino soldiers (Philippine Scouts) in the US in 1904. Some came for short visits but others, like Ramon Rojo, served for a long time with the US military and were probably stationed in many other locations in the US and overseas.

According to census records, Ramon Rojo in 1930 was 33 years old, single, and was born in the Philippines. His father was born in Spain while his mother was born in the Philippines. He was able to read and write English. As a soldier in the US Army, he was a veteran of the First World War. Based on that census information, I concluded that Ramon Rojo was a member of the US military by 1917 when he was about 19 or 20 years old, most probably recruited during the early American consolidation of colonial rule in the Philippines.

Photo shows Philippine Scouts marching in the 1904 Louisiana Purchase Exposition in St. Louis, Missouri.

Filipino American Military Service. It was serendipitous to find that the first Filipino resident of Fairfax County was a soldier. Filipino Americans have long served with great distinction and pride in the US military – and the stories of Bataan and Corregidor are milestones in the heroic alliance of Filipinos and Americans during World War II. A member of the Philippine Scouts Jose B. Nisperos was the first US soldier of Asian heritage to be awarded the US Medal of Honor for heroic action on September 24, 1911.

However, many Fairfax County Filipino Americans had become involved very actively in the legislative battle spanning several decades that was aimed at correcting the injustice suffered by Filipino American veterans of World War II. This controversy was finally settled when equity payments for Filipino American veterans were made part of the January 2009 stimulus package to address America's economic crisis.

In 1941 over 200,000 Filipinos were drafted into the US Armed Forces and served honorably during WWII. In what appears to be an act of perfidy, Congress passed the Rescissions Act of 1946 that authorized a $200 million appropriation to the Commonwealth Army of the Philippines conditioned on a provision that service in the Commonwealth Army of the Philippines should not be deemed to have been service in the active military or air service of the United States.

It would take Congress more than four decades to acknowledge that the Filipino WWII veterans had indeed served in the US armed forces. The Immigration Act of 1990 included a provision that offered the opportunity to obtain US citizenship. And 19 years later, the American Recovery and Reinvestment Act (ARRA) of 2009 included a provision that authorized the payment of benefits to the 30,000 surviving Filipino veterans in the amount of $15,000 for those who are citizens and $9,000 for those who are non-citizens.

The 2009 equity payments to Filipino American veterans resulted from many decades of marches, demonstrations, and political lobbying by the Filipino American community. In one bold action, Filipino American WWII veterans, elderly men in their seventies and eighties, marched on Washington, DC in the July 1997 summer heat and chained themselves to the fence surrounding the White House, many proudly dressed in military uniform. They were calling on Congress to end its stalling and give the estimated 70,000 then-living Filipino American WWII veterans the pensions and benefits that every other allied veteran who fought under US command has received.

FCAAHP was privileged to interview a remarkable Filipino American veteran Alberto Bacani of Alexandria, Virginia who was 98 years old on April 8, 2009 when he received one of the first equity compensation payments for his US military "active service" during the Second World War.

Fighting for Civil Rights in Fairfax County. The fight for equity for Filipino American veterans underscores the Filipino American community's long involvement in working for civil rights in the American society. And in Fairfax County, this civic activism is personified by the story of the family of Cecilia Suyat Marshall-- widow of late Justice Thurgood Marshall -- that is included in this book.

Some historical footnotes may be useful to provide context for the civil rights struggle in Fairfax County. There were local units of the Ku Klux Klan in Fairfax County in 1868. The high tide of the Klan in Northern Virginia came in the aftermath of World War I. That was the period when town commercial interests and newcomers who worked in Washington, DC challenged groups whose political and economic influence was based on their farmland. Although membership in the Klan was secret, local units used public events to show off their numbers. There were periods of massive resistance in Fairfax County to integration of black and white schools and to the Civil Rights Movement.

Nevertheless, minorities continued to make progress in voting and ending discrimination in housing, public facilities, and employment. The 1964-1965 school year was the first year that the public school system was fully racially integrated, following the 1954 US Supreme Court decision (Thurgood Marshall's great civil rights victory) that declared segregated public schools unconstitutional. The Fairfax County branch of the NAACP was the first rural affiliate when it was established in 1915.

As Cecilia Suyat Marshall remembered, her family was invited in 1968 by then-Attorney General Ramsey Clark, a friend of late Justice Thurgood Marshall, to "come and integrate the county." Her memories did not include racial harassment and discrimination in Fairfax County. Her neighbors were very welcoming and in 1999, when the Lake Barcroft Foundation was established, it included the Thurgood Marshall Scholarship Fund. A road near her home was also renamed in honor of Justice Marshall.

Of course, the Marshalls could have been arrested if they had moved to Fairfax County or any other place in Virginia earlier than June 12, 1967. Before that date, state governments, notably Virginia, were able to deny marriage licenses to interracial couples and punish them with fines, imprisonment, and hard labor if they got married in more progressive areas of the country, like the District of Columbia. Richard and Mildred Loving were dragged out of bed by Virginia state police and arrested for being married outside of their race in DC. When the Supreme Court ruled in their favor in *Loving*

v. Virginia on June 12, 1967, interracial relationships were legalized nationwide. And without the Supreme Court decision in *Loving v. Virginia,* the Foley family would probably not have been able to live in Burke, Virginia – and I would not have been able to sit in my Fairfax County home to write this pioneering book on the Fairfax County Asian American History Project.

<u>Post-1965 Immigration Reform and Filipino Americans.</u> After the 1965 immigration reform, many Filipino American professionals in the health care field came to the US and Fairfax County. Among them is Epifania Edralin Legaspi Balintona de la Cuesta – a pharmacist who arrived on December 28, 1968. She worked at the DC General Hospital and US Department of Health and Human Services from October 1969 and retired in 1991 after her husband, Agustin de la Cuesta, died in 1987. Eppie moved in October 1995 to the Burke Lake Gardens Apartments beside Nativity Catholic Church where in 2010 she has served in the choir and as a Eucharistic Minister.

Eppie de la Cuesta shared two photos with her doing pharmacy work in 1983, and in 2009 with her family.

<u>In Fairfax County, Filipino American Stories of Patriotism and Civil Rights.</u> As part of the Fairfax County Asian American History Project, we are sharing stories of Alberto Bacani, 98 years old in 2009 when he received US equity compensation payment as a WWII US veteran; and of Cecilia Suyat Marshall, a second-generation Filipino American born in Hawaii and widow of legendary civil rights pioneer, the first African American Supreme Court Justice Thurgood Marshall. Also included is the story of Pacita Aguas, who helped me interview Alberto Bacani.

Alberto Bacani – Filipino American World War II Veteran
By Corazon Sandoval Foley

On August 10, 2007, Alberto Bacani (then 96 years old) and his wife Nina (then 94 years old) very graciously participated in one of the earliest oral history interviews that I conducted for both the Filipino American National Historical Society of Northern Virginia and the Fairfax County Asian American History Project. I was accompanied by Pacita Aguas and Flora Golayan, who are both longtime Fairfax County Filipino American residents very active in Catholic Church programs. Flora Golayan was a former student of Nina Bacani in Isabela province in the Philippines. The Bacanis were very kind in sharing stories, photos, and a family book to assist me in the history project.

Left to Right: Alberto Bacani in the center between Pacita Aguas and Flora Golayan ; two paintings depicting the life story of Alberto and Nina Bacani; Pacita Aguas and Flora Golayan standing at table where Nina and Bert Bacani are seated during FCAAHP interview in 2007.
(Photos by Cora Foley)

The photo collage underscores the Bacani family's commitment to family and country with Bert's service in the military and Nina's contributions to the church and community. Alberto Bacani has long been honored as a hero in the Filipino American community in the Metropolitan Washington DC area. On March 18, 2007, 96-year old military veteran, Alberto Bacani, received an outstanding ovation from some 200 people as he received the 2007 *Dakila* Achievement Award for Education. Named after the Filipino word for 'greatness' the *Dakila* Award reflects the awardees' outstanding contributions to the Filipino American community and to the mainstream American community.

In 2009, 98 year-old Alberto Bacani was one of the first Filipino American WWII veterans to receive the equity compensation payment of $15,000 from General (retired) Antonio Taguba, the second Filipino American General and 2007 Outstanding American By Choice Award recipient -- whose story is included in this book's chapter on patriotism and Fairfax County Asian American soldiers.

Memories of WWII Valor and Suffering in the Philippines. Alberto Bacani shared with FCAAHP his story as a soldier fighting for the US Government against the Japanese during WWII in the Philippines:

December 22, 1941. In the field (at Palattao, Naguilian, Isabela), Alberto Bacani was inducted into the USAFFE by Lt. Col. Glen R. Townsend, CO, 12th Infantry Regiment, 11th Division, covering the Cagayan Valley (Northeastern Luzon). The Colonel immediately designated him S-2 (Intelligence) Officer of the Regiment, hurriedly instructed him on his duties, put him in charge of the HQ Office and its staff of 20 men, including officers.

His Office HQ became the enemy's target. His group was continuously on the alert; always ready to move the Command Post anytime, anywhere, by day and by night, mostly by night, southward, in the direction of Bataan.

Christmas Day 1941. At breakfast time, his HQ at Pallatao was heavily raided by Japanese planes based at Tuguegarao, Cagayan Province.

December 31, 1941 and New Year's Day 1942. Bacani's group reached Mexico and Arayat (Pampanga) and established the Command Post near Mt. Arayat. Air raids became frequent, with the enemy cutting deeper into their position. Frequent changes were taking place in the group's upper command.

By the end of January 8 - 12, 1942, the 12th Infantry Regiment was no longer operating as a unified body, but broken into splinter groups. Dawn on January 12, 1942, a composite group of the regiment (about 50 more or less) were deployed in a defensive position along Layac Creek (at Km 95) on the Highway between Pampanga and Bataan. Alberto Bacani was in that group.

A brief lull gave the enemy the chance to penetrate their position, and then completely surrounded them. There were three times the number of men in Bacani's group; they were armed with bayoneted rifles, and some of them with machine guns and auto-rifles.

Bacani's group ran out of ammunition. They were greatly outnumbered and outflanked. They had to surrender – 52 of them with 12 officers. They were now Prisoners of War. The enemy disarmed them, ordered them to keep their hands clasped at the back of their necks, and to stay where they were. Eight in the morning of that day, they were all herded to one side of the highway (Km 95), hogtied at their backs, some three or four together – ordered to squat on the shoulder of the roads the whole day under the scorching heat of the sun, with 2 fully loaded machine guns mounted 30 feet in front of the group, guarded by a squad of heavily armed Japanese soldiers.

Next: their captors relieved them of everything they had with them – valuables as well as non-valuables, even their shoes. Those who resisted seizure of items on their body were kicked, slapped or pushed hard so as to fall.

When Bacani's time came, the confiscating soldier got almost everything – his wedding ring, his watch, coins, etc. He was about to leave Bacani when he noticed the left pocket of his khaki shirt bulging with a few 10-centavo coins and a small black rosary that his mother gave him many, many years ago. He took the coins and squeezed the rosary back into Bacani's pocket. (Note: As of 2007, Alberto Bacani still has the rosary with him, although the beads are falling apart.)

At 5pm on January 12, 1942, Bacani's group was moved to their garrison at the San Fernando (Pampanga) Hospital; they had not eaten the whole day. At the garrison, they were given one or two pieces each of hard Japanese biscuits; and they passed the night under heavy guard.

The next 3 to 5 days, they were subjected to rigid questioning and intensive investigation, the main focus of which was on their jobs: what they did before the war; what their military background was; why and how they got into the army.

On the basis of the investigators' findings, that not one of them was a professional soldier, that they were teachers, farmers, students, or plain citizens recruited for the army, they were all released at 6:30 p.m. on the 6th day following their captivity. They were given clearances and "passes" to "go directly home." Bacani's group broke up, went their ways in different directions; hiked all the way through, everyday, crossing acres and acres of farms and rice fields, avoiding the highways and principal roads...with occasional periods of brief rest for food and sleep.

From the day they were released, Bacani began having some awfully bad feeling...tired, chilly, feverish at times...yet he had to keep going on and on with the rest. He did not want to be left behind; but no matter how hard he tried to conceal his condition, he knew and his companions knew that he was sick -- so very sick because he was running a fever and suffered chills.

After five days of continuous hiking, Bacani's group of 10 reached a small barrio 2 miles south of San Jose (Nueva Ecija) called Camanacsacan...just as the sun was about to set. Here, Lt. Jorge Cancio (a co-officer of Bacani) and Bacani advised the group to pass the night in the barrio – clearly 120 miles from where they started in San Fernando, Pampanga. It was at the home of a very simple, gentle, and kind-hearted family of rice farmers – Bernardino Llena, his wife Catalina Castillo, and their four children. The group stayed for at least two more days.

Bacani's companions left him behind; and he stayed in the farming community with the Llenas, a total stranger, sick and haggard looking, with almost nothing except his soiled clothes. For Alberto Bacani, this was the most pathetic and trying moment of his life –because his wife Nina and his family did not know at all where he was nor that he was very ill and fighting hard for his life against disease.

The Llenas had a very sick person at the brink of death in Alberto Bacani. And they generously took him in, fed him, and gave him the best care they could give – because of his weakness and helplessness, they lifted and carried him in their arms from his sickbed to bathe him with warm water.

Alberto Bacani noted that: "In all my life, I have never met a family like this one -- the Llenas, so kind, so simple, so humble, and so compassionate. One thing I shall never forget: I owe them my second life."

Bacani was on sickbed, totally helpless, for three-and-a-half months (from 17 January 1942 to about the end of April). At the height of his illness, he was practically reduced to bones covered with skin, with a minimum of flesh. With the kind of care given him by the Llenas, with all the necessary precautions he had to undergo, such as light daily exercises plus prayer, it took him the whole month of May to recover.

Leaving Camanacsacan (barrio of San Jose, Nueva Ecija) on June 1, 1942, and hiking all the way to Isabela (a distance of approximately 200 miles), with a lone traveling companion (a young man from Aritao, Nueva Vizcaya), on the road by day, walking through unpaved roads and mountain trails, sleeping anywhere by night, with a minimum of "carretela" and banca rides, Bacani reached home (in Cabagan) at exactly ten o'clock on the evening of June 18, 1942 – the biggest surprise to his family.

Alberto Bacani's wife Nina concluded that "When Bert was captured early in January 1942 before reaching Bataan, the Lord meant to save him from the horror that was to come -- the "Death March" where 76,000 POWs (among them 12,000 Americans) were in the long line and 10,000 died during that fateful march. More succumbed while in camp. Were he in the "Death March," Bert would have been a goner."

The Bacanis shared the hardships of the war years, including escapes from Japanese soldiers. Bert Bacani then shared memories about war's end in the Philippines: "By December 3, 1945, I was at Army HQ in Camp Murphy for processing before I could be discharged, then go back to my old job of teaching. With my discharge on December 12, 1945, I joined the ranks of the "Honorable USAFFE Veterans of World War II." Five days later, I was back in the classroom, this time no longer facing guns and enemy soldiers, but in front of bright and sweet-smiling faces of young men and women. What a change, and what a relief!"

Alberto Bacani receiving one of the first compensation equity payments for US military "active service" in WWII.
(Photo from US Veterans Affairs)

It must be noted however, that Alberto Bacani's World War II battles continued through early 2009 as a Filipino American resident of Alexandria, Virginia. He played a leadership role in winning the battle for recognition of the honorable US military service by Filipino veterans of WWII denied them by the Rescission Act of 1946 – with its provision that service in the Commonwealth Army of the Philippines should not be deemed to have been service in the active military or air service of the United States.

Celebrating 70 Years of Marriage. During our FCAAHP interview, Alberto and Nina Bacani shared with me the June 7, 2007 *Arlington Catholic Herald* interview entitled "Filipino American Couple in Northern Virginia Celebrates 70 Years of Marriage" that celebrated the commitment by Alberto and Nina Bacani to faith and family.

"In gratitude for their 70 years in matrimony, Alberto and Nina Bacani, of Alexandria, gathered with family and friends to renew their marriage vows. The Mass at St. Rita Church was concelebrated by Father Denis Donahue, pastor of St. Rita, and Filipino American Father Art Mallari, who was recently ordained for the Diocese of Rockford, Illinois.

"Married on May 26, 1937, Alberto and Nina, ages 96 and 94, respectively, expressed profound joy as they surveyed their children and spouses as well as their "additional olive shoots around their table" (Psalm 128) – 15 grandchildren and 21 great-grandchildren – and many family friends who traveled for the Memorial Day weekend event.

Alberto and Nina Bacani celebrating their 70th wedding anniversary in May 2007 (Courtesy of the Bacani family)

"The necessity of building a marriage on one's faith is paramount," said Alberto, a World War II veteran, when asked about success in marriage. Without their faith, enduring World War II, the loss of two of their children to cancer, and a stroke with its 20 years of debilitating effects would have been impossible, the Bacanis said. "The issues may change, but one thing never does: when the going gets tough, the tough pray," he said.

"As they recounted their years together since their first meeting in the Philippines, Nina smiled as she talked about their first encounter. "I'm sure my husband doesn't even know this story, but four months before Bert and I met, I asked St. Anthony to send a good husband into my life if it was God's will that I be married," Nina said. "Four months later, Bert arrived as a boarder in my parents' home."

"Both Bert and Nina agreed they have "been blessed with a wonderful family and the most supportive of friends." The Bacanis are parishioners of St. Rita Parish with their daughters Lyda Miranda and Mimi Cabagnot and families. Granddaughter Marla Mooney and family are parishioners of St. William of York Parish in Stafford. Granddaughter Teresina Thomton and family are parishioners of Holy Trinity Parish in Bristow. Granddaughter Karen Avis and family are parishioners of St. Raymond of Peñafort Parish in Springfield in Fairfax County, Virginia."

Another Filipino American Renewal of Wedding Vows: Pacita and Doroteo Aguas

Pacita Aguas assisted me in the oral history interview of Alberto and Nina Bacani. She and her husband Doroteo also renewed their wedding vows on the fortieth year of their marriage that they celebrated in Fairfax County – their home since 1986.

Pacita Aguas was one of the first Filipino Americans to participate in an FCAHP oral history interview, perhaps because she knew my father when they were professional colleagues in the Philippines. They were part of the first group of officials of the Philippine Central Bank in 1949 when it was established as an agency of the Republic of the Philippines that became independent on July 4, 1946.

In Fairfax County, Pacita Aguas has been a longtime respected leader in the Filipino American Catholic ministry. She has been vice president of the Legion of Mary in the Nativity Catholic Church located beside her home in Burke Lake Gardens Apartments.

Pacita Aguas has lived with two other Filipino American friends in the apartment complex – Corazon Alvano and Eppie dela Cuesta. The story of Eppie, a pharmacist, is in the overview on Filipino Americans. The three Filipino American ladies in their 80s made their housing decision based on their commitment to serve more actively in the Catholic Church mission through the Nativity parish.

Courtesy of Pacita Aguas, the attached photos were taken on December 3, 1989 when Pacita and her husband Doroteo Aguas celebrated their 40th wedding anniversary by renewing their marriage vows in St. Mary's Church, the oldest Catholic Church in Fairfax County. That church was built in 1858 to serve Irish Catholics who came to work on the railroads. Standing at the right side in the back of the bottom photo is their grandson Charles dela Cuesta who in 2009 has been a teacher at Thomas Jefferson High School and is featured in the section on Education in this book.

The Aguas history in Fairfax County began when their daughter moved to the US in 1970 to join the World Bank. Her siblings later followed. And in 1986, Pacita and Doroteo Aguas moved from the Philippines to Fairfax County, Virginia. Doroteo died in 1996 at the age of 82 and was buried in Fairfax Memorial Park in Braddock Road.

During her first ten years in Fairfax County, Pacita Aguas worked for the Girls Scouts of America. She retired when her husband fell ill with cancer. After his death, she has devoted her life to Catholic Church activities, including daily mass at Nativity Church, and leadership in programs of the Filipino Ministry of Northern Virginia.

Over several years, she has organized *"Simbang Gabi"* (Christmas Evening Masses) in Nativity Church, followed by receptions with Filipino food donated by many of Pacita's friends in the community.

Pacita Aguas has also been actively engaged in physical fitness activities with members of the Lorton senior center. She has worked with me in organizing the innovative public-private partnership called the Burke/Springfield Senior Center Without Walls to develop wellness programs for the growing numbers of seniors in the county. An estimated 9% of Fairfax County residents in 2009 were senior citizens (65 years and over).

Photos below were taken by me, Cora Foley, showing the daily life in Fairfax County for Pacita Aguas and her Filipino American friends – visiting and comforting sick patients in Burke Health Care, enjoying Filipino food in gatherings with friends, exercising at Lorton Senior Center, and playing bingo at a luncheon in Nativity Catholic Church.

In addition to Pacita Aguas, many Filipino Americans assisted me in the research for this project, including: Wilna Ray, a diplomatic official with the US Department of State; Rolly and Tessie Saldana, a couple very active in the Fairfax County Filipino Catholic Ministry and the leaders of the Monthly Filipino Mass at St. Bernadette's Church in Springfield in Fairfax County; Bing and Nanette Crisologo; Cora Alvano, Cora Arca, Julieta Fuster, Flora Golayan, and Eppie De la Cuesta.

Cecilia Suyat Marshall: Filipino American Civil Rights Champion
By Corazon Sandoval Foley

Cecilia Suyat Marshall and Justice Thurgood Marshall in 1967 when he first took his seat in the Supreme Court. (Supreme Court of the U.S.)

1968 was a milestone in Filipino American arrivals in Fairfax County when Lake Barcroft in Mason District became home for Mrs. Cecilia Suyat Marshall, a second generation Filipino American born in Hawaii and wife of the late Supreme Court Justice Thurgood Marshall. Her oral history interview was made on September 26, 2005 with Naomi Sokol Zeavin of the Fairfax County History Commission.

Cecilia Suyat Marshall told Naomi Zeavin that she, her husband and two sons moved to Fairfax County because then-Attorney General Ramsey Clark – a dear friend of Justice Marshall – invited them to "come integrate the community."

Fairfax County in 1970 had 445,000 residents with racial and ethnic minorities comprising 6.8% of the population (much smaller than current estimates of over 40% by 2010).

Cecilia Suyat Marshall said that she found Lake Barcroft in Fairfax County to be beautiful and that her family was right at home with neighbors who welcomed them with open arms and parties. The Marshalls bought a home and became members of the community. Mrs. Marshall said that there were never any problems of integration for them or their two sons during their life in Fairfax County. She said that "she has had a wonderful life living here in Mason District and her neighbors are just like family."

In 1993, the portion of Columbia Pike from Little River Turnpike down to the Arlington County line was named the Thurgood Marshall Memorial Parkway by then supervisor Tina Trappnel. There is also an ongoing Thurgood Marshall scholarship at JEB Stuart High School. Justice Thurgood Marshall lived from July 2, 1908 – January 24, 1993.

As for her early life, Cecilia Suyat Marshall said that both her parents were born in the Philippines while she was born and raised in Hawaii. She described her life in Hawaii as one without prejudice where all types of people integrated well. Her father had his own printing company. Her mother died when she was young and having many siblings, she felt she should go and take care of herself.

Her father then encouraged her to go to New York in her early twenties and she went to work for the NAACP. Her first job there was to picket the movie theater where "Birth of a Nation" was being shown. She said it did stop showing shortly after their protest.

She worked her way up from stenography pool to the private secretary of the head of the NAACP organization, Dr. Gloster B. Current from 1948-55. This was an important position due to the fact that he was head of 1,500 NAACP groups throughout the USA. She did much traveling in her position. Their main job was to promote racial integration of schools, education and stores. At that time, they had to stay in Black hotels only and all conventions and meetings had to be held in Black churches.

Cecilia Suyat Marshall and her family
(Library of Congress collection)

She met and on December 1955, she married Thurgood Marshall who at that time was chief counsel for the National Association for the Advancement of Colored People (from 1938-1961). They lived in New York for a while and one of their overnight visitors was a special guest Rosa Parks, as she could not stay in a hotel due to being black.

They were living in New York when Thurgood Marshall was appointed to the U.S. Court of Appeals, second circuit by President John F. Kennedy. In 1965 President Lyndon B. Johnson appointed him Solicitor General of the United States. And later in 1967, he was appointed by President Johnson to be the first Negro to serve as an Associate Justice of the Supreme Court of the United States. Mrs. Marshall said Thurgood Marshall preferred to be called Negro.

As for the early years while living in Washington in the early 1950s and 1960s, Cecilia Marshall remembered that you could not try on dresses or any clothing items in the department stores such as Woodies and Garfinkels. If they did not fit, you could not bring any items back. All the bathrooms were one for blacks and one for whites. The dining rooms and soda counters were not open to blacks. And getting water sometimes was impossible in terms of getting to a black store for a drink. Union Station was the only place for African Americans to eat at that time. In his younger years, Thurgood Marshall could not get in the University of Maryland Law School due to his color. Years later he made it his business to sue the University of Maryland and won.

Cecilia Marshall has been a warm, nurturing and very proud mother to the two Marshall sons. John William Marshall was a Virginia state trooper. He served as the United States Marshall for the Eastern District of Virginia and as Director of the United States Marshalls Service. He also served as Secretary of Public Safety for Governor Mark Warner and Governor Tim Kaine of the state of Virginia.

John Marshall, Virginia Secretary of Public Safety (2002-2009)

Meanwhile, the eldest Thurgood Marshall Jr. while in high school, summer interned for Senator Carl Albert of Oklahoma. During college years, he worked for 14 years for Al Gore when he was Senator, then as his legislative liaison to Congress when he was Vice President. After graduating from University of Virginia Law School, President Clinton appointed him as assistant to the President and secretary to the cabinet. Thurgood Jr. went to prep school at Phillips Exeter Academy in New Hampshire.

Cecilia Suyat Marshall shared with Naomi Zeavin her great pride in her husband's record. To her, he was a person down to earth, very friendly and would listen to all views with an open mind. A very humble man, he felt the "real heroes were the people he represented." He could take off and go home after a case and they were left to face the music. His mentor was Charles H. Houston. She is extremely proud of her husband's victory in winning the *Brown vs. Board of Education* case. This ended segregation not only in schools but also in restaurants and hotels.

Naomi Zeavin and Cecilia Marshall in November 2006

Naomi Zeavin sponsored a follow-up reception celebrating African American Heritage on November 13, 2006 at historic Clark House – a 1902 Victorian farmhouse in Fairfax County. Mrs. Cecilia "Sissy" Suyat Marshall shared with the participants her belief in the importance of "preserving our history not for our generation but for the younger generation... to keep reminding them and telling them the history of where we came from...it was not very easy."

I should note that I first met Cecilia Suyat Marshall at a memorial service in the US Peace Corps building for my friend and her nephew, Stanley Suyat (shown in photo), one of the leaders of the Asian American interagency community in the federal government. Many of us in the community still remember his generous contributions to civil rights and the Asian American community with leadership awards that have been named after him in order to keep his memory and legacy alive.

Stanley D. Suyat served as the Director of Civil Rights for the Energy Department from December 1997 until his death in July 1999. He previously served as Associate Director for Management of the United States Peace Corps where he had worldwide responsibility for the Agency's management support functions. Stan Suyat was very proud of his service as a Peace Corps Volunteer in the Republic of the Philippines.

Stanley Suyat (Courtesy of Cora Foley)

Historical footnote on the Marshall family's Lake Barcroft neighborhood .

The Lake Barcroft community was named in memory of Doctor John W. Barcroft who built his home and operated a mill in 1849. Lake Barcroft was created in 1915 by placing a dam across Holmes Run at the Old Bacroft Mill and Columbia Pike near Bailey's Crossroads to provide a reservoir for the Alexandria Water Company.

In the 1940s, the reservoir became too small to serve Alexandria. In 1950, the reservoir and its surrounding land were put up for sale; a partnership of developers from Boston bought the lake and 680 acres of land for about one million dollars. They created a community of miniature country estates around the lake. Over a few short years, the number of families living in Lake Barcroft increased from 368 in 1956 to 650 in 1958 and 783 in 1960. Eventually, the Lake Barcroft community grew to over 1,000 families.

Lake Barcroft Estates was one of the first major real estate developments in Fairfax County. The community achieved upscale status in the beginning of the 1960s. Notable politicians became residents, including President Kennedy's press secretary Pierre Salinger, Congressman Wayne Hays, Melvin Price and Charlie Bennett – and former Attorney General Ramsey Clark, the friend who invited the family of late Justice Thurgood Marshall to move and "integrate" Lake Barcroft and Fairfax County. ##

From 1930 - Japanese American History in Fairfax County
By Corazon Sandoval Foley

My own understanding of the Japanese American experience was deepened when I worked as a Congressional Fellow in 1992 with then-Congressman Norman Mineta and became the office's lead staff officer in the successful passage of the legislation establishing in the nation's capital the Memorial to Japanese American Patriotism in WWII. I worked with Senator Inouye's legislative staff officer Marie Blanco, a Filipino American and longtime Fairfax County resident, and Kaz Oshiki of the Go For Broke Japanese American veterans' association in that successful project.

My work was also greatly aided by Kennon Nakamura, a third generation Japanese American Fairfax County resident, who was a senior legislative staff officer for then-Congressman William Broomfield. Ken's parents were forcibly relocated to the World War II internment camps for Japanese Americans; after WWII, they rebuilt their lives with great dignity in Seabrook, New Jersey. The stories of Ken's family and the patriotism of Japanese American soldiers in WWII are included in this chapter.

I worked in 1992 with Marie Blanco of Senator Inouye's office (top photo) and Kaz Oshiki to achieve successful passage of legislation for the Memorial to Japanese American Patriotism.
(Courtesy of Cora Foley)

1930 and Japanese Residents in Fairfax County. From two Japanese residents in 1930, the Fairfax County Japanese Americans totaled some 2,210 in 2007. In 1930, the Census recorded two Japanese American residents in Fairfax County who were servants for a private family living in Providence District – but details were rather skimpy:

- K. Ito was 35 years old, male, single, working as a butler for a private family. He was born in Japan and both of his parents were also born in Japan. K. Ito entered the US in 1916 when he was 21 years old. He was able to speak and write English, as well as speak Japanese. He was not a veteran.

- Sam Waka 30 years old, male, single, working as a cook for a private family. He was born in Japan and both his parents were born in Japan. Sam Waka was able to speak and write English, as well as speak Japanese. He entered the US in 1907 when he was about seven years old. He was not a veteran.

Asian Pacific American Heritage Month celebrations are held in May in part to commemorate the first recorded immigration on May 7, 1843 of a Japanese national to the United States. Large Japanese immigration began in 1868 when the Hawaiian consul general in Japan transported 148 Japanese contract laborers. In 1884, the Japanese government permitted Hawaiian planters to recruit contract laborers. By 1900, the Japanese population had reached 138, 834 concentrated mainly in the Pacific Coast states, especially in California, where 42% of total continental population lived in 1900 and 70% some thirty years later. By 1930, the Japanese were almost evenly divided between *Issei,* or first generation, and *Nisei,* second generation. Some 40% of Japanese migrants had made America their permanent home, and together with their children, they were ushering the Japanese American community into the era of settlement.

The Internment of Japanese Americans in World War II. On February 19, 1942, President Franklin D. Roosevelt issued Executive Order 9066 that targeted Japanese Americans for special persecution and deprived them of their rights of due process and equal protection of the law. They were relocated into internment camps with some 2/3 of the 120,000 internees who were American citizens by birth.

Some 30,000 Japanese Americans served in the US Army during WWII, with 13,000 in the segregated 442nd *Nisei* Regimental Combat Team – the most highly decorated unit in US military history for its size and length of service.

When WWII ended, about 45,000 Japanese Americans were still interned. Many were unsure where to go, their homes and livelihoods lost and their communities poisoned by neighbors who had turned against them. Some followed relatives to the East Coast.

On July 9, 2009, Robert Nakamoto, longtime Fairfax County resident and President of the Japanese American Veterans' Association (front row third from right), joined other JAVA officials (Terry Shima and Dr. Ray Murakami) in the briefing of visiting Japanese military officials on the Japanese American experience during WWII at the National Memorial to Japanese American Patriotism in Washington, D.C. (Courtesy of Terry Shima)

Did any Japanese American move to Fairfax straight from Internment Camps? Our FCAAHP research indicated that at least one family of Japanese American internees moved to Fairfax County straight from the camps – and ended up building the gardens of what is now Clemyjontri park. The park was the former estate home of the family of Mortimer Lebowitz, a civil rights pioneer in Fairfax County.

An E-Mail about the Ishiyamas. On August 21, 2008, I received the following letter from a longtime Fairfax County resident Ms. Claudia Chaille:

"These are early childhood memories of mine and I have not researched the spelling of the names. My parents bought the Rare Plant Gardens nursery in Vienna (near Oakton on Rt. 123). My father moved to Vienna after he got out of the Navy in World War II.

"He built a small house on the property for a Japanese family. The Ishiyamas moved there about 1947 and lived there until they moved to McLean about 1950. During the War they had been interned in a camp.

"Nonkie T. Ishiyama, his wife and two daughters, Hiroko and Kyoko, moved in to the small cottage. Mr. Ishiyama was a gardener who built magnificent gardens and taught my father much about gardening and plants. Although my father worked at the Department of State all of his career, he and my mother also ran the nursery with Mr. Ishiyama's help in the early days. The nursery became Vienna Gardens.

"Mrs. Ishiyama helped to take care of my sister who was born in 1949. About 1950, the Lebowitz family in McLean offered to house the family at their estate. They loaned them land so that they could open their own nursery on the property. The property is now a park near the Kennedy estate. Our gardens that Mr. Ishiyama built were destroyed when Gulick houses were built there. I imagine that some of Mr. Ishiyama's gardens still exist in the McLean area. He was truly a genius when it came to knowing and loving plants.

"Memories of the Ishiyamas: (They moved when I was about six, but my father quoted him often.) My father told me that he did not like fall because the leaves were dead. Also, he did not like bonsai because he felt that the trees were being crippled. He did not believe in building fences around yards. He said that you open sight lines so that it looks like all of the land that you see is yours."

Ms. Chaille later wrote me that Mr. Ishiyama may well have built the gardens of the Lebowitz estate home – the 18-acre property was donated in March 2000 to Fairfax County by Mrs. Adele Lebowitz to become the Clemyjontri Park in McLean, Virginia – not far from the Hickory Hill, the former estate home of Robert Kennedy and his family. The Lebowitz family lived in the 13-room home since 1947 and the park's name of CLEMYJONTRI is derived from the first names of the four Lebowitz children: Carolyn (CL), Emily (EMY), John (Jon), and Petrina (Tri).

Adele Lebowitz is the widow of Mortimer C. Lebowitz who used part of his first name for the Morton's department store chain he founded in the Washington area in 1933. The stores closed in 1993 but Lebowitz is still remembered by many longtime area residents as a civic leader who championed racial justice. In the 1930s and 40s, two decades before the civil rights movement, the specter of segregation was very much a part of the Washington landscape. However, Mr. Lebowitz refused to conform to the racial practices of the day and was one of the first to fully integrate his stores for customers and staff alike. A very modest man, he was driven by a sense of fair play and justice. He joined the NAACP in 1942 and the Urban League in 1952, for which he served as President. As a civic leader, Mr. Lebowitz worked untiringly to improve the economic standard of the citizens of Washington DC until his death in 1997.

Adele Lebowitz, through Clemyjontri Park on which the Ishiyamas worked, has taken up the cause of accessibility for disabled children, saying "there should be a way that handicapped children should be able to feel less handicapped." She donated property that was worth as much as $30 million, depending on the zoning.

Sumiko Biderman.   I also heard about Sumiko Biderman, a longtime Japanese American activist in the Fairfax County Democratic Party, as a possible interviewee for FCAAHP.   But I was too late, for Sumiko Biderman, 84, died on March 2, 2009.

In 1958, she and her husband, social scientist Albert Biderman, moved to Falls Church and in 1965 to McLean where she began her long involvement with the local Democratic Party.

She was born Sumiko Fuji in Hayward, California where she was valedictorian of her 1942 high school class. Her family was interned at the Topaz relocation center in Utah.

Sumiko Biderman (Courtesy of her family)

FCAAHP research showed that there were other Japanese Americans who were interned in WWII and then chose to become residents of Fairfax County. William Marumoto moved to Fairfax in 1977; his family spent three years in a relocation camp in Gila River, Arizona. Robert Nakamoto, whose story is in this chapter and in the chapter on Asian American businessmen, was ten when he was sent for three years in an internment camp. And Nori Nakamura was born in an internment camp in Tule Lake, California.

As I collected stories about other Japanese Americans, it is clear that the Ishiyamas were followed as Fairfax County residents by other Japanese Americans who were either incarcerated themselves or whose parents were in the camp. But like Sumiko Biderman, they did not come to Fairfax County straight from the camps. Some of their stories are included in several sections of this book.

It is also important to note the Civil Liberties Act of 1988. The Act signed by President Ronald Reagan mandated a historic national apology and reparations to Japanese Americans unjustly interned by the US government during World War II.

Declining Japanese immigration to the US. After 1965, the second wave of Asian immigration has included proportionately fewer Japanese. Only about 4,000 have been coming annually, far below the 20,000 quota allotted to Japan. Between 1965 and 1984, only 93,646 Japanese entered the US representing a mere 3% of all Asian immigrants. Their numbers have been declining; in the first half of the 1980s, Japanese immigrants dropped to only 1.7% of the total immigration from Asia.

Without an influx of new immigrants from Japan, Japanese Americans have become predominantly a native-born population; in 1980, 72% were citizens by birth. Japanese Americans are largely English-speaking; very few *Sansei* and *Yonsei* (3rd and 4th generation) know any Japanese.

Many Japanese Americans like the Nakamura family and Yukiko Orlandella (shown in photo) share their heritage with their neighbors in Fairfax County by promoting classical dance, music, and other traditions.

In Fairfax County, Japanese American Stories of Patriotism and Civic Pride.

As part of the Fairfax County Asian American History Project, we are sharing with you four Japanese American stories. Grant Ichikawa shared his story of patriotic military service in World War II and the Korean War, CIA service in Asia -- and community service in Fairfax County. Carolyn Sam of Springfield District, a third generation Japanese American and wife of Fairfax County Chinese American Terry Sam, narrated her biography and the story of her uncle, American hero Ben Kuroki of World War II. Kennon Nakamura, a third generation Japanese American learned lessons from his parents who rebuilt their lives after being detained in an internment camp in Arkansas. Ken shared his family's life in Fairfax County, particularly their involvement in the founding of Ekoji Buddhist Temple and celebrating their heritage with neighbors. FCAAHP is grateful for the support of Robert Nakamoto, President of the Japanese American Veterans' Association (JAVA), who very kindly shared the story of the contributions of his family to the prosperity of Fairfax County, Virginia.

Yukiko Orlandella teaches classical Japanese dancing to share the culture in Fairfax County. (Courtesy of Yukiko Orlandella)

Grant Ichikawa:
Patriotic Service in WWII, Korean War, Vietnam – and Fairfax County
By Corazon Sandoval Foley

The Japanese American Veterans' Association (JAVA) very kindly agreed to share the 2003 interview of Grant Ichikawa for inclusion in the FCAAHP book. Grant Ichikawa was born in 1919 in Suisun, California, near San Francisco. He served in the Army for two tours of duty: first, 4.5 years during WWII in Military Intelligence Service; second, 2.5 years during the Korean War. He was discharged as a First Lieutenant. As exciting as his military tours of duty were, they were precursors to his challenges as a professional civilian in the Central Intelligence Agency. Grant also talked of his community service in his home in Fairfax County after he retired from the CIA in 1975 soon after being evacuated from Vietnam.

Grant Ichikawa described how the family became Fairfax County residents: "My son Bryan kept on asking me "Where is my home?" So we decided we had better go back to the States and put down some roots for the family. We bought this house (in Vienna) in 1961, this house was one-year old when we bought it, and we loved it so much, we are still living in it (in 2010)." (Note: In 1955 the family lived in a Fairfax rented home.)

Unfortunately, I missed a chance to interview Grant's wife, longtime Fairfax County Japanese American resident Mildred Ichikawa who died at the age of 91 on January 10, 2010 at Fairfax Hospital. She left behind her husband, Grant, son Bryan, and daughter Lona. Mildred Ichikawa served as a linguist with the assimilated rank of 2nd Lt. with the first group of Japanese American women deployed to occupied Japan during WWII. She also served as a dedicated CIA wife. Her family requested that contributions in her name be made to the Japanese American Veterans' Association (JAVA), for the NARA Digitalization Project to collect all relevant data on the 442nd Regimental Combat Team and

Grant and Mildred Ichikawa in 2003 (Courtesy of Grant Ichikawa)

the *Nisei* who served in the Military Intelligence Service during WWII.

Grant Ichikawa described his reaction to the internment of his family in WWII: " What are they doing to us American citizens? Then we received our Evacuation orders in mid-April 1942. I couldn't believe this was happening. I was devastated because here I am an American citizen being treated like an enemy alien. It just truly devastated me. I had to sell my car which was not too old for a song... We were all sent to Turlock Fairgrounds where we were assigned to a horse stall; two families to one horse stall. A family of five and a family of three; we put a sheet across the room to separate the two families... And then, about three months later, we were sent to Gila River Relocation Center in the Arizona desert."

On volunteering for US military service in WWII: "In November 1942, I saw posters all over the camp asking for volunteers for the Military Intelligence Service – you had to be a Japanese linguist… I went home and we had a family conference. My father said, "It's up to you. This is your country. If you want to volunteer and fight for the Army, go ahead. One thing I ask. Do not bring shame to the family name." I went back and volunteered. Around the end of November 1942, 29 of us volunteers from Gila River were put on a train for Minnesota… I felt free. There were no more guards hovering over us with guns pointed in our direction… I felt free like a US citizen again."

2nd Lieutenant Grant Ichikawa

On wartime experience in Manila: "On August 6, 1945, the atom bomb was dropped in Hiroshima; on August 9, another dropped on Nagasaki. Japan surrendered unconditionally on August 15. We jumped for joy. It was a great day. Our mission changed in the 38th Division. Japanese soldiers were now surrendering according to the edict from the Emperor. So we were picking up surrendered prisoners… Then one day, we got word that 200 of them were surrendering at a certain point. We went and saw the Japanese hiding around in the woods. They had white flags tied to their bayonets, but they would not come out. So, I, as the linguist, started walking to the middle of the field to meet them. They were not exactly ready to surrender yet. I had to talk to them. They finally surrendered…We disarmed them – all the guns and rifles were well-oiled… this unit was ready to fight. Thinking back, that was a real close shave. If somebody got a little itchy finger or moved something, we would have been mowed down."

On getting married in Japan: (Grant Ichikawa's unit was transferred to Japan to survey the results of the atomic bomb.) "When we first got to Japan...we were housed temporarily in a building where women were housed... Among the women were thirteen Nisei women from Hawaii; they were linguists, and they were the first censors to come into Japan. I sat next to one of them, a very pretty girl, and I started making conversation about her perfume and things like that. She didn't give me the time of day. Salem Yagawa, my old tent mate in Australia met Elaine, another one of the girls. She wouldn't go out with him except on a double date. I guess she didn't trust him. Salem got me as his double date, and Elaine got Millie as her double date. We became a pair. After a short courtship, we decided to get married. We had to get General McArthur's approval to get married. I sent my papers for approval, first. That got lost. So, I sent another one and that came back approved. We were married on April 2, 1946. It was the first marriage in Japan. We had a great write-up in the papers. The ATIS Officers Club threw a reception for us; we had a nice reception that didn't cost us a penny."

On being evacuated from Vietnam: "That day, April 29, 1975 (the day of the evacuation) I was outside meeting an agent. I didn't know that the evacuation was being called. When I tried to come back into the Embassy, it was mobbed by Vietnamese all clamoring to get in so they could be evacuated. I didn't have a chance of getting in there. Then, I saw a number of other Americans; they spotted me and put me inside the wedge and we forced our way through the Embassy Gate...We waited until nightfall. It was a mess. Helicopters were leaving from the Embassy ground and the Embassy roof... I began to wonder thinking of the fifty thousand odd US Army soldiers who died in Vietnam. Here we are just giving up... It depressed me to think that we were leaving Vietnam like this...I was physically and mentally burned out because of my Vietnam experience... So, I opted to retire at the age of fifty-six at GS-15."

On life as a Fairfax County resident: "Right after I retired in 1975, on my own, I worked to help Vietnamese families resettle in this area. We sponsored a Vietnamese family. They lived with us for a little while until they moved on. I bought a van and collected a lot of furniture and when they moved into an apartment, I got them furniture. I did a lot of work like that... I even got a letter of appreciation from the White House on that.

"The first evacuees from Vietnam were all in the elite educated class. Pretty soon, they found themselves a place in the American society, found a job, they were able to buy a house... My next job was to teach them how to be a "do-it-yourselfer."... I helped them and trained them to work around the house; plumbing, auto mechanic, carpentry roofers... I enjoyed working with my hands again. I did that for quite a while. I still do that.

"A few years ago, I felt I should leave a legacy. One of the things that bothered me were lists of people who went to the Army's Military Intelligence School. The only lists that we have had last name and a first initial instead of the first name. That's a poor record of people who attended the MISLS (Language School). Myself, Paul Tani, and Seiki Oshiro – the three of us started working on a list complete with serial numbers, where they were assigned, their present location, their campaign... We still have a long ways to go. At least, we got most of the full name and the serial numbers of these people. We now (in the year 2003) have over 7,000 names in the "MISLS REGISTRY." We realized that there were many MISers who did not go to this school; they were left out. So we started another registry called "SUPPLEMENTARY REGISTRY"; that one has over 3,000 names. We're still working on that... Without computers, we could not even begin to make a dent."

On being a Japanese American. "I am proud to be a Japanese American. After retirement, I have become a Japanese American again. All during this time I was working with the Agency, I felt no discrimination. I did not dwell on my Japanese heritage. I didn't even think about the way I look, except when I was on some operation where I would blend in better because of my Japanese face. Other than that, I didn't even think about being a Japanese American. I had no interest in Japanese Americans, until after I retired. I became a Japanese American because of my involvement with the Japanese American Veterans' Association (JAVA).

"To give an example, I brought up my son in a non-Japanese American atmosphere. As he was growing up, he didn't know what his face looked like. When he was going to high school (in the States), he had a bunch of friends in the neighborhood, and they sneaked into a members-only swimming pool. One day, they got caught. All of his friends gave false names. When it came to my son's turn, he gave a name something like Smith, a non-Asian name. Right away, they picked him up and called home. We told my son "How stupid can you get? Take a look in the mirror. You don't look like a Smith.""

Grant Ichikawa summarized his life experiences as follows: "In summary, I was mentally devastated when I was forced to evacuate in April 1942 to a concentration camp in Arizona as an enemy alien, deprived of all the rights of a US citizen. I then volunteered in the US Army as a linguist, which in effect, served to restore my rights as a US citizen. I served in the Pacific Theater and was given a field commission; I was discharged as a First Lieutenant. I was recalled during the Korean War which eventually led to a fascinating career with the Agency. Out of this discrimination, loss of civil liberty, incarceration, misery was born a very patriotic person who was given the opportunity for a full, exciting, adventurous, and satisfying life."

We asked Robert Nakamoto, President of JAVA and Chairman of Base Technologies, a McLean technology firm, to give his observations of Grant. Nakamoto said, "Grant and his late wife Mildred are two outstanding patriots. Grant has made it his personal mission to publicize to the American public the story of the Japanese American experience during World War II and the impact of that experience on future generations of Japanese Americans. He is invited to speak at Fairfax County public schools, Montgomery County, Maryland, public schools, government entities, and civic organizations; he is interviewed by radio and TV. Mildred accompanied Grant on some speaking engagements to speak of Japanese American women contribution to the war effort. Grant's motivation to speak at middle and high schools stems from his desire to describe factually the unconstitutional act against the Japanese Americans during World War II.

"At the outbreak of the war, Japanese Americans were viewed as saboteurs and collaborators of the enemy. There was mass hysteria, which the national government fanned. Denied the right to fight for their country, they protested, obtained approval and the 442nd Regimental Combat Team, a segregated Japanese American unit, was formed. The *Nisei* who fought in Europe and the Asia Pacific Theater had one purpose: i.e. to prove their loyalty. US Army record shows they succeeded in establishing a combat performance record that has not been surpassed. Grant wants to talk to as many middle and high school students as possible because they will be leaders of the nation one day. When and if they are faced with a situation as seen in 1941 these future leaders will know instinctively what to do and what not to do.

To Grant Ichikawa
With best wishes,

"In this connection, Grant also likes to talk of the Greatness of America: i.e. a nation which is willing to apologize at the highest level for its mistake and institute reforms that benefited not only Japanese Americans but other minorities as well. We are today a better nation for it, Grant concludes." ##

Uncle Ben Kuroki, An American WWII Hero and My Biography
By Carolyn Sam

My grandparents, Naka and Shosuke Kuroki, came from Japan to the U.S. early in the 20th Century. My mother was born in Wyoming. Some of her nine siblings were born along the way as they migrated from the West. The family settled on a farm near Hershey, Nebraska. A man named Hershey originally owned the small farmhouse the family lived in. Corn, potatoes and sugar beets were raised. The potato crops were so large that a truck could drive into an earthen storage area. A few Kurokis still live in Hershey. The town was small when I visited it as a child in the 1940s. I remember seeing a train slowing down, not stopping, to toss the mailbag onto a hook next to the railroad tracks. Passengers had to board trains in nearby North Platte, NE. Hershey is still a small town, but it now has one stoplight. Every Kuroki child was given a Japanese name, which was difficult for people to pronounce. Someone gave them American names, except for my mother, Fuji. My parents named me Kaoru Carolyn Joyce Enari. I was always called Carolyn. I didn't know that it was not my legal first name until as a teenager when I received a copy of my birth certificate to acquire a work permit. My sister was given two middle names also, but not my two brothers.

The Kuroki family with Terry and Carolyn Sam standing on the left side of the photo in back row. (Courtesy of Terry Sam)

My uncle, Ben Kuroki, was the first and perhaps only Japanese American in the U.S. Air Force as a bomber crewman in combat during World War II. His father urged Ben and his brothers to enlist, because the US was their country. Grandfather Kuroki and my father, Ken Enari, were among many foreign born Asians who by law were not allowed to become citizens until after the war. Uncle Ben was a gunner with the 8th, 12th, 9th and 20th Air Forces. He was on the war fronts in North Africa, Europe and Japan. After a crash landing in North Africa he was captured by Spaniards, tried to escape, was re-captured, and smuggled out of Franco Spain to freedom. He received a Distinguished Flying Cross for the air raid on Ploesti, Romania, which had devastating losses. Servicemen could return home upon completion of the required 25 air missions. To prove his patriotism, Uncle Ben flew the required 25, and then volunteered for five more missions in the B-24 Liberator. Then he completed 28 missions in the Pacific over Japan in the B-29 Superfortress. The Enola Gay was parked back-to-back to his plane.

Ralph G. Martin wrote a biography of Uncle Ben, *Boy from Nebraska*. Uncle Ben was present in Washington, DC, at the Smithsonian National Air and Space Museum program for the Smithsonian APA Heritage Month kickoff event on May 1, 2008. The program featured a showing of the documentary film about him, *Most Honorable Son,* followed by a Q & A session with Uncle Ben. The film denotes his trials and tribulations of trying to gain acceptance for combat duty during war service. The producer of the film, Ken Kubota, was inspired to produce the film after reading *Boy from Nebraska.* It was also aired on PBS. Awards of several war medals have culminated with Uncle Ben receiving the Distinguished Service Medal.

My mother and some of her siblings eventually moved to Chicago, Illinois. I was born, raised and educated there. In the city I was able to go to Lincoln Park to roller skate, ride my bike, climb trees, ride horses, ice skate, play tennis, and see the wildlife in Lincoln Park Zoo. Avoiding the shallow waters of the beach, I would swim in the deep water of cold Lake Michigan at North Avenue next to the Outer Drive. This area is often seen in movies, because the lake, street traffic and downtown Chicago in the background are all visible.

Ben Kuroki (2nd from right) at the Smithsonian in May 2008 with Carolyn Sam in the middle wearing a white jacket and Terry Sam in the left corner beside Mrs. Kuroki holding the flower bouquet. (Courtesy of Terry Sam)

My family and relatives in Nebraska and Illinois were not sent to internment camp during WWII, because they were not on the West Coast. The only relatives of my father, the Yenaris, were interned at the Arkansas internment camp. We have photographs of my imprisoned great-aunt, Kaoru Yenari, and great-uncle, Daisuke Yenari, standing in front of tar-papered internment housing with their sons in American army uniforms. I believe I was named after my great aunt. In our Fairfax County home I have a bas-relief carving of a fierce fish made by my great-uncle while he was interned. The wood he used came from a packing crate. (See Sam Family photo gallery page 43.) After the war the Yenaris moved to New Orleans. My great-uncle had a backyard filled with bonsai. Midori Yenari Tong, Daisuke and Kaoru Yenari's granddaughter, is an Associate Professor and research neurologist at University of California-San Francisco. She comes to DC, National Institutes of Health, and Baltimore for her research projects. We met Midori, her husband, and son for the first time on November 19, 2008 when she traveled to Washington DC for a research project meeting. (See Sam Family photo gallery page 43.)

In Chicago during the war, we moved from a spacious, nicely decorated apartment to one room in the back of my father's sign shop. Although there are numerous pictures of my older brother and me, there are only a few pictures of my sister who was born during the war. My father's camera had been confiscated. (See Sam Family photo gallery page 43.) My parents attempted to teach us to read and write Japanese by themselves. Then they sent us to Saturday language school. English was the main family language. Eventually, both parents, who were fluent in English, only spoke Japanese to each other. My family attended and was baptized at the Second Evangelical United Brethren Church. I did learn some Japanese dances for the Obon Festival held at a Buddhist church. *Sumi-e,* Japanese brush painting, was taught to me by Ryozo Ogura.

I graduated from Northwestern University, Evanston, IL. While I was a substitute teacher in Chicago, I attended the School of the Art Institute of Chicago. Then I taught art in a Detroit, MI, public junior high school. I met Terry Sam, a Detroit native of Chinese descent. He had been sent to Saturday Chinese school. English was the main language at his home, because his mother wanted to practice her new language. We married while I was attending graduate school at Wayne State University, Detroit. We lived a few months in Detroit's new Chinatown, which was smaller than the old one that had been displaced by urban renewal. After we married, Terry returned to the University of Michigan, Ann Arbor, MI, to resume his education after a hiatus from when his mother died. His father had died when he was in high school. I taught art and Spanish at Plymouth, MI, senior high school near where we lived in Ann Arbor and took a few courses at the University.

We lived in the Detroit area for a short time after Terry graduated. Then we moved to the Washington, DC area. A friend from Chicago lived in Ann Arbor when we were there. She settled in Vienna, Virginia and recommended living in northern Virginia because of the good public school system. We moved to Burke, Virginia in 1975. Our subdivision of townhouses, Greenfield Farm, was so new that units were still being completed. We were the first Asians in our section until a family arrived from Guam. Usually, we were the only Asians in our neighborhood from childhood to adulthood. Our daughter, Mika, was born at Columbia Hospital for Women, Washington, DC. Then our son, Kenneth, was born at Fairfax Hospital, Falls Church, Virginia. Kenneth is named after his maternal and paternal grandfathers.

In 1979 we moved near Centreville, Virginia, which is still considered to be way out in spite of development over the years. At that time the area was a mix of country and suburban housing and viewpoints. Occasionally, there would be a racial incident such as rude noises being made while passing someone in a restaurant, or slurs yelled out of a passing vehicle. We were the first Asian family in our Willowmeade subdivision. A few years ago, four Korean families moved into the neighborhood after a Korean church was built at the Willowmeade entrance. I think our children were the only Asians at Centreville Elementary for several years. Definitely, there were not any Asians on the staff. I integrated the school as a volunteer art teacher. Staff and students were generally very amiable towards our family. At Back to School Night, the family of our son's fellow kindergartner introduced themselves. They left the area when our sons were in third grade. We remain friends to this day even though they moved to Maryland and then Montana. At Centreville Elementary, a boy refused to let Kenneth sit next to him on the school bus. A friend of our son stood up for him.

After second grade our daughter attended the Gifted and Talented Center at Greenbriar West Elementary, Rocky Run Junior High and Thomas Jefferson High School for Science and Technology, where there were a large number of Asians. Kenneth went to Lanier Junior High where friends stood up for him when someone would give him flack. Fairfax High School (FHS) had a fair number of Asians due to the ESL center. At FHS the defensive backs on his junior varsity football team were Asian. They named themselves *The Asian Persuasion.* I called them *The Pacific Rim* since they were the last line of defense.

I am a breast cancer survivor. I noticed in the statistics presented at a lecture that I was one of two Japanese who had breast cancer surgery in 2003 at Inova Fairfax Hospital. Upon completion of treatment, I became a Life with Cancer (LWC) participant and volunteer. LWC is an Inova non-profit organization funded primarily by community contributions, which provides information, education and support free of charge to survivors, their families and friends. Anyone in treatment or remission may attend classes regardless of where or when treatment is received. As an LWC volunteer, I was a member of the ad hoc Inova Community Advisory Council on Cancer, which among many things, helped to develop and manage the first Inova Cancer Survivorship Conference. I teach crochet and origami at LWC. I have been the facilitator of the monthly Knitting and Crocheting Circle since its inception in 2005. I have also helped with mailings, fundraisers, health fairs, setting up for the Chair-Based Exercise class, plus other classes, and manned the reception desk. I have not seen very many Asians at LWC. Perhaps this is due to minorities being fewer in number or for cultural reasons. In 2007, Inova Cancer Services and Life with Cancer presented me with an appreciation award for my many volunteer services. ##

President George W. Bush Salutes Carolyn Sam's Uncle Ben Kuroki on May 1, 2008

President Bush saluting Ben Kuroki at White House on May 1, 2008. (The White House)

President George W. Bush said:
"I do want to point out one soul who's joined us – and Ben is not going to be happy about it, Ben Kuroki. He probably doesn't want to be called out but I'm going to do it anyway, Ben. I got the podium and you don't.

"Two days after Pearl Harbor, Ben volunteered to join the Army, where there is no doubt he met prejudice at nearly every turn. Still, he became one of the few "Nisei" admitted to the Army Air Corps. He flew 58 missions over Europe and Japan, and he earned three Distinguished Flying Crosses. When he came back home, he turned to another mission: working to overcome the intolerance he had experienced during his early days in the Army. Ben edited newspapers. He spoke to audiences around the country. He became a strong advocate of racial equality. He knew something – and he knew the subject well, unfortunately. Sixty years after the Japanese surrender, Ben received the U.S. Army Distinguished Service Medal. And at the ceremony, here's what he said: "I had to fight like hell to fight for my country – and now I feel completely vindicated." We are glad you feel vindicated, but I am proud to tell you America is a better place because of you, Ben. Thank you for coming." ##

Kennon Nakamura, a Third Generation Japanese American
By Corazon Sandoval Foley

One of the first friends that the Foley family made in Fairfax County was the Nakamura family of Burke, Virginia whom we met in 1980 when their children, Maya and Greg enrolled at the same preschool, Springfield Academy, in which our own Joshua and Melinda studied for a couple of years.

The Nakamura family goes back two generations in Fairfax County, Virginia.

Melinda and Maya took ballet lessons together in Rolling Valley Mall in Burke, Virginia – near the *"Les Trois Continents"* pizzeria once owned by the former police chief of Saigon, General Nguyen Ngoc Loan, made world famous by the Pulitzer prize-winning photo of him executing a Viet Cong in Saigon in 1968. (Note: On July 16, 1998, General Nguyen Ngoc Loan died of cancer in his home in Burke, Virginia.)

In addition to our family friendship, Ken and I shared professional interests for he too was involved in international affairs as a Congressional staffer for former Congressman Broomfield and later, as legislative counsel for the American Foreign Service Association. And in 1992 when I became a State Department Congressional Fellow for then-Congressman Norman Mineta, Ken's advice on legislative procedures was invaluable in my work to win passage of legislation for the National Memorial to Japanese American Patriotism in Washington, DC.

Kan Nakamura has been one of the strongest supporters of the FCAAHP efforts. He agreed to participate in the FCAAHP interviews at the Ekoji Temple of which he was one of the founding members in 1981. He also welcomed Francine Uenuma, a Japanese American reporter of the *Washington Post* who joined me in interviewing the Nakamuras on July 14, 2008.

The *Washington Post* Fairfax section on August 21, 2008 ran a front-page story on FCAAHP entitled "Asian Americans Carve a Place in History" that featured photos at the Ekoji Buddhist Temple during the interview of Maya Masami Nakamura Horio, her husband Brant Horio, Kennon Haruo Nakamura, and Gregory

Washington Post **interview of Nakamura family at Ekoji Temple for August front-page article in the Fairfax section.** (Photo by Cora Foley)

Kiyoshi Nakamura. Ken was a founding member and past president of the temple. Greg has served as vice president of the Ekoji Buddhist temple for several years.

When asked about the importance of the FCAAHP oral history project, Ken said: "I think it's something that's really, really important. In some respects, Asian Americans are still viewed as very much an immigrant population that's brand new here. Cora's work will . . . help show the diversity of the county and that we were here, we are here, and we've been here for a long time."

Maya and Brent Horio, Ken and Greg Nakamura, and Cora Foley during the FCAAHP interview of July 14, 2008 at Ekoji Buddhist Temple. (Photo by Cora Foley)

Kennon Nakamura is a third-generation Japanese American whose parents were interned in Rohwer, Arkansas. His wife, Nori, is a second-generation Japanese American born in the Tule Lake, California internment camp.

During the July 14, 2008 interview, Ken described the impact of the internment experience on the Japanese American community. His parents were sent from their homes (they were not married yet) in Central California to the camp in Jerome, Arkansas, and later when that camp was closed, they were moved to the larger camp in Rohwer, Arkansas. Ken's mother was part of a committee of three from the internment camps who explored the possibility of moving to Seabrook, New Jersey. After looking at the area and talking to community leaders, they decided that it would be a good place for Japanese Americans to start all over again. She was part of the Japanese American team that led over 2,500 Japanese Americans from the camps to Seabrook, New Jersey. Ken's parents got married in Rohwer before leaving for Seabrook.

After being released from the internment camp, his parents moved to start a new life. They were instrumental in starting the Seabrook Buddhist Temple and the local Japanese American Citizens League in Seabrook. Ken's mother, Ellen, became the moving force in the Seabrook Educational and Cultural Center – a Japanese American Museum that describes how Japanese American internees made a new start in their lives and helped develop the community of Seabrook, New Jersey and in 1996, she was recognized by the State of New Jersey and the Government of Japan for her work

Ken and Nori Nakamura moved to Burke in Fairfax County in 1974. Their children, Maya and Greg, were born in Fairfax County and graduated from Lake Braddock High School. Ken in 2008 was working for the Library of Congress' Congressional Research Service after having worked for former Congressman Broomfield and the American Foreign Service Association (AFSA).

Maya and her husband Brant are U.S. federal government officials while Greg has served as an elementary school teacher with the Fairfax County Public School system. Brant Horio was born in Hawaii and moved to Fairfax County when he was eight years old; he graduated from Robinson High School. Brant's mother was a long-time public servant with the Fairfax County Planning Commission. Greg, Maya, and Brant lead the Nen Daiko taiko drummers who regularly perform at several events during Washington's Cherry Blossom festival and in the Ekoji Buddhist Temple's annual Obon festivals.

On July 18, 2003, Ken, Nori, Greg and Maya were featured in a discussion of the Buddhist Obon Festival in National Public Radio. The Bon or Obon is also called the Feast of Lanterns when Buddhists pay special tribute to the dead.

Ken explained that when the Ekoji Buddhists celebrate Bon, they do not think of spirits coming back but of a memorial service, a time to remember those who have passed on. Greg added that Obon is a reminder that we are here because of our ancestors, because of the way that they chose to live their lives, and the way they taught us. For him, it is a reminder that they continue to live on through our actions. Ken said that the Ekoji Buddhist Temple has a board that people can put the memorial plaques or the Buddhist name that's given at the time of the person's death.

The Ekoji Buddhists call themselves "householder Buddhists" because they do not have a monastic tradition. Ken said that they are very much involved in the life we lead, which includes ego, self, ambition, attachments, love for family. He adds that the more popular sense of reincarnation is that there is a spirit that transmigrates upon death from one entity to another. They look at reincarnation not so much in the transmigration of the spirit, but the sense that we, in our daily lives, go up and down this whole realm of good and evil. The hard part is to hit the realm of the Buddha and stay there.

For Maya and Greg Nakamura, the Buddhist temple was a place of comfort where they and their Buddhist friends could feel secure and laugh at uncomfortable situations that sometimes confront religious and ethnic minorities. During the 2008 FCAAHP interview, Greg Nakamura laughed when he recounted questions from his school friends: "Do you worship that fat guy with the big belly? No, we do not. Why do you celebrate Christmas? To get presents...."

Maya and Greg Nakamura have tried to improve their classmates' understanding of the difficult experiences of Japanese Americans. Their grandparents had been very open about talking of their internment camp experiences and had shared artifact from that difficult period. Maya used to bring some of the artwork created by the Japanese American internees to her classes in Lake Braddock High School in order to sensitize more Americans about the difficulties that her grandparents endured in World War II.

Ken Nakamura shared with FCAAHP his memories of the history of the Ekoji Buddhist Temple of Fairfax County, Virginia.

Ekoji Buddhist Temple – "The Temple of the Gift of Light"
By Kennon H. Nakamura

Sunday, September 13, 1981, the doors of the Ekoji Buddhist Temple opened, welcoming a gathering of Buddhists from the local area, and as far away as New Jersey, New York City, and even Oregon, for the first service of a new Buddhist temple in Fairfax County, Virginia.

In 1981 the temple, a part of the Jodo Shinshu denomination of Buddhism, took up half of the first floor of the Cary Building II office condominium in Springfield, Virginia, where it served its Sangha, or fellowship, for the next 17 years. In 1998, the Ekoji Sangha moved to a new site in Fairfax Station. Ekoji started with a membership of about 30 people, mostly Americans of Japanese ancestry. Today (in 2010), it has about 175 members -- about 60 percent who are Japanese Americans and about 40 percent who come from other races and ethnicity.

INNEN
A Japanese Buddhist phrase, *Innen,* refers to the causes and conditions that come together for something to happen. Those causes and conditions, the Innen, for Ekoji to exist go back decades to Japan, Toronto, Canada, and Washington, D.C. before they flowered on that Sunday, September 13th.

Innen: Japan. In the early 1920s, Yehan Numata, the son of a Jodo Shinshu priest, came to the United States in his late teens to study. He worked as a domestic for $2.00 a week plus lodging to pay for his education, first at a high school near Fresno, CA, and then the University of California at Berkeley. It was a hard life for a foreign student who initially spoke very little English. During that time, he fell gravely ill, and thought he would die alone in a foreign land. In his illness, he found solace in his religion, and it deepened his faith. While at Berkeley, he started a small publication, *Pacific World,* which eventually failed because it was undercapitalized. In 1928, Yehan Numata graduated from Berkeley and returned to Japan. In October 1934, Mr. Numata started the Mitutoyo Corporation. Mr. Numata, with his deepened faith that developed during his illness as a student, dedicated his life to spreading the teachings of the Buddha. But this goal was also tempered by his experiences with the *Pacific World* publication and the importance of adequate funding. With the economic growth of Japan following World War II, Mr. Numata's company, Mitutoyo Corporation, eventually became one of the world's largest manufacturers of micrometers, with offices around the world. It also made Mr. Numata a millionaire several times over, and gave him the financial means to support the spread of the Buddha's teachings through his religious foundation, Bukkyo Dendo Kyokai (BDK).

Innen: Toronto, Canada. While Mr. Numata was in pre-war California, Takashi Tsuji was growing up on a farm in western Canada. Tsuji decided to become a Buddhist priest and went to Japan to study for the priesthood. As the winds of war were stirring in the 1930s, Tsuji was advised to leave Japan and return to Canada before there was war with the western nations. After his ordination, Rev. Tsuji caught one of the last ships leaving Japan and returned to Canada. World War II came, and he and all Japanese Canadians, like Japanese Americans living in the United States, were relocated from their homes to camps in the interior. After the war, Rev. Tsuji and his wife Sakaye moved to Toronto and started the Toronto Buddhist Church with the help of many other Japanese Canadians who decided to make new lives for themselves in Toronto and other eastern Canadian cities. Because the temple was just starting and all the members were starting over again, Rev. Tsuji served as spiritual leader on Sundays and when needed, and as a short order cook, dishwasher, and whatever other jobs he could find to put food on the table for his growing family on the other days. While in Toronto, a traveling Japanese salesman, Yehan Numata, selling micrometers that his company manufactured and searching for markets, came to Toronto and found Rev. Tsuji and the Buddhist Temple there. Rev. Tsuji and Mr. Numata became friendly acquaintances as Mr. Numata continued to market his micrometers. In the mid-1950s, Rev. Tsuji left Toronto to become the first western-born Director of Buddhist Education for the Buddhist Churches of America (BCA), which was headquartered in San Francisco, California. Later, he was to become the first western-born Bishop (or Socho) of the BCA, and upon taking that position was given the Buddhist name, Kenryu

INNEN: The Washington, D.C. Sangha Dharma School

In 1959, Rev. Shojo Honda and his wife June moved from New York City to Washington, D.C. Rev. Honda took a position as research librarian in Buddhism with the Library of Congress. He also organized an informal group, the Washington, D.C. Sangha, which met regularly at the Hondas' home in Arlington, VA. In this way, Rev. Honda kept Buddhism alive for other Japanese American Buddhists who had left World War II relocation camps to start new lives in the Washington, D.C. area. Because of Rev. Honda's efforts, these families, like the Fukudas, the Kitaharas, the Ushiros and the Matsumotos, had a place to practice their faith and raise their children as Buddhists.

Nearly two decades later, in 1978, Ken and Nori Nakamura, who had moved to Virginia in 1974 and whose two children were almost 1 and 2, felt the need to provide a religious experience for their children. At the encouragement and support of now Bishop Kenryu Tsuji and the Board of the BCA's Eastern District Council (EDC), Ken and Nori contacted other Buddhists in the area who had young children about starting a children's Dharma School. Now adults, these were the children who had grown up in Rev. Honda's Sangha. A group of five families with 13 young children – Dr. Norman and Gail Kitahara Kondo, Jessie and Sachiko Matsumoto Shimabukuro, Shigeki and Ruby Fujiwara, Dr. Herbert and Lillian Oie, and Kennon and Noriko Nakamura, with the advice of family friends, Shigeki and Kimiko Sugiyama and Mitsu Yasuda Carl -- began discussing the idea of a Dharma School, and how it would operate. It was agreed to try and hold a service every other week and rotate the service in each other's homes. Classes were organized and it was agreed who would be teaching which class. Ken Nakamura was to serve as Coordinator for the group.

In January 1979, the first service of the Washington, D.C. Sangha Dharma School was held at Ken and Nori Nakamura's home in Burke, Virginia. Rev. Arthur Vergara, from the New York Buddhist Church, came to provide both encouragement and lead the first service. Rev. Vergara talked about why it was important to have a Dharma School to help the children, and we parents, develop a "third eye," a Buddhist eye with which to see the world, life, and our relationship to the transcendental.

That was the Dharma School's beginning with services twice a month. Because no one knew how to chant and lead a service, Nori Nakamura, who was the daughter of Rev. Shingetsu Akahoshi, minister at the Seabrook Buddhist Temple in New Jersey, led in the chanting. Guitars were used to accompany singing gathas (Buddhist songs), and the parents taught the classes and gave Dharma talks as agreed. Each second meeting of the month, following the service, Shig Sugiyama would run a Dharma class for the parents so we could keep one step ahead of the children. As the year went on, other Buddhist families with young children joined.

Bishop Tsuji made sure that the small Dharma School had sufficient service books and other materials with which to teach. During that time, the BCA also sent ministers from the West Coast to visit temples that were in other states besides California. Bishop Tsuji made sure that Washington, D.C. was always on the itinerary, and that the expenses were covered. One of the first ministers to make that trip to Washington, D.C. in October 1979 was Rev. Kosho Yukawa, who led the service at Shig and Kimi Sugiyama's house. We were still so new and nervous about this Dharma School effort that, during the lunch that followed, we asked him to help us design Dharma talks, and what we should teach. Rev. Yukawa's response to us was very basic. He said that we would never go wrong in talking to the Dharma School children about the Golden Chain, in its totality and its various parts.

I am a link in Amida Buddha's Golden Chain of love that stretches around the world,
I must keep my link bright and strong.
I will try to be kind and gentle to every living thing and protect all who are weaker than myself.
I will try to think pure and beautiful thoughts, to say pure and beautiful words, and to do pure and beautiful deeds, knowing that on what I do depends not only my happiness or unhappiness but also those of others.
May every link in the Buddha's golden chain of love become bright and strong, and my we all attain perfect peace.

He then suggested that as we became more comfortable with teaching, we could teach Buddhist etiquette, the lives of Siddhartha and Shinran Shonin, the founder of our denomination, and their teachings. But start with the Golden Chain.

Beyond holding services and Dharma classes for the children, the parents worked to give them a fuller Buddhist experience – an experience drawn from our memories as we grew up in the faith. In April 1979, the Dharma School parents organized the first Buddha-day or Hanamatsuri service celebrating the birth of the historical Buddha. It was a traditional service with a potluck lunch and entertainment, including performances by the children. The parents rented the cafeteria at

North Lake Elementary School in Rockville, Maryland, and invited Rev. Honda's Sangha and friends to participate. In July, the Dharma School organized its first O-Bon memorial service and festival, again at North Lake Elementary. Again, friends and supporters of Rev. Honda's Sangha helped and participated, and members of the Sangha from the Seabrook Buddhist Temple came and joined in the observance.

In 1980, Bishop Tsuji called Ken and Nori and said that the Shin-Monshu, Koshin Ohtani, the son of the spiritual leader of the worldwide Jodo Shinshu movement based in Kyoto, would be coming to the United States later in the year to visit various Buddhist temples. Bishop Tsuji would like to bring the Shin-Mon to Washington to hold an affirmation service. Invitations could be sent to the Seabrook Buddhist Temple and the New York City Buddhist Church to participate in the service. A visit by the family of the Monshu is generally reserved for the larger temples because of the expenses, rituals and logistics involved. Bishop Tsuji said the BCA would take care of the expenses, and that he would be available to help with the rituals. The evening prior to the affirmation service, an informal reception was held at Shig Sugiyama's house for the Shin-Mon and his retinue with the members of the Dharma School Sangha and Rev. Honda's Sangha. On November 16, 1980, the affirmation service was held at the Kay Spiritual Life Center on the campus of American University, with a reception following. With that, a memorable weekend, and certainly an honor for the small Dharma School, came to a conclusion.

At the beginning of 1980, with the encouragement and financial support of the BCA's Eastern District Council, the Dharma School moved to Walter Johnson High School in Bethesda, Md. It was felt by the EDC that holding services in people's houses could sometimes act as a barrier for growth because people might hesitate to go to a stranger's house. The small Dharma School, while still ethnically basically Japanese American, was also growing well beyond the seven original families.

The Flowering of INNEN:
The Beginnings of the Ekoji Buddhist Temple

In the spring of 1981, Bishop Tsuji called Shig Sugiyama and said that he was coming to Washington and would like to meet privately with Shig, Dr. Norman Kondo, and Ken Nakamura for dinner. During the dinner, he said that he would like to see a temple started in the Washington, D.C. area to serve both as a home temple for the Jodo Shinshu Buddhist population in the D.C. metropolitan area and as a study center for those interested in Buddhism in the area and the southeastern United States. We would have a full time resident minister as well as a temple building. He asked if the parents and supporters of the children's Dharma School would be able to support this initiative. The three of us expressed our concern that, while this would be great, we were not strong enough as an organization to afford such an endeavor. Bishop Tsuji assured us that we would not have to worry about the expenses, and that we were being asked to provide the personal support. He did not ask for an immediate response, but suggested that we talk it over with the members of the Sangha, which we did. The Dharma School parents thought if this could be done, it would be a great start for our children and ourselves and agreed to Bishop Tsuji's proposal.

Prior to the Washington dinner with the three members of the Dharma School, Bishop Tsuji, who had gone to Kyoto for meetings, met with Yehan Numata, the Japanese industrialist and Buddhist philanthropist whom he had befriended in Toronto decades earlier. He told Mr. Numata that he believed that there should be a Jodo Shinshu temple in Washington, D.C. that could serve as a home temple for Buddhists in the area and as a center for the expansion of Buddhist teachings. He also told him that there was a small Sangha in Washington, which might serve as a nucleus for such an effort. Mr. Numata was intrigued and asked Bishop Tsuji to explore this possibility. He would provide the finances for a temple and a resident minister to lead the temple and Sangha. Since then, the Numata family, through BDK, has also supported the founding of temples in Germany and Mexico, provided assistance to other temples such as in Toronto, Canada, and established several professorial chairs in Buddhist studies in several nationally known universities.

In the spring of 1981, Rev. Tsuji had completed his third term as Bishop of the Buddhist Churches of America, serving 15 years in that position. He had decided that if the Washington D.C. Dharma School parents agreed to his proposal, he would lead in developing a Jodo Shinshu temple in Washington. A few years after the temple was started, Rev. Tsuji talked about why he decided to start a new temple instead of going to a larger, established temple in California, any of which would have welcomed him with open arms. Rev. Tsuji said that after his term as the BCA Director of Buddhist Education, and later during his many years as Bishop, he had begun to feel like an administrator and not a priest as he had planned. He said that he wanted to become a minister again and share the teachings of the Buddha and Shinran in a new place.

In July 1981, Rev. and Mrs. Tsuji drove across the United States to Norman and Gail Kondo's house in Springfield, Virginia, to meet the parents and children of the Washington, D.C. Sangha Dharma School. Rev. Tsuji talked of what might be as the parents and he and Mrs. Tsuji, together, started the Ekoji Buddhist Temple -- the Temple of the Gift of Light.

Shig Sugiyama worked with Rev. Tsuji and representatives of BDK in searching for property that could become the first temple and worked with the other members of the Sangha on the By-Laws of the temple. Ken Nakamura worked with Rev. Tsuji and members of the Sangha on services and plans for the Dharma School. The members of the Dharma School, who had been meeting every other week, inquired as to how often we would be meeting. Rev. Tsuji said every week, of course, and also insisted that the Dharma School provide a substantive education going well beyond arts and crafts. It was his belief that our children needed a strong religious education because, in many instances, they would be the only Buddhist in a group at school or gathering. They should be able to explain their religion, and more importantly, understand why they are Buddhist.

Over the next few weeks, things moved quickly. With the help of Springfield attorney Greg Harney, the By-Laws for the temple were drafted and filed with the State of Virginia. Shig Sugiyama and Norman Kondo were named as Trustees of the temple. A parsonage was bought in the Cherry Run development in Burke, and half of the first floor of the Cary Building II on

Old Keene Mill Road in Springfield, Virginia was bought to serve as the site of the temple. An altar was sent from Japan by Mr. Numata. All was ready for the September 13th opening of the Ekoji temple, and the flower that was the result of the seeds of Innen, planted decades ago, started to bloom. At its first service, Rev. Tsuji shared his vision for the temple. Our temple newsletter reports of that service and Rev. Tsuji's message saying,

He reminded those in attendance that the temple, despite its beautiful appearance that day, was not a temple, not without true and earnest seekers of the Dharma to participate and make it one. He said, Shinran Shonin said there should be no distinction between monk and lay person. He expressed his own hopes to put those concepts into practice at Ekoji, where we will all eventually be leading services, discussing the Dharma and putting the Nembutsu into active use. Rev. Tsuji spoke of himself as not a monk but a farmer in priest's robes. "We will all be priests, disguised as workers, homemakers, fathers, and yes, even children," he said. "Ekoji will be a place where the differences of races, color or creed will disappear," he said. "Ekoji will be open to all who earnestly seek the Dharma."

The official dedication of the temple on took place on November 8, 1981. From Kyoto Japan, His Eminence Kosho Ohtani, the retired Go-Monshu or head of the worldwide Jodo Shinshu denomination represented his family at the dedication of Ekoji. Also in attendance were representatives from Canada, Hawaii, Europe, and Rev. Dr. Yehan Numata, Ekoji's benefactor, with Rev. Tsuji and Rev. Honda leading the service.

EKOJI TEMPLE – The Early Years. Led by Rev. and Mrs. Tsuji, Ekoji served the temple Sangha as their religious home with the development of a sense of a Buddhist community. As almost an extension of the Temple, one felt that the Tsuji home was always open for the Sangha to drop by and talk, for it seemed Rev. Tsuji was always available as a friend and religious advisor. Ekoji started to grow slowly as it worked to become a temple open and welcoming to all, as Rev. Tsuji said in his first Dharma talk, "open to all who earnestly seek the Dharma," and not only Japanese Americans.

At this time, Ekoji was also establishing a role for itself in the BCA's Eastern District (an area that covered all of the United States east of the Mississippi River). Ekoji, with BDK's support, sponsored an annual Eastern District seminar so that the Eastern District ministers could come together and talk about issues that affected their temples, have guest speakers for ministerial in-services, and work on common projects such as the translation of a ancient Buddhist chant into English. Shig Sugiyama, Ken Nakamura and later with fellow Ekoji Sangha members Dr. Gordon Bermant and Dr. Erick Ishii also represented Ekoji on the Eastern District Board and eventually all served many years as District officers, as well as active members of several BCA Boards of Directors. Dr. Bermant eventually became the first, and so far, only non-Japanese American President of the Buddhist Churches of America.

Rev. Tsuji also extended his ministerial work in Washington. He developed an original English chant for Ekoji's Dharma School children, *Gassho to Amida*, so that they would have something written for them that they could understand. The need for such a chant was obvious, and *Gassho* to *Amid*a is now used throughout Jodo Shinshu temples in the United States, Canada, and Hawaii. Ekoji also started holding regular seminars, inviting guest speakers for its own members and for others in the community who were interested in learning about Buddhism. Ekoji joined ecumenical organizations in Fairfax County, and began to send speakers, either Rev. Tsuji or other members of the Sangha, to talk about our faith and our religion to those who invited us. The temple also served as host to students and members of other churches who wanted to get a sense of the Buddhist religion.

EKOJI TEMPLE: Fairfax Station and a New Chapter. By 1995 it became clear that Ekoji had outgrown its original facility in Springfield. Again with the support of BDK and the Numata family, the members of Ekoji began searching for another site upon which to build a temple. After a long search and a couple of false starts, a five acre site was found in Fairfax Station. Architects and a construction company were engaged, and construction was ready to begin. Among the participants at the ground breaking in September 28, 1997, were Congressman Tom Davis, and Chairwoman of the Fairfax County Board of Supervisors Katherine Hanley. While Springfield Supervisor Elaine McConnell was unable to attend, she also sent a congratulatory message. The construction of the beautiful, multi-building facility was completed in 1998, with the dedication service of the new building held on November 1, 1998.

On July 31, 1999, our founding minister, Rev. Kenryu Tsuji, retired after 18 years as the resident minister and guiding spirit of Ekoji. Rev. and Mrs. Tsuji moved back to California to be close to their family, and in September 1999, Rev. Shojo Honda became the part-time resident minister. On June 1, 2001, Koshin Ohtani returned to Washington, now as Monshu Koshin Ohtani, the leader of the world-wide Jodo Shin denomination, to conduct a Buddhist naming ceremony – Kikyoshiki – for Buddhists in the eastern area.

Reverend Honda served on a voluntary basis as the part-time resident minister after he retired as a research librarian in Buddhism with the Library of Congress. Though officially the Ekoji position was voluntary and part-time, he conducted services each Sunday, provided services for all of the important life changes from the Hatsumairi service, or the first service for an infant, to weddings, funerals, and memorial services. He was there when a person needed to just talk, and he was there to provide guidance when some of the lay leaders shared the Dharma talk responsibilities with him in his later years. Rev. Honda was particularly interested in the children's Dharma School and wanted to help in whatever ways he could. Under Rev. Honda's leadership, Ekoji continued to hold services every Sunday, conduct special classes, and continued to grow both in size and diversity. On June 30, 2009, Rev. Honda retired from his position as minister of the Ekoji Buddhist Temple for a well-deserved rest.

EKOJI TEMPLE: Continuing to Share the Dharma. July 1, 2009 saw Ekoji's second, full time resident minister take the spiritual leadership of the temple, Rev. Kazuaki Nakata. Young and full of energy and vitality, Rev. Nakata and his wife, Michiko, bring a new spirit to Ekoji. Prior to coming east, Rev. Nakata served as the assistant minister at the Sacramento Buddhist Temple in California. Unlike many Buddhist temples on the west coast, Rev. Nakata comes to a temple that is growing and diverse. Yet in its diversity, it also has tradition from its Japanese origins. The services are often different from our sister temples on the West Coast, but a visitor would also have a sense of familiarity. Our potlucks have a mix of ham, collard greens, and potato salad next to sushi, teriyaki chicken, and nishime. And then we celebrate *O-Bon* in July, our memorial service with a festival which includes Japanese folk dancing and taiko, Japanese drumming, the night before a very solemn memorial service on Sunday.

The Ekoji Temple Nen Daiko Group (Courtesy of Ken Nakamura)

Rev. Nakata also encountered an active, growing children's Dharma School program led by Superintendent Maya Nakamura Horio, one of Ekoji's and the Washington, D.C. Sangha Dharma School's original Dharma School students. There are regular classes in Buddhism led by Director of Buddhist Education Mark Lawall, who also leads a meditation class every week. There are regular discussion groups, visitations by college and high schools students, invitations to speak at other churches and organizations, and an active, welcoming outreach program. Nen Daiko, a popular, often heard Japanese taiko (drums) group in the area, is also affiliated with Ekoji and practices in its facilities.

The Ekoji Sangha welcomed Rev. Nakata and his family, as it welcomes all residents of the Washington Metropolitan area, with open arms, inviting everyone to join us.

The Ekoji Buddhist Temple of Fairfax County is located in 7500 Lake Haven Lane, Fairfax Station, Virginia 22039. Its website: www.Ekoji.org.

Robert Nakamoto:
Korean War Veteran and Fairfax County Business Leader
By Corazon Sandoval Foley

The Fairfax County Asian American History Project (FCAAHP) has benefited tremendously from the support of many Fairfax County residents, particularly Robert Nakamoto, a Korean War Veteran, who in 1971 chose Fairfax County as his residence when he accepted an offer of employment from the Federal Government. He has been a business leader in Fairfax County and has very generously shared with us his story and that of his children, including Robert Nakamoto Jr. whose military service is detailed in the chapter on Patriotism by Fairfax County Asian Americans.

A Fairfax County Civic Leader. Robert Nakamoto shared with FCAAHP his perspective on his own contributions as a Fairfax County resident: "I have been involved in a number of non-profit and volunteer activities as a longtime Fairfax County resident. Among them are the American Legion, Veterans of Foreign Wars, Armed Forces Electronic Association, Chamber of Commerce, Business Executives for National Security, Japan America Society, and British American Business Association, just to name a few.

Most recently for the past three years, I have served as President of the Japanese American Veterans' Association (JAVA). We are a nationwide organization headquartered in McLean, VA and hold many of our meetings in Fairfax County. JAVA preserves the legacy and spirit of the Japanese Americans who served in World War II and veterans since that time in promoting historical lessons as well as to assist current youth and families in need. There are over 360,000 Asian American Veterans."

Robert Nakamoto with Veterans Administration Secretary Retired US Army General Eric Shinseki (Courtesy of Robert Nakamoto)

Robert Nakamoto's Internment, Public Service and Business Success. Robert Nakamoto was born in 1931 in Sacramento, California. He is a third generation Japanese American and the oldest of eight children. During World War II, his family was interned in a camp in Utah for 3 years starting when Bob was ten years old. Bob was educated in the California school systems and graduated from California State University at Sacramento.

Robert Nakamoto volunteered for military service during the Korean War and was assigned to Hill Air Force Base near Salt Lake City, Utah and Tokyo, Japan for 2 years. He managed a personnel office in the Air Force.

After graduation he was employed by Sacramento County as Supervisor of Programming. He was then employed by the State of California as a Manager of Data Processing. The Federal Government then recruited Robert Nakamoto in the late 1960s; he came to Washington, D.C. as a Computer Specialist with the mission of introducing technology to state and local governments.

In 1971, he bought a home in Fairfax County and has maintained his residence for many years.

In 1972, Robert Nakamoto accepted an assignment from the State of Texas as Deputy Commissioner of Planning and Systems. He was awarded the Honorary Citizen of Texas by the Governor and an Honorary Citizen of Bexar County by the Mayor of San Antonio.

In 1977, he returned to Fairfax County and resumed public service with the Federal Government where he was Director of Systems for Medicaid and Medicare Program.

In 1982, he was recruited by MCI Communication Corporation as Director of Corporate Systems. He was responsible for the development and installation of all internal systems.

In 1987, Bob started Base Technogies, Inc. (BTI) in Tysons Corner; BTI celebrated 23 years as a successful business enterprise in Fairfax County in 2010. Among its customers BTI is an information technology company that has a multi-year contract with a partner with the State of Virginia to issue drivers licenses.

The company has grown incrementally and successfully over the years. In 2009, Base Technologies Inc. won three prestigious awards:

-- BTI was named one of the top 500 Minority Owned Business from over 650,000 business from DiversityBusiness.com;

-- Contractor of the Year Award from the Annual Greater Washington Government Contractor Awards; and

-- one of the Top 100 Minority Business Enterprise Award; The annual awards program honors outstanding women and minority business owners in Maryland, Virginia, Delaware and the District of Columbia.

A Nakamoto Family Affair with Civic Involvement: Bob Nakamoto's family has been involved heavily in numerous business and civic activities that have helped promote the prosperity of the Fairfax County community.

His wife Laurie is a graduate of University of Washington, MSW from St. Louis University and holds a Gerontology certificate from University of Michigan. Laurie consults with a number of nursing homes and does case work in Fairfax County.

His son Robert S. is a graduate of the U.S. Military Academy at West Point, and earned an M.B.A from Ohio University. He moved to Nashville, Tennessee to start a music career but is now a professional engineer for the State of Tennessee. A recent veteran of the Iraq conflict, Robert S. Nakamoto is now on 60% disability. His wife Sheri is a graduate of Belmont University is a fulltime housewife and home schools five children.

His son Gary is a graduate of Ohio University, Chairman of Base Technologies, and was also past Chairman of the Fairfax County Chamber of Commerce. In 2010, he is on the board of INOVA Hospital, American Red Cross, AAA, and a Trustee of Ohio University. His wife Kelly, a CPA, is a graduate of Fairfield University and holds a B.A. from American University. She is a Partner at Price Waterhouse located at Tysons Corner. They have one son.

His daughter Mae holds a BA and MBA from University of Maryland, and is the President/Owner of A Solution, Inc. located in Tysons Corner. Her son Michael is a graduate of Herndon High School and is now a junior at James Madison University.

His son Michael is a graduate of Marshall High School and earned a B.A. from the University of Virginia. He is employed at the Nature Conservatory. His wife Chizuko – PhD from Gallaudet University--is now employed there as a professor. They have one son.

His daughter Amy is a graduate of Marshal High School, and earned a B.A .from North Carolina State, M.A. from University of North Carolina, M.A. from University of Pennsylvania. Formerly Head Soccer coach at Bryn Mawr Collage, Amy is now Executive Director of D.C. Scores – a non profit agency who house 750 children in after school programs. Her husband Jeremy is a graduate of Haverford University and earned an M.A. from Stanford University. He is a teacher and Executive Director of Sports Challenge. They have one son.

From the 1950s: Korean American History in Fairfax County
By Corazon Sandoval Foley

According to the report of the Fairfax County Demographer Anne Cahill included in this book's appendix, there were some 31 Korean immigrants in Fairfax County who entered the US before 1950 based on the 2000 Census results. It is not clear when these early Korean immigrants came to live in Fairfax County.

By 2007, Korean Americans were estimated to be the second largest Asian American group in Fairfax County, totaling some 38,553 residents. Their community has been highly visible in Fairfax County where numerous signs in Korean language are often displayed. Ethnic solidarity appears quite strong in their community in part because of the need to resolve problems caused by language difficulties.

The Annandale area is often referred to as Koreatown. Signs with large Korean characters – subtitled with English words – fill Annandale's urban streetscape. They advertise a wide range of businesses: lawyers and realty offices, doctors, restaurants, electronic stores. In 2005, the Giant Directory – one of four Korean telephone books in the region – listed 929 businesses in Annandale that catered to Koreans, nine times as many as in 1990 and about one-third of all Korean businesses in the Washington area. An early Korean business was Taekwondo schools started by Jhoon Rhee who moved to the Washington area in 1962 and to his current residence in McLean in Fairfax County.

Korean American churches have also grown in numbers in Fairfax County. As I walk out of my home in Edgewater community in Burke, Virginia, I am reminded of how the landmarks in Fairfax County have changed, particularly in terms of the increasing numbers of Asian churches. I often walk by a historic building on Burke Lake Road that has now become the home of the Korean American Happiness Presbyterian Church.

Happiness Presbyterian Church on Burke Lake just outside Edgewater neighborhood. (Photo by C. Foley)

The Korean American church is leasing the building that was erected in 1891 by former African American slaves for the "Little Zion Baptist Church." Reverend Lewis Henry Bailey mortgaged his home for $50 so that the church could be built. In 1990, the Baptist church moved to a new building in Sideburn Road.

Fairfax County Korean American Residents in the 1950s. FCAAHP research in the Fairfax County Asian American History Project has benefited from many residents who are not Asians themselves. I met Ms. Lois Brown at a May 2009 luncheon of the nonprofit group, the Shepherd's Center, in the parish hall of St. Mary's Church. The luncheon discussion focused on the Fairfax County Asian American History Project.

Lois Brown on May 22, 2009 sent me the following note on her Korean American friends who lived in Fairfax County in the 1950s. "To me this project is fascinating because the first family I met when I moved to Fairfax County in July 1957 was a Korean mother with three young children (same ages as my children). The husband/father was working in Japan. The mother learned English (informally) from me. We became and are still best friends! The youngest son, Thomas Ahn, is now a head physician at Cedars-Sinai Hospital in L.A."

The Ahn family from Korea and the Brown family met in 1957 while living in the Belle View Apartments, south of Alexandria, near the Potomac River. They quickly became friends and the Browns were delighted to familiarize the Ahn's with American customs and culture. Lois Brown sent two photos with Mary Ahn in one and the other with Gaby Ahn, Lucy Ahn and Jackie Brown.

A Fairfax County Korean American Doctor in 1954. On June 6, 2009, Lois Brown sent me the following information on Dr. Chae Chung Choi from Korea who practiced in Fairfax County in the 1950s.

1957 - Lois Brown and Mary Ahn in Mount Vernon
(Courtesy of Lois Brown)

"Dr. Chae Chung Choi from Korea came to The Medical College of Virginia in Richmond and was in my sister's class there in the 1920s. In the 1950s he was my family physician and had his office at his home on Mt. Vernon Ave. (Near Fort Hunt Road). Later he bought a house further down off Fort Hunt Rd. He had several children, and one was a daughter, named Virginia. His wife was also from Korea. He was up in his 90s when he died not so many years ago. I understand that his children set up a Foundation in his memory for scholarships for school for needy children."

On June 12, 2009, Lois Brown sent me the following obituary of May 12, 2004.
OBITUARY FOR CHAI C. CHOI, PHYSICIAN

Chai C. Choi, 98, a retired Alexandria primary-care physician who was founding presiodent of the Korean American Medical Association of America and its Washington chapter, died of cardiac arrest May 7, 2004 at his home in Alexandria. (i.e., in Fairfax County south of Alexandria City)

Born in Kaesung, Korea, Dr. Choi was about 20 years old when he immigrated to the United States to pursue his education. He graduated from Emory University in Atlanta and the Medical College of Virginia in Richmond. He also received a master's degree in public health from John Hopkins University. After he interned at Charity Hospital in New Orleans, he returned to Korea to teach at a medical school in Seoul. In 1946, he served as deputy minister of health and welfare in Korea of the US Military Government.

Dr. Choi, who also was the author of "American Medicine in Korean Medical History" (1996), opened his medical practice in Alexandria (that is: Fairfax County, south of Alexandria) in 1954. He retired in 1978 and was associated with Inova Alexandria Hospital during his 24-year career. His wife, Soon Hak Kim-Choi, died in 2001, after 55 years of marriage. Survivors include three children, Walter Choi of Alexandria, Virginia Lee of Washington and John Choi of Columbia, and four grandchildren.

Historical Note on Fairfax County in the 1950s. By early 1950s, Fairfax County was reaching critical stages in its development with pressing needs for water, sewer, and transportation. A 1953 consultant study indicated that 90% of residents were federal government employees. It projected that Fairfax County growth would level off at 320,000 residents by 1980. That projection is definitely off-the-mark as we look back in hindsight at dramatic growth way past 1980 to reach over a million residents by 2007.

2003 and 100 years of Korean Americans in Hawaii. Dr. Yearn Hong Choi – the leader of FCAAHP

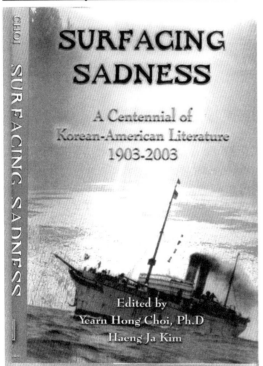

Literary Club – is an editor of the book *"Surfacing Sadness"* that was published in 2003 to commemorate the centennial of the first landing of Korean immigrants in America.

On January 13, 1903, one hundred and two people from Korea disembarked from the merchant ship *Gaelic* in Honolulu, Hawaii. They were the first group of Koreans to work on the sugarcane plantations in search of a new and better life. Many others have followed in waves of immigration as Korean Americans have spread throughout the United States. In Fairfax County, the Korean American community has been very prominent in the business and political arena – and not the least, in literary creativity.

As the book *"Surfacing Sadness"* demonstrates, "despite the fact that the language barrier has by and large hampered the majority of Korean American immigrant authors to write their works in English – therefore making it difficult for them to enter the mainstream American literary scene – their literary voices deserve to be heard, and their art deserves to be recognized. All that does not glitter may be gold."

Jeung-Hwa Elmejjad-Yi's Research on Korean American organizations in Fairfax County and Northern Virginia. Fairfax County Korean American civic leader JeungHwa Elmejjad-Yi provided FCAAHP the following information about Korean American leaders and organizations in Fairfax County to complete this chapter.

Saint Paul Chung Catholic Church was established on September 25, 1986 in 4712 Rippling Pond Drive, Fairfax, Virginia 22033. The number of registered Korean congregation was approximately 6,400 as of December 2009. The webpage for the church is www.stpaulchung.org.

Saint Paul Chung Catholic Church is part of the Catholic Diocese of Arlington and is a parish uniquely established to preserve Korean customs and traditions while providing Mass services in Korean. As a Korean-speaking Catholic parish, Saint Paul Chung Catholic Church has the largest congregation in the United States. The Catholic Diocese of Arlington has worked together with the Diocese of WonJu to provide priests to provide Mass services in the Korean language. Furthermore, this parish provides Mass services in English for members who were born in the United States or those who immigrated at a young age and are not comfortable with the Korean language.

This Catholic Church not only administers Mass services, but also operates a Korean language school which provides 2nd generation Korean youngsters the opportunity to learn the language, history, and culture of Korea. They also provide Korean elderly a wide variety of programs through its Senior Center. As the church prepares to celebrate its 25th anniversary they are looking ahead to the next 50 years, even 100 years, to determine how the church can best meet the needs of the community. The Saint Paul Chung Catholic Church not only strives to meet the spiritual needs of its congregation, but also endeavors to cultivate admirable American citizens while preserving the cultural identity of Koreans living in America.

Korean American Association of the Washington Metropolitan Area (KAA) was established in 1950 and is located in 7004-L Little River Turnpike, Annandale, Virginia 22003. The President is Young Cheon Kim. KAA represents approximately 200,000 Koreans living in the Virginia, Maryland, and Washington, D.C. area.

KAA Purpose: To protect the well-being and interests of the Korean community and to expand and advance the status and prosperity of Koreans living in the Washington, D.C. metropolitan area. KAA endeavors to increase awareness of Korean culture and traditions to Korean Americans and impart a sense of cultural pride in the 2nd generation. KAA hosts an annual Korus Festival to encourage cultural interaction and exchange between the many ethnicities represented in the Washington, D.C. area. KAA provides a variety of cultural programs to promote camaraderie and unity. KAA makes inquiries, examines and researches all necessary resources for the advancement of the Korean community. The KAA Board consists of 80 sitting members.

Jae Ok Chang -- Korean American Culinary Scholar (Author of *"Vignette of Korean Cooking I, II, and III"*). Mrs. Jae Ok Chang immigrated to the United States in 1970. She then began her career by giving lectures on Korean cuisine and became an exceedingly popular and sought-after culinary specialist in the United States. Mrs. Chang wished to pass on the cultural legacy of healthy Korean foods to her daughter, and began to write her recipes in Korean and English. This ultimately went on to be published as the *"Vignette of Korean Cooking I, II, and III"* cookbooks, which is the only Korean cookbook translated in English. The *"Vignette of Korean Cooking I, II, and III"* sold over 100,000 copies and became a best-selling cookbook.

Mrs. Chang in 2010 has worked with the Korean Embassy in Washington, DC -- featured as a culinary specialist at the Korean Culture Center. She also collaborates with the US Department of State as a specialist in Korean Cuisine Education. Mrs. Chang has provided special culinary lectures that are broadcast via radio (AM 1310) and television (WKTV – Washington DC affiliate of MBC America for Koreans), and also in major libraries across the Washington DC metropolitan area and America. Mrs. Chang's vision, dedication, and steadfast devotion have made it possible for future generations of Korean-Americans to learn and continue to carry on the legacy of Korean cuisine -- and make Korean cuisine more accessible to people of all cultures and backgrounds.

Kyung-Shin Lee, DMA, Director of the Washington Korean Symphony Orchestra (WKSO). The WKSO (consisting mostly of Korean professional classical musicians and young promising talents) has been very active in serving both the Korean and American communities in this area. The WKSO's performances include many benefit concert events such as: the WKSO Inaugural Concert in 2002 at the Kennedy Center featuring world renowned pianist, Richard Joo; a candlelight concert in memory of the victims of September 11 at the Thomas Jefferson Memorial in 2002 in partnership with the Korean Concert Society and the National Korean United Methodist church; Asian Chamber Music Festival sponsored by the Asian American Music Society at the Kennedy Center in 2004; the National Minority Enterprise Development (NMED) Awards Gala in 2003, 2004, and 2008. In addition, WKSO and KASF held a joint scholarship fund raising concert at George Mason University in 2003 featuring a world renowned soprano, Young Ok Shin, and guest conductor, Shinik Hahm.

Dr. Kyung-Shin Lee has been recognized and revered as one of the top artists of our time in Korea. She has appeared on various Korean television and radio programs. She has also performed numerous recitals and concert series in Korea, Japan, Russia, Europe, and the United States. Dr. Lee is also well known as a member of the Kyung Trio. The Kyung trio has performed throughout the globe including Carnegie Hall's 100 Year Music Festival with the New York City Symphony. In 1992 she performed in a private concert for Pope John Paul II in Vatican City, Rome, Italy. Dr. Lee is currently the Music Director for the Washington Korean Symphony Orchestra (WKSO).

National Institute of Family Counseling (formerly the Korean American Family Counseling Center) is located at 1952 Gallows Road #204, Vienna, Virginia 22182. Its website is www. kafcc.org. The National Institute of Family Counseling is a non-profit organization that serves the Asian American community in the Washington DC area by helping children, youth, parents, and families overcome the many linguistic and cultural challenges they face in America by providing a wide variety of programs such as individual and family counseling, group mentoring, and education seminars, to establish well-adjusted families and advance the promotion of healthy families.

In 1974, a group of concerned Korean-American women opened a branch office in Washington D.C. to provide financial assistance to the Korean Legal Aid Center for Family Relations based in Seoul, Korea. The Legal Aid Center in Korea was established to help Korean women better understand their legal rights and gain access to legal service. In 1985, the Washington D.C. office expanded its scope to meet the needs of the rapidly growing population of Korean immigrants in the Washington metropolitan area, and was named the Korean American Family Counseling Center (formerly the Korean Family Counseling & Research Center) and appointed Soon Young Lee as the first chairperson. In 1997, the Korean Family Counseling and Research Center (KFCRC) relocated to Vienna, Virginia and changed its name to the Korean American Family Counseling Center. In January 2010, KAFCC changed its name to the National Institute of Family Counseling (NIFC). As of 2010, NIFC is the only non-profit organization in the Washington DC area that provides professional counseling at no cost to low-income minority families.

AM1310 WDCT Radio is located at 3251 Old Lee Highway #506, Fairfax, Virginia 22030. Its audible range: diameter 208 km (Southern Maryland, Northern Virginia, Washington, DC). AM1310 WDCT Radio, founded by Kyung Sup Shin and HyunAe Shin, was the first Korean radio broadcast station that began to air 24 hours a day in 1995. WDCT radio offers five types of programs: News, Resources, Education, Entertainment, and Spirituality. The radio broadcast, which began for the benefit of immigrant Koreans, now stands as a point of connection between 1st and 2nd generation Korean immigrant families that must integrate the Korean and English languages. This station uniquely endeavors to not only impart news and information, but to provide critical and useful resources for families trying to adjust to immigrant life in the United States.

Korean American Women's Chamber of Commerce (USA). The Korean American Women's Chamber of Commerce (USA) is an organization that was founded in December 2006 by Linda Han with a group of 20 successful women from all walks of life who were committed to working together to instill a sense of enduring pride and identity within the hearts of young 1.5, 2nd generation Korean businesswomen. KAWCC-USA functions as the "hub" of bringing together all generations of Korean businesswomen scattered throughout America and the world. The vision/dream of the founder, Linda Han, and its founding members, has been to pass on the cultural, social, and financial heritage of 1st generation immigrant women to future generations of Korean women, thereby empowering them with the knowledge, experiences, and resources of previous generations so that they may thrive in their time and create greater opportunities for future generations.

Korean American Association of Northern Virginia is located in 6131 Willston Drive, Falls Church, Virginia. It was founded in December 1986 and its website is www.vakorea.org. William Won K. Hwang is President and thee Vice Presidents are Jae In Lee, Sang Jun Han, Eun Hee Krieger. The Association's major projects include: a Job Fair in June; Korean Traditional Cultural Night; and Sisterhood Relationship with Culpepper County.

The Vocational School of Korean American Association of Northern Virginia was founded in March 10, 1989 and is located at 6131 Willston Drive, Falls Church, Virginia. The Chairman of the Board is Hyung Joon Kil and the Principal of the School is Chong Ho Yuk. The school has 600 -700 students yearly during its spring, summer and Fall semesters. The curriculum includes Language (English and Spanish); Technical License Course (Heating and A/C, Pharmacy Technician, Construction License); Computer (Basic, Intermediate, Internet and Photoshop); and Job Skills

(Alteration, Tailoring and Home Fashion). The school's budget is supported by the Fairfax County Government, the Korean Government, board members and sponsors' group.

In Fairfax County, Korean American Stories of Cultural Pride and Civic Engagement.

FCAAHP's research work on Korean American History has been enriched tremendously by the assistance of Jeung-Hwa Elmejjad-Yi -- an outstanding community leader and the founder of the Korean American Cultural Committee that has been the leader in the creation of the Korean Bell Pavilion Garden in Meadowlark Park. JeungHwa Elmejjad-Yi has generously shared her own story in this FCAAHP book. Ilryong Moon of Braddock District in Fairfax County in 2010 has been the first and only elected Asian American School Board Member. Yearn Hong Choi of Springfield District in Fairfax County is a recognized poet who has written several books and fascinating poems/stories about the 100 years of Korean American history.

Creating a Fairfax County Landmark – The Korean Bell Garden
By JeungHwa Elmejjad-Yi

My name is Chun Elmejjad, also known as JeungHwa Yi in the Korean community. My parents gave me a name that means, "Spring." Spring is the season that follows winter and ushers in new life and hope. Many people change their native names to more "Americanized" names when they are granted citizenship in the States, but I wanted to retain my heritage as a Korean American.

I was born in Pusan, South Korea, as the oldest child. When my father passed away when I was in high school, we decided to immigrate to the United States to give ourselves more opportunities and a better education. My mother (Okcha Kim) had sisters already living in the States and we came to live with them here in Fairfax County.

When people see my name, many of them comment that I have a family name, or last name, that does not reflect my Asian appearance. I've been married for 21 years to a wonderful man, Jamal Elmejjad, who is Moroccan. We met here in Fairfax County, got married in Fairfax County, and had a lovely daughter, Sonia, here in Fairfax County. When my husband and I went to get our marriage license, the clerk told us that we were the first Korean-Moroccan union in the county. I've lived in Fairfax County since I first arrived here in America, I began my family here in Fairfax County, and I plan to die in Fairfax County. I have visited several different counties and none of them come close to sharing the amazing cultural diversity that can be seen in Fairfax County.

I am so proud to have a multicultural background. I grew up in an environment where sharing was the norm, and I want to continue that custom today in our community. I am so fortunate to have a multicultural familial and professional background. I have been working in the field of finance for 16 years where there is a plethora of diversity. I have been honored to work together with people from all different walks of life that have contributed to deepening my appreciation for people of all different backgrounds. Furthermore, I deeply value the importance of serving the community.

I do my very best to give back to the community by serving in the community as:
> Chairperson of the Korean American Cultural Committee
> Chairperson of the Korean American Family Counseling Center
> Executive Board Member of the Vocation School of Korean American
> > Association of Northern Virginia
> Asian Liaison for the Virginia Asian American Advisory Board

I am also part of something called the "sandwich generation." I have the privilege of serving as a bridge between the 1st generation of Koreans (Koreans who immigrated to the US as adults) and the 2nd generation (Korean Americans who were born here in the US). I consider it a noble calling to be the bridge that passes on values of hard work, love and concern for our neighbors, and the sharing of joy and happiness to our future generation.

In commemoration of 100 years of our immigrant history, we created plans to build the Korean Bell Garden in Meadowlark Park. Our vision and hope for this Bell Garden is to share the legacy of Korean culture, traditions, and customs with the community and also with the future generations of Korean Americans. We had nothing when we began this endeavor, but God surrounded us with so many wonderful people like Penny Gross, Paul Gilbert (NVRPA), Sue Webb, Sharon Bulova, Chap Petersen, and all the members of KACC that have supported and provided the resources necessary to make our dreams a reality. I would also like to give a special acknowledgement of thanks to Professor David Chung who provided the conceptual design for the Korean Bell and Dr. Chang Ho Ahn who shared his insight, vision, passion, and prayer in support of this great undertaking. Without such individuals this historical landmark would not have been possible.

Finally, I believe that all of the hard work, toil, tears, and efforts of previous generations will be the soil that will enable our children and future generation to grow and thrive as Korean Americans. I want them to know what we have sacrificed and what we have done so that they can have the lives they are living today, and remind them to work just as hard for the future generation, and to give back to the community what was given to them. But most importantly, I hope they become people who have faith in God and I believe He will continue to bless them as He has blessed us.

Jamal, JeungHwa, Sonia Elmejjad of Fairfax County (Courtesy of JeungHwa Elmejjad-Yi)

Ilryong Moon: Korean American Leader in the Fairfax County School Board
By Corazon Sandoval Foley

As of 2010, Ilryong Moon remains the first and only Asian American elected member of the Fairfax County School Board. He has encouraged political involvement by Fairfax County Korean Americans with this frequent advice: "Do not live in a self-imposed isolation. You need to step out of your small ethnic community and try to learn to live together with others. Do not give up learning English. Language acquisition does not happen overnight. Remember that a few votes can make a difference in any election. Politicians will listen to you only if you vote."

Ilryong Moon's Fairfax County saga began in 1974, when at the age of 17, he moved from Seoul, South Korea to Northern Virginia. He has often discussed his memory of the culture shock during his arrival when he saw so many cars in the airport parking lot and his father, who had immigrated earlier than the rest of the family, arriving in his own car to pick them up. For in Korea, his family had lived

Young Ilryong Moon in 1977 sitting at the bleachers in T.C. Williams High School. (Courtesy of Ilryong Moon)

in an apartment with only one room besides the kitchen. The apartment had no hot water or shower and only one outhouse that six or seven households had to share. His father never learned more than a few words of English and was an auto mechanic.

Ilryong Moon arrived as a 17-year old rising junior, but repeated the 10th grade to learn English as an ESL (English as a Second Language) student at George Washington Junior High School in Alexandria, Virginia. From 1975 -1977, he studied at T.C. Williams High School, where he was then one of the few foreign-born students. Some of his teachers took him under their wing, tutoring him each morning before classes or making vocabulary lists for him to memorize. He also played bingo to improve his English.

Ilryong Moon remembered that, "I felt badly about my heavy accent until one teacher took me to the office of the principal who was from New England, and had him read, 'Go park your car.' Then the teacher said, 'See? You're not the only one with an accent.' It made me feel better. I still have an accent, but I survived."

After graduating from T.C. Williams High School in Alexandria, Ilryong Moon went on to become a *cum laude* graduate of Harvard University and then to William and Mary Law School. He has been a partner in the law firm of Moon, Park &

Ilryong Moon with family at son's graduation in 2007. (Courtesy of Ilryong Moon)

Associates in Annandale in Fairfax County and his main practice area is business law, dealing primarily with Korean American business clients. He has held key positions, including At-Large Commissioner on the Fairfax County Planning Commission; Vice President of a local Rotary Club; and member of the Virginia Advisory Committee of the U.S. Civil Rights Commission. His wife, Haewon, has been coordinator of the piano department at the Duke Ellington School of the Arts. Ilryong Moon's joys include: cheering at his sons' soccer and basketball games; and singing in the choir of his church, the Korean United Methodist Church of Greater Washington.

The *Washington Post* October 22, 2007 endorsement of Ilryong Moon for the School Board, noted his contributions: "Mr. Moon, on the board since 1995, has a record of solid achievement. He was instrumental in the expansion of foreign-language instruction, and his experience emigrating as a teenager from South Korea gives him insights into the needs of English-language learners."

When I interviewed Ilryong Moon, he shared his belief that: "the diverse communities in Fairfax should all work together to build a better community and they can certainly build a better community by working together. Although the county enjoys the best reputation as a model of education in the whole country, we need to improve what we have. As Fairfax has the most diverse student body and an increasing population, I want to hire more bi-lingual staff and teachers. I want to get more resources to raise the standard of teachers' training and pay them better. I want to decrease class size as class sizes are a factor in success and a key to reduction in disparity." He shared with me his dream that his children will grow up and live here (in Fairfax County) not just as "hyphenated" Asian Americans, but as "full-pledged" Americans.##

Ilryong Moon standing left side in the front row in 2008 with the elected 2007 - 2010 Fairfax County Public School (FCPS) Board. (FCPS photo)

A Literary Life in Fairfax County
By Yearn Hong Choi

(FCAAHP Note: Yearn Hong Choi, an accomplished poet and author, has requested inclusion in the FCAAHP book of the following excerpts of his publications and poems on his life as a Korean American and a Fairfax County resident, as well as a poem entitled *"Immigrants' Dream"* that he wrote for the May 29, 2009 Naturalization Ceremony sponsored by the Fairfax County Asian American History Project.)

The Voice of America and the 2003 Centennial of Korean Immigration to Hawaii. "In 2003, I spoke on the Voice of America's "New American Voices" on the subject of Korean American life. It was a centennial celebration of the first Korean immigrants to Hawaii sugar plantations. They left Korea in December 1902 and arrived at Hawaii in January 1903 by ship. They were the first Korean Americans.

"All-in-all I am positive towards U.S. society and the U.S. government and the American people as the leading nation and the leading people of this world society in the 21st century," I told the host. "Sometimes I see the glorious aspect of American life, sometimes I see some of the tragic, or arrogance-of-power side, sometimes I see the human-being dominated, or law-dominated society, and I try to reflect this in my poems."

On the 1960s and 1970s: "I was so attracted to the United States. What made the United States great was that kind of vitality. The civil

Yearn Hong Choi when he left for the US in 1970. (Courtesy of Yearn Hong Choi)

rights movement for human equity and equality, and the environmental movement for the man and nature relationship, and the anti-Vietnam war movement, an unjust war the young people tried to stop. I think all these three movements that I observed in the first part of my American life were unforgettable, and I believe that such power and such forces still remain somewhere in this country."

On discrimination in the United States: "Well, I shouldn't say this, but during my Pentagon experiences NATO people couldn't come to my office, or they were led to another room, skipping my office. I felt some bias and prejudice still existing in this country. All these kinds of things are still in my memory, but I still say this country is greater than any other country in accepting and accommodating foreign people, and that it is the land of hope and opportunities."

On poetry: "It's more or less personal poetry, it's basically my life, my 30-some years of American life reflected in 50 poems. I try to show my anger and my happiness, my pathos, almost everything is there. But poetry and literature is what I have been dependent on in a sense to sustain my life.

"The VOA host said this about my poetry: "One of Mr. Choi's early poems, entitled "My Sail" (excerpted below), shows his dichotomy of feeling on leaving Korea to come to America."

"A gull/ and solitude with the solidity of a thing./ My sail shines fresh venturing along/ In the shadow of the Pacific./ What am I searching for in a distant land?/ What have I cast off in my native land?/ The waves are playing, the winds whistle,/ And the mast bows and creaks./ Alas! I am searching for happiness! / Below the soul a stream of glistening azure/ Between the vast expanse of the sky and the waters."

Yearn Hong Choi and family in Fairfax County. (Courtesy of Yearn Hong Choi)

"For the past three years," the host continued, "Dr. Choi has been commuting from his home in a Washington suburb to Seoul, Korea, where he is a professor and chairman of the environmental policy program in the University of Seoul's Graduate School of Urban Sciences. He accepted the job, he says, because he has an aged mother in Korea, and as the eldest son he has a duty to take care of her. Dr. Choi says that after 30 years in the United States, he still embodies strong Korean, as well as American, values."

On Filial Piety and Family: "I've been Korean in the sense that I am going back to Korea to take care of my mother, that's the Korean aspect, filial piety, but I enjoy my freedom of thinking and freedom of expression, as a poet and writer I appreciate the country I am living in…Married to a Korean American woman, I have two grown children both of whom work on Wall Street, the financial district of New York.

"My children's values are quite different... They are American. They are not Korean American; they are totally American. It's a totally different world they live in. This is their country; English is their mother tongue. Probably the language and the value systems they acquired from kindergarten and all the way... They are good American citizens... It is somehow ironic that in Korea I am often seen as an American.

"Well, some people think I am a foreigner, some people think I am too pro-American, but it's all right with me. I have two countries I'm living in. And maybe this is still much freer and more comfortable than my home country. Both sides have virtues and things I care about and value highly. I've been very fortunate to live in two worlds, and get good things from two worlds. I appreciate my life, I thank you to the society I have been in, and I'm grateful particularly in this centennial year of Korean immigration."
***

Poetry Reading in the Library of Congress. "On April 28, 1994, I was invited to read my poems in the Library of Congress under the auspices of the Gertrude Clarke Whittall Poetry and Literature Fund. As the first Korean American poet who was invited to read my poems, I was deeply honored. The Library of Congress invited Dr. Seung Soo Han, the Ambassador from Korea. He was out of town for his attendance at former president Richard M. Nixon's funeral in California, but deputy ambassador Ki Moon Ban, who later became U.N. Secretary General in 2006, came to my poetry reading and delivered a short congratulatory speech.

"I like to think of Korean American poets and writers as a forest – a forest with its many different elements of nature coming together to make one. All kinds of trees and plants, creeks, rocks, birds, deer, morning glory, waterfalls, and sounds of water, a diversity of trees or plants, squirrels, and deer make up the forest of Korean American literature. Diversity makes one picturesque forest.

"Korean American poets and writers have a great sense of loss and sense of deprivation. The loss is the loss of their home country, their mother tongue, their relatives and friends, and their past. Literature fills the void or the loss.

"Insofar as Korean American literature is based on sorrow, nostalgia, pathos, yearning, and tears over joy, laughter, victory and happiness in a New Land, it reminds us that the new land is still very foreign to the first-generation Korean immigrants. Some resorted to Christian literature as a comfort to the people with sorrow. Oscar Wilde said, "sorrow is the most beautiful thing in the human heart." Yearn Hong Choi is "Going Home" constantly. We all together make one forest.

"In the Library of Congress, I read my poems in Korean, and the poet laureate read my poems in English. That is a tradition of the Library of Congress poetry reading. Several Nobel laureates did read their poems in their mother tongues, and their American friends read their poems in English."

Second Poetry Reading in the Library of Congress. "In January 2003, I was invited to read my poems at the Library of Congress a second time, this time on the celebration of the centennial year of Koreans' laborers' landing in the Hawaii sugar plantations in the early 20th century. In the same year, I edited *Surfacing Sadness: A Centennial of Korean-American Literature* (Homa and Sekey Books). Here are some of the poems I read, many reflecting on my American life.

Journey to Korea
Even though only an empty house
Awaits me, I go.
I beg pardon to my ancestors,
Buried in my family cemetery
Up in the mountains.
I beg for forgiveness; a son living abroad
So long in a foreign land.

Reminiscence
A certain coquettish Korean girl
Is my only memory of my Indiana University.
Oh, how flirtatious she was!
I cannot even begin.
She sang always, dreaming of
Being an opera singer someday.
I applauded her dream.
By time and tide
I am older and wiser since my university days.
Even if I see her now
I doubt I would blush as I used to so often then.
My heart yearns for those carefree days---
The innocent days of my youth so long ago---
Wishing to become as a young man once again.
The beautiful campus is still vivid in my memory.
I wonder if the splendor of the green field
Is still the same.
Music by Bach that she and I used to appreciate
May still permeate the fresh air on campus.
There was a beautiful prelude of a young couple.
There was nothing but an overture of young lovers' opera.

Korean American Life in the Metro Washington Area. "The Korean American community did not exist when I first came to the Washington area in 1981. There were just a handful of Korean churches, grocery stores and restaurants. Now, there are two Korean community centers: one in Annandale and another in Centerville. Koreans are now one of the largest minority groups in Fairfax, Virginia.

"There is one Korean-American school board member and many with influence on the congressional elections, both among Democrats and Republicans. Regionally, we have two daily newspapers--the *Korea Times* and the *Korea Daily,* plus one weekly magazine, the *Korea Monitor.* One major television network (NBC) even has a Korean lady as an anchor. Virginia Cha is an anchor/reporter for CNN.

"The problem is that Korean Americans are too often isolated as an ethnic group, or assimilated completely. It is not always easy to enter into the so-called "mainstream" America. Many new arrivals end up isolating themselves. But then some second-generation Korean-Americans ignore their heritage completely. Many feel they do not need the Korean community or the Korean churches. There is a happy medium. That, at least, is what I strive for.

'I had a poetry reading in the Korean community in spring of 2008. I tried to get a couple of lines printed in the *Washington Post's* Literary Calendar in its Book World, but failed. A Korean Buddhist Temple, Borimsa at Fairfax, organized the 49th day ceremony for the victims of the Virginia Tech in 2007. I tried to get a couple of lines printed in the *Washington Post's* Religion Page Saturday, but failed. I thought they were newsworthy, but the *Washington Post* did not think that way.

The Korean American people who aimed at the main stream could be frustrated. The urban riots in American cities in the 1960s were erupted from the African American people's frustration. So my concerns on the Korean American community can be a serious one: Is it a self-isolating move? Or is it an acceptable move? Depending upon who views from what angle, this can be a serious issue."
***

Yearn Hong Choi during FCAAHP interview in November 7, 2008.
(Photo by Cora Foley)

A Poem written by Yearn Hong Choi for May 2009 First Naturalization Ceremony at the Fairfax County Government Center initiated by the Fairfax County Asian American History Project

Immigrants' Dream ---For My Fellow immigrants
By Yearn Hong Choi

We came to this country with new hope, dream and ambition.
We came to this country with much bigger hope, dream and ambition.

In May 1968, I came to Seattle with $70 in my pocket.
I finished my studies, while washing dishes
and working in factories every summer.

Teaching in the fall of 1972
Found the" immigrant" enveloped within
The great heart of the University of Wisconsin.
The enormity of the Pentagon, HUD and NASA
Might have further diminished "the immigrant".
It didn't. It raised his stature to giant dimensions.
 2006 welcomed the new journey into the immense universe of retirement.

This is still an open country
A vast country from the Pacific to the Atlantic.
This is an open country for you.
Please embrace your dream.
Sky is the limit.

You had a bold dream for a richer, affluent and prosperous life,
With great hope and greater courage
 You made this new country your hearth and home.
Your dreams deserve this country of opportunity.

The immigrants
The immigrants they made America Great.
The immigrants are Us.
We are America.

Our dreams, our sweat moves this, our country this country, forward,
This world moves forward
The Depression we see today
Our children and their children will not witness tomorrow
The immigrants will move this Country forward as in the past.

My fellow new citizens,
Let us do our very best.
God will help those who help themselves.
Let our sons and daughters see our dream
Let our sons and daughters witness
The achievement of this dream.

The Lady of Freedom offers Her light and guidance
Her torch, Her light is the ray of hope
Sailing from the darkened sea of night

Welcome home brothers and sisters!
Welcome to our harbor
Of New Hope, New Dream and New Ambition.
Welcome fellow immigrants no longer.
Welcome fellow Citizens.

New Americans at the First Fairfax County Naturalization Ceremony
May 29, 2009

Photo by Terry Sam

From 1970s: Vietnamese American History in Fairfax County
By Corazon Sandoval Foley

Fairfax County Demographer Anne Cahill's report noted that in the year 2000, there was no record of any Vietnamese American resident in Fairfax County who entered the US before 1950. There was a record of 22 who entered the US before 1950 and 1959; and 137 between 1960 and 1969. There was an explosion of Vietnamese residents in Fairfax County who entered the US from 1970 to 1979 – and the numbers have continued to increase. What is not clear from Anne Cahill's report is when those Vietnamese moved to Fairfax County after they entered the US.

By 2007, Vietnamese residents in Fairfax County have grown to 24,236, making them the third largest group in the county, after Asian Indian and Korean residents.

Eden Center and a 2009 Smithsonian Exhibit. On June 22, 2009, I visited Eden Center, in part to see the Smithsonian Institution exhibit at an old warehouse on Vietnamese American history titled *"Exit Saigon, Enter Little Saigon."* Since it's founding in 1984, Eden Center has acted as a venue that has enabled Vietnamese residents, many of them from Fairfax County, to celebrate their ethnic heritage.

In her 2003 academic paper *"Pho and Apple Pie,"* Jessica Meyers wrote a good paragraph describing Eden Center.

Eden Center June 2009 Exhibit *"Exit Saigon Enter Little Saigon."* (Photo by Cora Foley)

"Eden Center is the largest Vietnamese commercial center on the East Coast of North America. Set on the corner of Wilson Boulevard at Seven Corners in Falls Church, Eden Center serves as the most visible point of interaction among the dispersed Vietnamese community in the Washington DC metropolitan area as well as for other Vietnamese Americans along the East Coast. The complex boasts throngs of shops selling *pho,* a traditional Vietnamese noodle soup flavored with anise and a signature meal in Vietnam. Vietnamese run and own the businesses, which also include an extensive array of regional restaurants from Vietnam's numerous provinces, jewelry boutiques, bakeries, delis, music and video stores, travel agencies that offer transportation to and from Vietnam, and money wiring offices where one can carry out all business in Vietnamese. The center also houses an assortment of barbers, electronics outlets, nail salons and two Vietnamese markets to total over 120 stores."

Eden Center with South Vietnamese flag and US flag. (Photo by Cora Foley)

Jessica Meyers added that: "Despite the Passats and SUVs residing outside store entrances, Eden does feel like a miniature replica of a Vietnamese city. Young Vietnamese men gaze sleepily from behind café shop windows as mothers scold their children from across the parking lot in the multiple tones that characterize the Vietnamese language… Two stoic lions guard the entrance and between them, a red arch frames the complex and calligraphic gold letters announcing the name "Eden Center." One might assume that the sign provides entry to a sleepy Chinese palace sitting on a hill outside of Beijing or a thriving Buddhist temple along the Mekong River in Laos. However, a glimpse to the left reveals a newly renovated GAP and the Seven Corners junction that joins several major roads in Northern Virginia."

Historical note on Seven Corners. Eden Center is located in Fairfax County's first regional shopping mall that was developed in 1953 on a 34-acre tract of land at Fort Buffalo, locally called Seven Corners. The land was owned by the heirs of Frederick Foote, a black man with some white and Indian ancestors, who had purchased it for $500 in 1864. The shopping mall at Seven Corners marked the beginning of Fairfax's substantial retail community. By the 1990s, Fairfax County would have more retail space than almost any jurisdiction in the US and attract shoppers from around the world.

Seven Corners (Courtesy of Virginia Room)

The Waves of Vietnamese Arrivals to Fairfax County. There were three major phases in the Vietnamese immigration into the US and Fairfax County. Prior to 1975, few Vietnamese settled in the DC area. The first massive wave of immigration occurred with the fall of Saigon to Communist troops on April 30, 1975. From April to December of 1975, 125,000 Vietnamese fled to the US and of those who settled in the metropolitan DC area, most settled in Arlington County due to placement by US sponsor services. The first wave consisted of fairly well educated and Westernized Vietnamese who practiced Roman Catholicism and came from urban areas. Sponsored by families or agencies, many were thrust into a foreign environment with few resources on which to draw. "Little Saigon" in Clarendon, Virginia (Arlington County) developed as a result of the growing need for familiarity. Many then moved from Arlington to Fairfax County as they got jobs and their economic situations improved.

The second wave of refugees began in 1978 and the "boat people" arrived steadily until 1985, like the family of Lan Du who gave an FCAAHP interview in 2008 at Pohick Library. Around 75,000 boat people arrived in the US with this wave, including many ethnic Chinese. Generally, they were less educated, spoke little English and considered themselves Buddhist. Many Vietnamese-run small businesses were started after the arrival of the second wave because the refugees could not find jobs in the area and started marketing to the growing Vietnamese population.

The third wave of immigrants came from 1989. Although categorized as "boat people," most came to the US through government-sponsored programs, namely the Orderly Departure Program (ODP) and the Humanitarian Operations (HO) Program. In 1987, a smaller wave of AmerAsians, people with American fathers and Vietnamese mothers, arrived in the US with the Homecoming Act, providing reunion of children with American GI fathers. .

Many groups have been created to address issues arising from the waves of Vietnamese refugees. The Vietnamese American Youth Education (VYEA) was founded in 1977 to help in the adjustment of the Vietnamese refugee population to American society. Boat People S.O.S. was formed to offer mental health, recreational programs for torture survivors, educational information, and legal services to the 10,000 HO people in the DC area -- many of the 180,000 HO refugees who came to the US were survivors of torture and face different adjustment difficulties.

The waves of Vietnamese refugees drew a mix of people – as you will discover in the set of stories in this book. While the first wave refugees distinguished themselves as Westernized and the second wave less so, the third wave has contained people from various economic and social backgrounds.

I have summarized below some of the responses to the FCAAHP oral history interviews that provide better understanding of the adjustment to American life by Fairfax County Vietnamese Americans from the different refugee waves to our area.

1975 and Nhi Anh Chu's student visa to the US. Nhi Anh Chu, PhD, is an engineer and member of the Vietnamese Youth Educational Association of Washington (VYEA).

The first wave of political refugees from Vietnam included Nhi Anh Chu – but he and his siblings came with F-1 (Student) visas just days before April 30, 1975. They came as foreign students, half knowing and half guessing during the last year before their departure that big changes were on the way for their future lives. His father always thought of their destination to be "Washington DC" and Fairfax County was thought of as a DC suburb that attracted him as a "Shining City on a Hill." His father consistently stated that the US was the technological center of the world, and that opinion shaped his desire to send his children to the US to acquire knowledge and skills.

Nhi Anh Chu's earliest idea of the US was through a picture of his mother with the kids at the Dalat market (his hometown) taken by an American G.I. Growing up, they looked at the black-and-white 1964 picture often, when his mother would talk about the kind Americans. The picture made him put himself in the position of the American behind the camera, looking at them from the outside world. "That's it, the Americans were to me a kind people, but a people different from us."

He described the period between 1975 and 1979 when his family lived in an apartment complex in South Arlington. "Too poor to buy and too unsettled to invest in a new car, and too busy to care for the used cars that we had, we literally went through a couple of Volkswagens or Pintos or Ford station wagons per year. (Pinto is a cheap Ford car that is the ultimate lemon of all time!) One summer, our Ford LTD station wagon broke down with a busted water pump, I was struggling with the self-repair job when a man who lived in the nearby apartment came out and offered to help. He looked like Jimmy Connors, the tennis star. He ended up teaching me about water pump, thermostat, rubber hose, even loaned me the tools. He drove with me to the parts store…and he wanted NOTHING in return. This was one of the great many stories of our life in the US where people are simply generous in small and big ways."

On life in the US: "Personally, life in the US has been great. To me, it is in fact a paradise on earth where people respect one another out of innate appreciation of what's right, if not just because the law requires it… However, my parents did encounter hardship. My mom was not able to continue with her career as an educator, or my dad. My dad worked as a draftsman and the comedown on status probably drove him into over-compensating with 12-hour-a-day volunteer work at home that took a toll on his health. But we were all free to enjoy or to suffer or both, that was clear."

His family participated substantially in the activities of the Vietnamese Youth Education Association (vyea.com) that has been holding a 6-week Summer School for about 300 Vietnamese American Youths every year since 1977.

On Vietnamese American contributions: "Statistics would correct the general and false impression of the great success of Vietnamese Americans as seen in the disproportionate presence on the top rung of the education systems from grade school to Stanford… Nevertheless, the symbolism of the apparent success of the elite Vietnamese Americans serves to exemplify the basic American Way: Everyone is given a fair chance to succeed and the better ones are rewarded accordingly. At the bread-and-butter level, Vietnamese Americans contributed positively to American society without creating problems. Vietnamese Americans are the next door workers: grocery store clerks, nail salon workers, restaurateurs, teachers, engineers…"

Nhi Anh Chu's advice to younger generation: "Pay attention to the political process, or process in general, to be applied in every societal activities… The process must be right in order for the good to rise above the bad."

1975 and Professor Nguyen Thi Kim-Oanh. In July of 1975, after several months of living in refugee camps and shelters, including Guam and Camp Pendleton in California, Professor Nguyen Thi Kim-Oanh came to live in Fairfax County.

On leaving Vietnam: "I left Vietnam on April 23, 1975, before the fall of Saigon, not knowing the fate Vietnam was going to face in only a few more days. With me, I brought my nephew (14 years old) and a zither, one of my favorite musical instruments. When I heard of what happened to Vietnam a week later, I was very sad. I could not believe I had left my mother behind. I cried a lot and comforted myself with my own music. I didn't realize that my music also comforted other refugees in our camp."

On experiences in Fairfax County: "When I first arrived in July of 1975, I began babysitting and then got into lots of different jobs to support my teenage nephew and me. I remember using my art skills to exchange for furniture for our apartment. In 1976, my niece (16 years old) and another nephew (17 years old) joined us from another refugee camp.

"To support my niece and nephews with their studies, I took on many different jobs and projects. One time I remember doing a special project for a restaurant by writing their menu in calligraphy. Even though it was a lot of money for me, I was later told by a friend that I was underpaid. I took it lightly because it was a lesson learned, but was happy to be able to use my skills. I also took on a job as a waitress until I found a job as a cosmetics secretary. Through the years, I also worked as a hand engraver for Woodies before they closed their store. I also had a chance to try bookkeeping as well.

"At first, these odd jobs made me feel uncomfortable and sad because I felt I lost my dignity...it was hard to go from being a well-respected teacher/professor in Vietnam to starting at the "bottom" at the age of 40 something in a strange country. I missed my mom a lot and could not bear to think that I had left her in Vietnam. We finally reunited in 1983 and so did my sister with her children. I never talked much about the different jobs and struggles I went through with my mom and sister because watching my niece and nephews become successful was gratifying enough."

On the Asian American community in Fairfax: "As soon as I came to the US, I've tried to keep my Vietnamese traditions alive to help others around me cope with the changes. I celebrate our cultural traditions when I can. I have shared my music, songs, and dances with others. I have interacted with many children throughout the years to teach them about Vietnamese culture and tradition and I have found opportunities for them to perform and celebrate our heritage. The Asian American community was comforting in helping me get established in Fairfax County."

1976 and Nhon Phan Tran's Escape from Vietnam. Nhon Phan Tran's family first lived in Fairfax County from 1977 – 1978 to take ESL classes and be with more Vietnamese people; then they moved and returned from 1980-2003 when her husband had a medical practice in the county. In 2009, they had moved to Triangle but Nhon Phan Tran still volunteers in Fairfax County for the Fairfax Area Agency on Aging.

On escaping Vietnam: "In 1975, after the fall of Saigon, I began organizing an escape from Vietnam by boat while my husband was being imprisoned in the reeducation camp. My husband was a doctor and I was a pharmacist. We had four children. I lived in Nha Trang and bought two boats. For a year prior to our departure in 1976, every morning we (the whole family) would go to the beach to swim and pretend to learn how to fish. What we were really doing was learning to survive on a boat. Then on June 1976, our family of 11 people (my husband, 4 children, 2 younger sisters, 1 cousin, 1 sister-in-law, and 1 friend of a sister, and me) and 12 other close friends (23 of us in total) made our escape. During our six-day journey, we lost one boat (the bigger boat) because it was damaged during a heavy storm, a storm we thought we would never survive, but we woke up that morning we were all alive and close to the Philippines...We finally arrived in Hawaii on August 12, 1976. We settled in Prince William County where our sponsors lived. We lived in Fairfax County for one year before my husband was accepted to medical school in Michigan. Then, we moved back to Fairfax County where I managed his office from 1980-2003."

On American adjustment: "We felt very welcomed coming to the US, but there were hardships. Because we had such a large family, it was hard to find a place to live when we moved to Fairfax County. No one wanted to allow a couple with four children to rent an apartment. Our sponsors were really nice; they continued to help us get settled. When we first moved to Fairfax County in 1977, we applied for food stamps and other benefits. Our apartment was close to the children's school, so they could walk; they went to Timber Lane Elementary. The families in the apartment above and below us were Vietnamese, so we supported each other."

Scenes from adjustment of the family of Nhon Phan Tran in Fairfax County and American Life. (Courtesy of Nhon Phan Tran)

On the Vietnames community: Since her family was one of the first waves of Vietnamese refugees to come to Fairfax County, she has contributed to the establishment of the Vietnamese community. "When we returned to Fairfax County in 1980, we participated in groups like: Hoi Y Te (Vietnamese Medical Society), Buddhist temples, Hoi Cao Nien (Vietnamese Senior Association), Hoi Giao Duc (Vietnamese Cultural Society), and others." She thinks the community is missing collaboration and cohesiveness because of too many different political views and influences.

On generation gap: "Later when we started sponsoring more family members, I noticed that we all had different ways of thinking, especially with different waves of sponsorship…I tried very hard to help my children retain their Vietnamese language and being active in the Vietnamese community has helped. We still celebrate Vietnamese and Buddhist traditions in our family."

On her legacy: "I want to be remembered as a person with experience as a refugee who lived under the communist regime, which is what led me to want to find freedom for my family. I've always told my children, America is the land of opportunity and freedom. You need to work hard to obtain your dream. All my children have taken this to heart and I am proud of their accomplishments. If you don't work hard, you'll have nothing."

1980 and Amy Trang's family in Fairfax County. Amy Trang holds a PhD in Public Policy from George Mason University and works with the Fairfax Area Agency on Aging. She has been tutoring Vietnamese Americans in her community for over ten years while also actively involved with youth leadership programs such as Girl Scouts.

Amy Trang was about 18 months old when her family moved as refugees from Vietnam to Fairfax County where her father had relatives. Her father formerly worked for the Vietnamese government and her father was being politically persecuted at the time of her birth in 1979.

Amy grew up balancing several cultures: Vietnamese, Chinese, and American. Having an Asian American community in Fairfax County has helped Amy become aware of her cultural heritage and personal identity.

Amy Trang and family in Fairfax County. (Courtesy of Amy Trang)

The Asian American community is growing with businesses that contribute cultural flare and awareness for cultural diversity. Amy's family celebrates Vietnamese and Chinese traditions and holidays.

When she was growing up, there were many immigrant children in Annandale and Falls Church and they were all trying to assimilate into the American culture. There were fractions and friction in school and teachers were trying their best to minimize prejudice and discrimination. As she grew up and attended school, there were times when she felt un-welcomed and were called names. She believes that people in Fairfax County have become more tolerant of other countries than when she first arrived.

1990 and Thuan Ly's escape from Vietnam. In 2002, Thuan Ly moved to Fairfax County when offered a job as a police officer at George Mason University's Police Department; he was previously living in Hampton, VA.

On escaping Vietnam: "In 1990, when I was about 10 years old, I escaped Vietnam by boat with an uncle. My dad was already in the US; he escaped in 1985. I had lived with my mom, older sister, and older brother up until I left Vietnam. I ended up on a refugee camp for about two years in Indonesia; my dad sponsored me to the US. In 1993, I arrived in Hampton and started high school and finished college with an Engineering degree but I started my career as a police officer in Hampton…I didn't sponsor my mom and brother and sister until 1996…at that time we were already separated for 6 years and even longer for my dad."

On the Asian American community: "I supported Boat People SOS (BPSOS) youth program. I am also a member of the Asian Law Enforcement Society (ALES). They're good community support... I appreciate my life because of the hardships in Vietnam...When I was at the refugee camp sometimes there was no food to eat. I feel that family values are important...that's what I learned in Vietnam and I think the Vietnamese should carry those values with them wherever they go."

In Fairfax County, Vietnamese American Stories of Rebuilding Lives and Second Generation Americans. As part of the Fairfax County Asian American History Project, we are sharing with you two stories. A former refugee, Jackie Bong-Wright shared her story of escaping from Vietnam to becoming a civic leader in Fairfax County. The second story is a compilation of responses from second generation Vietnamese Americans that were gathered by Vy Nguyen, the youngest team leader in FCAAHP who graduated from Flint Hill High School in 2008 and has been studying international affairs at the University of Toronto. Vy and Dzung Nguyen are the daughter-and-father team who has helped FCAAHP understand the Vietnamese American lives in Fairfax County.

A Vietnamese Journey to Freedom
By Jackie Bong Wright

In 1978, I finally settled down in Falls Church, in Fairfax County, after three years of nomadic life in four countries and four different states in the U.S.

When the North Vietnamese Communists took over South Vietnam in April of 1975, I fled my country. I was a widow with three children under 10. Earlier, the U.S., our ally in the ten-year Vietnam War, had cut off aid to Vietnam and left us unable to defend ourselves.

As Chairman of the Board of the Vietnamese American Association (VAA) and its Director of Cultural Activities, I knew that the Communists would not leave me alone. They regarded the American "imperialists" and their "lackeys" as their number one enemies. My late husband, Nguyen Van Bong, leader of South Vietnam's main opposition party - The National Progressive Movement – had been assassinated by the Vietcong in 1971, a day after accepting the position of prime minister of South Vietnam.

I had become a widow at 30 with three children under five. My younger brother, a lieutenant in the South Vietnamese army, was executed at point blank by the Vietcong in 1965. My elder brother, a colonel, died in prison in the North of malnutrition and mistreatment in 1978. Thousands of family members, colleagues and friends suffered the same fate.

So, though I had only a $20 bill in my pocket, I felt lucky to be able to escape. It was mid-April 1975.

With the help of American friends at the U.S. Embassy, I was driven clandestinely to Saigon airport, ushered onto a C-130 American plane and flown to Clark Field Airbase in the Philippines. After four days at the American officers' dormitory, we were flown to Guam with hundreds of other Vietnamese.

We slept on cots under tents freshly set up by Marines while others cut more trees to set up more tents. We stayed there two weeks, wearing second-hand, oversized clothes from the Red Cross, and shared makeshift showers and portable toilets. I had to register as a maid, under the American "household help" category, to be able to reach the mainland at Camp Pendleton near Los Angeles.

Hundreds of us were given bunk beds in tin barracks and thousands were put under tents. I volunteered to make announcements over loudspeakers every morning and evening at the camp's Information Center to the thousands of refugees who came looking for lost family members and friends. During that time, my children played with other children their age under the supervision of parents who were happy to care for others' children as well as their own. My children felt like they were in summer camp all day long.

After having moved like bohemians to three countries and two refugee camps in seven weeks, I was fortunate to be sponsored by Sanford McDonnell, the CEO and Chairman of McDonnell Douglas

---

Aircraft in St. Louis. Nestled in their large house, we lived in a normal family atmosphere and a peaceful and serene community for two months.

But fate sent us then to the Washington area, where we lived in Old Town, Alexandria, for ten months, sponsored by former friends who had served at the U.S. Embassy in Vietnam.

I tried hard to find a job -- sent resumes, scoured bulletin boards, and replied to ads in the *Washington Post*. At interviews, I was usually told that I was either overqualified or under-qualified. I didn't know how to type and had no previous experience working in the U.S. I needed a chance to get a start so I could acquire some work experience. If employers were looking for some one with experience, how would I ever get a job? It was a chicken-and-egg puzzle for me, looking for work in the land of plenty.

My identity was printed on two small pieces of paper: my social security card and an I-94 form from the Immigration and Naturalization Service. The I-94 listed my status as a "parolee," the technical term for some one who is neither a citizen nor an immigrant. To my great consternation and anxiety, I found in the dictionary that I was "a person who has been released from prison on parole." I looked up the word parole and read: "the release of a prisoner whose sentence has not yet expired, on condition of future good behavior; the sentence is not set aside and the individual remains under the supervision of a parole board."

Starting my new life from scratch was not easy. I reflected that I had worn many hats in the space of three months: Chairman of the board and director of a prestigious center one day, then a refugee the next, later a "domestic" on Guam, and now a "prisoner under close examination." No wonder I couldn't get a job offer.

I started to develop fatigue and depression during that time of unemployment. I was affected by the traumatic moves from Saigon through three refugee camps to St Louis and then to Washington, within a span of four months.

Finally, friends told me to volunteer at the Indochinese Reception Center, an information and referral office helping refugees find jobs in the area. Two weeks later, I found an administrative position at a vocational school in Washington. I interviewed refugee applicants and placed them in courses they chose – keypunch, secretarial, accounting or TV and radio repair.

In Washington, I met Lacy Wright, a casual acquaintance in Saigon when he was at the American Embassy there. We went out, fell in love, and got married in mid-April 1976. That date ended exactly one year of refugee and parolee life for me, but it was also the start of a new cycle of nomadic existence. My horoscope seemed to be under the sign of the meteor, zigzagging from one corner of the earth to the other.

The children and I accompanied Lacy to Milan, Italy, where he was assigned to the U.S. Consulate General. We enjoyed eating Italian food, going to concerts, and, once, watching the famous Pavarotti perform at La Scala, the world's most famous opera house.

After two years, we returned home. We wanted the children to be rooted in the American way of life and to get an American education. We lived in Falls Church for seven years, where our children went to Jeb Stuart High School. This was the height of the Boat People refugees' influx, from 1978 to the mid-eighties. I volunteered at the school and was elected PTA treasurer. I was ready to learn the American schooling process and to be involved in community service.

During that tense period, my children, holding American citizenship and bearing "Wright" as their last name, were mistakenly considered "boat people." They told me they were insulted and asked to "go home" to Vietnam. They also saw the real boat people being beaten up nearly every day.

I myself was approached at a shopping mall by an American lady who told me, "You and your people came here as parasites for me to pay taxes for you and give you welfare money. You are nothing but a burden to our community. Just go back where you belong."

Proud to Live and Die in Fairfax County

Lacy was working at the Department of State in Washington, and I volunteered as an interpreter for boat people in Virginia who had been evicted from their apartments for overcrowding – that is, exceeding the number of residents that the law allowed. The hundreds of thousands of boat people who arrived from first-asylum refugee camps in Southeast Asia presented a huge challenge for the government and for American society.

An article in the *Washington Post* about the boat people described my work in helping to resettle them as well as the difficulties they encountered. Tom Davis, then Mason District Supervisor and later a U.S. congressman, called me and offered to help. He became the first official to support local programs to assist the refugees. After he was elected to Congress, he passed many bills in support of the Vietnamese and Asian community before retiring in 2008.

In 1980, the U.S. Congress passed the Refugee Act, which provided funding for voluntary agencies and private organizations to resettle the refugees. I received a grant to study counseling and help boat people refugees adjust to their new environment. On graduation, I interned at the Northern Virginia Family Service in Falls Church.

During my tenure, I created a support group that met weekly at Knox Presbyterian Church and provided food and clothing. I rented townhouses for the large families in the complex adjoining our office, and got American friends on weekends to carry furniture and donate kitchen and bathroom items. I also found the refugees entry-level jobs.

At the end of my six-month internship, I was hired as a caseworker at the Department of Social Services in Fairfax County. I helped hundreds of refugees get public assistance and health care. In Alexandria, however, the need was for people to assist those refugees who did not fit within the system. They were wandering the streets, unable to speak English or to find their way around.

At that point, I decided to establish a non-profit entity called Indochinese Refugee Social Services (IRSS), and opened a shelter for those who were falling through the cracks. I contracted with the Department of Social Services for funding to provide services not only for the boat people from Vietnam, but also for refugees from Laos, Cambodia, and Afghanistan.

Afterwards, I wrote proposals and received federal and state grants to provide the refugees with lessons in Basic English and with vocational training. I also worked closely with the Department of Employment to find jobs for hundreds of refugees in hotels, restaurants, poultry plants, and factories. The Department of Education gave IRSS funds for bi-lingual tutoring after school hours in math, social studies, and science at six middle and high schools in Fairfax County. I was the Executive Director of IRSS and supervised the three projects.

I was among the first Vietnamese refugees to become naturalized American citizens, and was proud to cast my first vote in the 1980 presidential elections. A year later, the fellow workers, colleagues and friends who had volunteered with my organization nominated me for a national award.

The U.S.-Asia Institute wanted to raise the profile and status of Asian Americans by honoring those who had made a significant contribution to American society in politics, the arts, business, architecture, and social services. I was the newest naturalized American in a group of awardees that included the famous Anna Chennault as well as Maya Ling Lin, who designed the Vietnam War Memorial. I invited Laotian, Cambodian, Chinese and Vietnamese social workers to the ceremony so they, too, could be recognized.

Other mutual assistance associations were formed to help resettle the refugees, and I saw that it was time for me to let younger people lead the effort. I had always wanted to understand why the U.S., the most powerful country in the world, lost the war in Vietnam. So, at age 41, after my children had left for college, I applied for admission to the Georgetown School of Foreign Service as a candidate for a Master of Sciences in International Relations.

The wounds of war were still deep inside the American psyche, and they were inside me as well. Feelings of guilt, anger, frustration, and humiliation were alive in both of us.

Upon my graduation in 1984, my husband was assigned to Bangkok, Thailand, and then to Mexico, Trinidad and Tobago, Jamaica, and Brazil, his last post. I worked during these years at different U.S. embassies interviewing visa applicants. I also raised funds for the annual Marine balls and for local charities. In 1989, the mayor of Kingston, Jamaica, presented me with the key to the city for my work in supporting Jamaican schoolchildren and orphans.

Then, in Brasilia, in November 1995, I saw on CNN former Secretary of Defense Robert McNamara, who had presided over the escalation of the Vietnam conflict, proclaim to the world that he had fought the wrong war. He even went to Hanoi to apologize for his errors of judgment and the "terrible mistake" the U.S. had committed, having known early on that the war was un-winnable. If that was so, his critics asked, why did he continue for so long, letting millions of North and South Vietnamese and 58,000 Americans die in vain?

I couldn't sleep that night, and went to my computer, starting what became a book three years later. It was about four generations of my family going through four wars in Vietnam. I called it *Autumn Cloud – From Vietnamese War Widow to American Activist.* My autobiography was published in 2001 by Capital Books of Leesburg, Virginia. We held book launches in ten states as well as in Jamaica, Australia, China, the Philippines, and Paris.

In 1997, Lacy retired after 30 years of diplomatic service in Asia, Europe, the Caribbean, and Latin America. We went to live in beautiful Lake Barcroft in Falls Church. I observed that the Vietnamese Americans in the Washington area had prospered, and thought it was time to urge them to participate more actively in the democratic process. I established the Vietnamese American Voters Association (VAVA) in Virginia and encourage Vietnamese Americans to register to vote. I was active in the League of Women Voters and began reporting regularly on the Vietnamese community for *Asian Fortune News.*

Jackie Bong Wright in 2008 registering voters for the Vietnamese American Voters Association. (Courtesy of Jackie Bong Wright)

In 2000, my volunteers and I registered more than two thousand people to vote; and, four years later, for the presidential elections, around 4,000. For these civic activities, The *Washingtonian Magazine* named me a Washingtonian of the Year 2003. That year, I produced my own radio program "Women Today" for Vietnamese Public Radio. A year later, I was the producer of the Vietnamese Public Television program "News of the Week," discussing U.S. and international happenings.

I was also a founding member of the Ethnic Coalition of Virginia (ECVA), teaming up with Asian, African, Hispanic, and Middle-Eastern associations as well as the NAACP to organize six annual Candidates' Forums in Fairfax County. The objective was to allow Virginia candidates to present their political platforms so minority constituents could make educated choices when casting their votes.

At a certain point, I became a Community Outreach Specialist for James Lee Senior Center in Falls Church. My job was to encourage older Asians to attend exercise, yoga, QiCong, Tai Chi, line dance, and other classes. The objective was to get Asian American senior citizens out of the house, combat loneliness, and promote mental and physical health. I was able to register hundreds of them, and was asked to replicate the same outreach program at other Fairfax County senior centers.

One day I happened to see a performance at the Center by the Cameo Club, which comprises former contestants for the title of Ms. Virginia Senior America. They urged me to enter the Pageant. I would show that Asians participated in community activities, share my Asian cultural heritage and, especially, combat the stereotype of Asians as primarily Medicare and welfare recipients.

To the great surprise of my family, the Vietnamese community, and myself, the six pageant judges not only gave me the Community Service Award, but also crowned me "Queen of Virginia." Their stated criteria were personality, charm, conversational ability, poise, grace, internal beauty (as evidenced by a contestant's philosophy of life), and, finally, evidence of some talent (mine involved performance of a traditional Vietnamese dance). My philosophy of life was: "Success is not how high and fast you go to reach the top, but how high and fast you bounce back when you hit the bottom."

Then I set my sights on a wider horizon. Human trafficking in the world had become so rampant that, in 2004, eBay advertised an auction of Vietnamese teenage girls, at a starting price of $5,400. My civic awareness expanded, and I began working closely with the Trafficking in Persons Office (TIP) at the U. S. Department of State, created to fight the trafficking of humans for labor and sex. This 21st century modern-day slavery now accounts for more than $25 billion a year in illicit business, exceeded only by arms and drug dealing.

Jackie Bong Wright Ms. Virginia Senior America 2004 (Courtesy of Jackie Bong Wright)

Of course, I was interested in Vietnam. According to UNICEF and Vietnam's Ministry of Justice, as many as 400,000 Vietnamese women and children had been trafficked overseas since 1990. That is around 10 percent of trafficked women and children worldwide. Alarmed by that fast-growing industry, I started writing articles, and, in 2006, organized the first Human Trafficking Conference at the U.S. Congress.

Congressmen Tom Davis (R-VA) and Jim Moran (D-VA) were the co-sponsors of that public awareness conference, which discussed the themes of prevention, protection and prosecution. I invited national and local officials, international experts, NGOs, community-based organizations

(CBOs) and the media to debate these heated issues. In 2007, I organized another conference – this time on the legal, labor and human rights implications of human trafficking -- at Chapman University in Orange, California. Last year's conference was held in Harrisburg, Pa., on the "Rehabilitation and Reintegration of Trafficked Victims." Recommendations were sent to the UN, Congress, the Administration and, especially, to Vietnam to take action.

This year, I started producing a television program in Falls Church on *SBTN-DC* (Saigon Broadcasting Television Network) Voice of Voters, a Vietnamese-language cable outlet with a national audience of over 275,000 viewers, including some in Canada. I interviewed experts to inform the Vietnamese public on local and national elections, congressional issues, and the domestic and foreign policies of the Administration.

My new life started 33 years ago in Fairfax County, where I saw my children grow up in a peaceful home with a loving husband, far from the war-torn country I left. My Vietnamese compatriots and my family had blossomed. Now, we continue to contribute to a nation to which we are grateful. We want to pay tribute to the generous Americans who changed our lives for the better.

Today, a new beginning awaits us. We are approaching our later years with a sense of assurance. We are proud of the United States as our adopted country, and happy to have made our lives in Fairfax County. ##

Dzung and Vy Nguyen – Stories of Second Generation Vietnamese Americans
By Corazon Sandoval Foley

Dzung and Vy Nguyen worked together as FCAAHP's father-daughter team focusing on the Vietnamese American community. Vy Nguyen, the youngest member of the FCAAHP team was honored with a recognition by the Fairfax County Board of Supervisors for her outstanding contributions to FCAAHP – especially for her creation of a Vietnamese American History website.

Recognition of Vy Nguyen by Fairfax Board of Supervisors in August 2008 for creating FCAAHP Vietnamese American website.

Moreover, Vy pursued the issue of a generation gap by focusing her interviews on second generation Vietnamese Americans like her who are children of refugees who have chosen Fairfax County as their home. All her interviewees expressed appreciation for the diversity in Fairfax population that appeared to help adjustment for refugee families. The women applauded opportunities that are greater here than in Vietnam. Some of Vy Nguyen's interview results are presented in this section while voices of other young Asian Americans are included in several chapters in the book.

Vy Nguyen's 2008 graduation
(Courtesy of Vy Nguyen)

Vy Nguyen's Idealistic Childhood. Vy Nguyen was 18 in 2008 and lived in Fairfax County all her life. She has gone to private schools, including Congressional and Flint Hill High School. She has never gone to school with many Asian peoples but thinks that she has grown up color-blind. "I think there is nothing wrong with having an idealistic childhood – no matter how unrealistic it is. Why would you want to grow up so fast anyway?"

She perceived growing up as pretty normal in Fairfax County except that everyone with whom she was around was unusually well off. She has personally not experienced discrimination but her family has experienced it in the workplace. She said that she has noticed more discrimination with Asians when they are in the group – "Then it's them discriminating against the rest of the population."

On generation gap: "Sometimes my parents will start off saying… When I was your age, I was already out trying to provide for the family…and that would be their effort in guilt-tripping me. Some of the things they say seem outdated. Especially their reasoning for why I can't do things. Sometimes their answer will just be "because you're a girl." I remember one time my grandpa turned to me and said "Why are you playing basketball? That's for boys. Girls should be gentle and learn to walk gracefully." Yeah. That's outdated."

On values from parents: Vy said that work ethic and education are key values from her parents, adding that her mother would often say that: "All we have is our education. People here aren't going to respect you – especially because we're Vietnamese. So make them respect you. Learn. Because education will get you anywhere."

Fairfax County resident Ms. Nguyen Van Su celebrated her 80th birthday in 2010 with her granddaughter Yvonne and her sons Hoang, Dzung, Man. (Courtesy of Dzung Nguyen)

Vy is most proud of membership in a club that has been a part of her four years in Flint Hill. It is called ACAP (All Cultures All People) that basically promotes cultural awareness and celebrates it. She has been involved in ACAP, student government, basketball/tennis, VYEA, tutoring, volunteering at the hospital and urgent care, cultural shows at the World Bank, Vietnamese Orchestra.

Vy's dad came by boat and her mother came a few years later from a refugee camp in the Philippines. She feels attached to her Vietnamese heritage, noting that there are festivals and cultural gatherings all the time. Fairfax County's Channel 30 has shows that keep people aware of what is going on in the community.

She wants to go into international relations so she could be involved in the grand scheme of things. She considers herself the black sheep in the family. She is the only one of her cousins on the maternal side who is not going to medical school. She has cousins who want to be surgeons, optometrists, pharmacists, biochemical researchers…so much pressure because she has to prove herself to the rest of the family.

On what to say to her elders: "Don't worry. I'll find a way."

Lam Bui, 16 years old, TJHSST. He did not feel different from his peers at the moment. "Now that I look back, I feel kind of embarrassed of the clothes my mom would dress me in and haircuts I was forced to get (boy haircut in fourth grade). My parents told me that in kindergarten when I was supposed to dress up like a pilgrim, they had no idea what a pilgrim was. Therefore they gave me an incense *(cay nhan)* to bring into school. Even they're embarrassed for me about that."

On parents' generation: "I think my parents' generation is definitely not as open minded as my generation is. Living in America has opened my eyes and I've grown to be able to accept many things that aren't conventional to my parents. I often find myself trying to teach them what I have learned from living here but they don't easily adapt to new principles."

On coming to America: "My mom escaped from Vietnam by boat and ended up being accepted into the Australian government. My dad received a full scholarship to the University of Tasmania when he finished high school in Da Lat. My dad eventually then got a job in the US and after my parents got married, my mom moved over here with him. I do not feel attached to my Vietnamese heritage, but I'm definitely proud of being Vietnamese. The growing population of Vietnamese people in Fairfax County has definitely helped with that. When I go out to the mail or grocery store, it is always nice hearing other people speaking Vietnamese because you know you're not alone."

Hoainam Nguyen, 21 years old, TJHSST & UVA. "I never felt discriminated against until I went to University of Virginia. In Fairfax County, the population was so diverse that everyone was used to interacting with people of many races. But at UVA it was different. I met plenty of people who had never gone to school with minorities until now, and they regarded Asians as totally different people sometimes. Even the most Americanized students were often grouped in with all the Asians as people who spoke a different language and did not understand the American way of life."

About feeling different from peers: "Maybe back in elementary school where we were always asked to do activities that made me stand out as being brought up differently, like bringing in things for show and tell that I would not have in my house and my parents had to go buy. But after elementary school, it has not really been an issue."

On Vietnamese heritage: "My mom came by plane and my dad escaped by boat and then came over to the US on a separate boat. In the last few years, I have felt much more attached to my heritage. Being in Fairfax County helps because I get to interact with many Vietnamese people."

Sayings from parents: "Homework first. But as I grew older, more things like "Never forget your family as you grow up and move on in life"."

Anthony Chung, 18 years old of Annandale High School: He has rarely ever felt discriminated but his parents frequently tell him that he has to work harder than Caucasians in order to be equal to them.

On the generation gap: "Probably both a technology gap and a cultural gap. My parents are not up to date with technology and they do not trust it as much. As for the cultural gap, my siblings and I have to find some sort of balance between the Vietnamese culture and the American culture. However, this is difficult to accomplish because the values of each culture differ greatly."

On coming to America: "My parents fled Vietnam to Malaysia when the Communists took over. They stayed in a refugee camp for almost a year until the US government allowed them to come into the country. Once in the US, my parents and their siblings worked their way up to the lifestyle we have today."

Van-Nhi Bui, 19 years old, Oakton High School. "Racial discrimination is when people act negatively as a result of prejudice, and I have not seen nor experienced this thus far in Fairfax County. It is not to say, however, that Fairfax County is free of racial bias. More often than not, I have observed a sort of self-imposed segregation inside and outside of school, where many individuals of a certain racial group band together and separate themselves from those of other racial groups. While this is most likely not intentionally done to be exclusive, it does become so and therefore fosters polarization and the potential for discrimination."

On generational gap: "The biggest difference between our generations is the extent to which we are Americanized – that is, the extent to which we have been immersed in American culture. My parents spent their childhood years in Vietnam and therefore have had traditional Vietnamese cultural beliefs and values built into their minds; American culture to them was more like a post script – it was an afterthought to their already strong Vietnamese background. I, on the other hand, grew up in America, so I simultaneously experienced both American and Vietnamese culture; as such, both cultures exert an almost equal influence on me. Because of the discrepancy in cultural backgrounds, my parents and I tend to be split in our world views – I am more liberal while my parents are more conservative."

On coming to America: "My dad came by boat, my mom came by plane through the ODP program. I feel attached to my Vietnamese heritage because of my parents and my involvement in Vietnamese cultural groups, including VYEA. Fairfax County has not really fostered this at all, unless you count the fact that such Vietnamese organizations are based in Fairfax."

Bao Vo, 19 years old of Chantilly High School. His parents escaped from Vietnam in 1987 and had him in 1988 in a refugee camp in Palau Bidong, Malaysia. After that, his grandpa sponsored them and got them to Fairfax County in 1990. He does not feel attached to his Vietnamese heritage.

Candice Chu, 18 years old, Lake Braddock High School. She believes that her parents' generation has a different view of American society than her generation. Her parents are generally more suspicious of other peoples' motives, more cautious in life, and just see things in a more conservative way than she does.

Chi Lan Vu, 21 years old, George Mason University. "There are more opportunities for me in this country than my parents' generation. Back then, girls were limited on their education than guys, if they were lucky they would have the high school diploma. The Vietnamese culture put more emphasis on men than on women; there were no such things as "being equal"."

Andre Nguyen, 18 years old of Fairfax High School: Eden Center has fostered attachment to his Vietnamese heritage.

Peter Nguyen, 19 years old, TJHSST. His mom left on boat and flew to the US. His dad was in a student exchange program and was still in the US when Vietnam fell. He does not feel attached to his Vietnamese heritage and noted that there is a relatively large Asian community in Fairfax County. He wants to be an engineer and was influenced in this decision by his parents who are both engineers. His greatest accomplishment so far was getting into TJHSST.

Jonathan Bradley, 18 years old, Fairfax High School. His dad escaped here. His grandfather took his mom and his whole family here on a boat. He wants to be a musician or a dancer and says that his parents support him 100%.

Man Minh Nguyen in 2009

Coming to America: Notes from Dzung Nguyen's brother Man Minh Nguyen

Man Minh Nguyen has been a longtime resident of Springfield, Virginia. He arrived at Washington National Airport in a snowy night on February 11, 1981 from the Philippines. He entered the US on February 10 and stayed at a military base one night in California.

Since his uncles, sister, and brothers (including Dzung) already resided in Fairfax and Arlington counties, Man chose to come and stay as a resident of Fairfax County. Man's family came to the US in different times: 1957, 1959, 1960, 1972, 1975 and 1978.

He felt very welcomed in Fairfax County. He first lived in a community full of newcomers to the US. When he arrived, Man Nguyen received welfare, free meals, and career training in high school. His very first job was as a bus boy at Chesapeake Seafood restaurant next to Dart Drug in Falls Church ("it is no longer there") from that program.

From his experience, Fairfax County has done a lot for the newcomers like him. He thinks the issue is how to reach out and let people know what Fairfax has to offer. For example, many Vietnamese do not know that they can contact Fairfax County Office of Community to borrow or rent public facility like school cafeteria. Many do not know that they can use computer/internet at public school locations throughout the county.

Man Nguyen in 2009 is a Fairfax County Public School employee. He loves the people, the workplace, and Fairfax County. Since all his relatives are here, he is here for good. He has observed so many changes in the county that he could not keep track of the changes -- the roads, housing communities, ethnic communities, people, etc.

The Asian American community is very important in Man Nguyen's life. His family celebrates Asian tradition like Vietnamese New Year, Ancestor Anniversary like *"Gio To Hung Vuong"* who is their father founder, *"Hai Ba Trung"* (women heroes who fight against invaders), *"Tet Trung Thu"* (mid-autumn festival for children).

On contributions of Fairfax County Asian American employees, he noted that "many Asian Americans, including me, have worked in Fairfax County or have been employed by the Fairfax County Government/Fairfax County Public School in the past and present, and I feel that is a great contribution to the growth of this county." Man Nguyen's community contributions include being an active Boy Scout Leader of Troop 904 in Arlington from 1986 to 2000.

Man Nguyen hopes that "the school system will add some of Asian histories in the curriculum, not a full-blown subject but just enough to encourage Asian American children to understand how and why they are here, to remember their roots."

Man Minh Nguyen arrival in 1981.
(Courtesy of Man Minh Nguyen)

Man Minh Nguyen and his brothers and sister in 1981.
(Courtesy of Man Minh Nguyen)

From 1950s: Indian American History in Fairfax County
By Corazon Sandoval Foley

According to the US Census, there was no record of Asian Indian residents in Fairfax County who entered the US before 1950. But 180 Asian Indian residents of Fairfax County in 2000 entered the US between 1950 and 1959. However, it is not clear when these Asian Indian immigrants moved to Fairfax County.

I should note that Asian Indian Americans have long played important roles in US history – the first Asian American Congressman was of Asian Indian heritage. In 1956, Dalip Singh Saund won a Congressional seat as a representative from California and served for three congresses. Born on September 20, 1899, to a Sikh family in Chhajulwadi, Punjab, he came to the US in 1920 to attend the University of California at Berkeley. In 1924 he graduated having earned MA and PhD degrees in mathematics.

Back in Fairfax County, by 2007, Asian Indians have grown to be the largest group in the Asian community in the county, totaling some 40,194 residents. FCAAHP research yielded interviews with some longtime Fairfax County residents in the Indian American community and their stories are presented in this chapter to be followed by two stories in their own words by FCAAHP team leaders Jaya Kori and Swati Damle.

Jaya Kori has described the Indian American community in Fairfax County as very diverse. India, being a diverse country with 28 states with each having its own dialect, cuisine and methods, there are many Indian organizations here in Fairfax County. The Indian community has grown dramatically in Fairfax County, with more Indian grocery stores, restaurants, boutiques, and especially, Indian cultural organizations.

Jaya Kori added that the Fairfax County Indian American organizations are all very active. During *Diwali* – the biggest annual festival for Indian Americans -- all the organizations and temples get together at the Chantilly expo center for a *Mela* – and it is a great event. She also noted that the Indian American community activities are evolving – initially the focus was on cultural activities but now she sees increasing community awareness of problems faced by older generation, politics, and health issues faced specifically by Asian Americans.

1959 begins the set of FCAAHP Indian American stories with the life and contributions of Gangadhar Kori, an elder brother of Jaya's husband, Raj Kori. The set of stories depicts the adjustment of many in the Fairfax County Indian American community.

1959 and Gangadhar Kori's Move to Fairfax County. Dr. Gangadhar S. Kori was born in Bijapur, India in October 1926 and moved permanently to Fairfax County in 1959 where he served as Professor of Management at the American and George Washington Universities, **Gangadhar Kori**

as well as serving as a management consultant to numerous multinational companies. He later served at both the US Department of Agriculture and the Environmental Protection Agency. He lost his courageous battle with cancer on December 19, 2004.

In 1968, Dr. Kori's wife Kanta and sons Suresh and Subash joined him to live permanently in Virginia. Kanta and Gangadhar befriended countless foreign students, immigrating couples, and visitors to the US. He was a founding member of Kaveri, the Basava Samiti of Washington, D.C., as well as the Veerashiva Samaja of North America. Through the years, these thriving organizations have continued to promote the culture, rich heritage, traditions, and religious beliefs for Indian American Kannadigas, Veerashiavas, and their families.

1970 and a Family of Indian American Medical Doctors in Fairfax County. The FCAAHP team leaders interviewed Dr. Baikunth Singh who moved to Fairfax County in 1970, one of the earliest Asian Indian county residents. In 1970, he had completed his advanced medical training and cardiology fellowship in George Washington University in DC and in the following year, he started his medical practice in McLean, Virginia. In 2009, Dr. Baikunth Singh decided to retire from his distinguished medical practice that provided compassionate and dignified care to many grateful Fairfax citizens, including FCAAHP official photographer Terry Sam.

Like the first Asian resident of Fairfax County, Chinese Dr. V.P. Suvoong, Dr. Baikunth Singh is a member of a family of medical doctors. He was born in Givzari, India and in 1960 received his medical degree in India. He is married to Mishu Singh, a medical doctor and pathologist. His children Alka and Anup Singh are both medical doctors.

The Asian American community was quite important in Dr. Singh's life and he was involved in activities in religious temples. When asked what he would advice the younger generation, the doctor in him said "work hard, keep away from cigarettes, and develop an exercise routine."

From India through Africa to Fairfax County. Our FCAAHP team interviewed another Indian American medical doctor – Dr. Tushar Patel who has a practice in Herndon, Virginia. He came to the US in 1965 from East Africa when his family was forced to leave Africa. He was a year old then. After completing his medical education in Connecticut where there was not much population diversity, he decided to stay in Fairfax County because he wanted to stay where he could engage with a more diverse population.

Raj and Jaya Kori, Tushar Patel, Swati Damle

The Asian American community has been extremely important in his family's life. He explained that we all define ourselves by what food we eat, what religion we follow, and who are our family members. The presence of Hindu temples like Rajdhani Mandir, Durga temple, and Mangal Mandir, as well as Indian grocery stores, has made his family feel comfortable and in touch with their heritage in Fairfax County. He belongs to the Asian American Foundation and has made significant contributions to the temples, cultural and educational organizations, and educational institutions.

Dr. Patel noted that traditionally, the welcoming of the new immigrants has been mostly left to the ethnic groups and he thinks that is the reason why the new arrivals tend to stay within their ethnic surroundings. They do not try to break out into the mainstream, e.g., Hispanic community, Vietnamese, Koreans, etc. They do not make an effort to learn English unless needed for jobs. This does not help their integration in America. Dr. Patel said it is important to create the feeling that "I am an American" in people's minds.

1971 move to Clifton by Jagdish and Shobha Berry. In 1971, Jagdish and Shobha Berry moved to Clifton because it is a developing county and the houses were cheap. Shobha Berry worked for Fairfax County in adult education and for the Voice of America. They felt welcomed by their neighbors while the Asian American community remained very important because it is all around them. They live in a joint-family arrangement with the families of the two younger brothers of Jagdish, as well as his mother. They have three daughters, one son, and four grandchildren.

1973 – Nine-year old Urvashi Mehra and family moved to Fairfax County. Urvashi Mehra's family immigrated to America in 1973 and within a decade, acquired land in McLean and built their dream home. She remembered that migrating to Fairfax County was a bit of a culture shock for they were not accustomed to the greater formality that is part and parcel of American culture – and unlike in India, work took precedence over relationships.

Urvashi was raised in McLean and left the area upon her marriage in 1991. She and her husband returned to Fairfax County – the place they call "home" – in 1998 to raise their own children.

A graduate of George Washington University, Urvashi grew in the management ranks of local information technology firms, focusing on the healthcare sector. Continuing her passion and dream to help with healthcare reform, she recently completed a graduate program at Harvard University focusing on disorders such as PTSD.

Urvashi shared memories of growing up with her parents maintaining a "tight leash" on her brother and herself. To her parents, the benefits of remaining Asian far outweighed the potential to forgo the past and embrace the American culture. She added that nowadays, the Asian American community plays a lesser, more diluted role for her as she raises her two children in America for she has adopted the goal of American assimilation, melding the best of both cultures. She believes that the next generation of Asian Americans will need to find methods that allow them to maintain their heritage and culture while simultaneously embracing certain features of American life. She added that: "Demonstrating citizen-centric leadership lies in neither being an Asian nor an American, but somewhere at the intersection of the two."

1977 and the Ullagadis. Saroja and CB Ullagadi moved in 1977 to Clifton because of the husband's employment. In the beginning, the Indian community was important – particularly the group belonging in the same state in India and spoke the same language as Saroja did because she could then be in touch with culture, happenings, festival celebrations. A little later, however, she found it more significant to associate with people belonging to the same spiritual/religious heritage. She has since became more active in writing about religious heritage -- forming a group that for 32 years has been her primary social network in the community.

She has developed a non-profit organization with a view of fostering universalistic and democratic values of Lingayatism through the teachings of its founders and its literature. She served as editor of the newsletter and this organization published in 1995 her book "In Search of Shiva." Her advice to the youth: get involved in the community.

1984 and Hindu Minister Amar Anth Gupta. The first Hindu minister of Fairfax County is Amar Anth Gupta who moved to the county on May 24, 1984. He described his community contributions: "I am working as a chaplain in INOVA Fairfax hospitals, correction centers, Fairfax County Schools for FLE, Assistant Chief election officer, first recognized Minister by Fairfax County as marriage celebrant, head priest of Rajdhani Mandir for Hindus, Holder of Ambassador of Peace Award. I got the opportunity to do prayer at Fairfax County Government Center when Honorable Thomas Davis was the Chairman of the County Board of Supervisors." Minister Amar Anth Gupta said that he expects to live in Fairfax County until his death.

The Durga Temple was presented with a Recognition Certificate by the Fairfax County Board of Supervisors on December 7, 2009 for playing a strong leadership role in supporting the develoment of the Burke/Springfield Senior Center Without Walls (BSSCWoW). Sherina Krup of Durga Temple is shown standing beside Fairfax County Chairman Sharon Bulova and holding the recognition certificate for the Durga Temple.

1986 and Sherina Krup of Durga Temple. Sherina Krup has lived in Fairfax County since 1986 and has played a leadership role in many community development programs -- and more recently, in the programs of the Durga Temple to support senior citizens. On December 7, 2009, Sherina Krup received a Recognition Award from the Fairfax County Board of Supervisors for the leadership role that Durga Temple has played in developing the innovative Burke/ Springfield Senior Center Without Walls (BSSCWoW). Sherina Krup kindly shared with FCAAHP the photo at right; and the Fairfax County official photo where she is shown holding the Recognition Certificate of December 7, 2009 and standing beside Chairman Sharon Bulova. The Durga Temple is the first Hindu Dharam Temple to receive a Recognition Award from the Fairfax County Board of Supervisors for its support of wellness programs for seniors in the county.

Sherina Krup has played a leadership role in senior programs of the Durga Temple. (Courtesy of Sherina Krup)

1999 and Pooja Arora, 15 years old in 2009. Pooja Arora assisted FCAAHP by interviewing her father, Vikas Arora, whose job brought the family to Fairfax County in 1999. Her mother is a teacher in Fairfax County. The family has observed Hinduism by going to temples and festivals. Interacting with other Asian Americans makes them feel more at home.

Pooja is a sophomore in Chantilly High School in 2009. She was born in Kansas and moved to Virginia when she was 5 years old. She never felt different from her peers because of her Asian American upbringing and she is involved in the Chantilly Youth Association. Her goal is to go to the University of Virginia and major in Business because she has always been interested in the commercial arena. Her parents have never forced her to be a doctor or engineer and they support her in whatever she chooses.

Pooja's advice to the elders: Listen more to what your kids have to say sometimes.

In Their Own Words: Fairfax Indian American Stories of Religion and Marriage.
On August 2, 2009, the *Washington Post* featured a wonderful story about love, Indian style – "Maybe this is meant to be." The story was about the marriage of Tej Sultana to Kivneet Kaur (26), a woman from India. Tej Sultana (28) did not think it would happen that way – he was born in Fairfax Hospital, spent his whole life in the States, graduating from a public high school and college, and traveling to India – the country his parents left 30 years ago – on only a handful of occasions.

In this book, we deal with similar themes. Our FCAAHP Indian American team leaders – Jaya Kori and Swati Damle -- shared their own stories of how love in an arranged marriage and strong spiritual anchors have enriched their lives in Fairfax County.

Yoga Eased Adjustment from India to My Home, Fairfax County
By Jaya Kori

Co-workers and friends always ask me "Jaya, you always seem calm and collected, what is your secret?" I tell them that there is no secret; it is my spiritual background that has allowed me to stay calm during calamities and to find effective solutions. I grew up in a small family in Mumbai, one of the major business hubs on the western coast of India. While I was in college I came in contact with Baba Muktananda, a spiritual master in India. I was very impressed with the environment and purity of his Ashram, a place where people perform spiritual practices under the Guru's guidance; and teachings.

After completing my bachelor's degree in Biology, I earned my diploma in Medical Technology from Bombay University. I came to United States in March of 1978. I landed in JFK airport in New York. Through the glass windows I looked outside and saw a lot of messy stuff like cement lying everywhere. I felt that America was supposed to be a clean country – here it looks very messy! After leaving the airport I realized it was not cement mess but actually messy snow; I got the first taste of snow in my life!

Raj and Jaya Kori with family after their wedding

I got married to my husband Raj in June of 1977. It was a semi – arranged marriage as was common during those days. Raj's sister-in-law had come to visit my family a couple months earlier. She was tasked with choosing brides for five of the men in her family – her own two sons and her three younger brother-in-laws. She traveled for two months visiting different towns and looking for suitable brides based on the ages and qualifications of prospective grooms. In India, some of these qualifications include family backgrounds and horoscope matching. This adds practical elements to marriage selection. Eventually for each brother – five prospective brides were selected.

My future sister-in-law brought all the brothers to visit their prospective brides, and that is how Raj came to Kolhapur, the town where I resided with my parents and two brothers. I distinctly remember how my brother-in-law described life in America – work very hard and live like a King!

The marriage was arranged in 10 days. In fact Dr. Gangadhar Kori – my oldest brother-in-law had already finalized the wedding date and had asked his family to make the wedding preparations. Thus five marriages took place on June 29th in Bijapur, the place where Raj and his other brothers were from. The wedding party included more than ten thousand people. It was a grand event and everyone enjoyed it, especially Raj's father who was about 80 years old and was happy to see all his sons and nephews getting settled in their lives. Parents in India think it is their responsibility to get their son/daughter married and settled in life.

India is a very diverse country with 28 states and each state has its own language. There are also thousands of dialects in all of India. My mother tongue is Marathi and Raj's mother tongue is Kannada. Since we were both taught English while growing up in India, and we have spent most of our married life in the United States, we became comfortable speaking English at home. However, we made an effort to teach our kids Marathi when they were growing up. I remember one time when my younger son was sent home early from kindergarten because he was speaking Marathi and not English to his teachers! This is when we started speaking English at home almost all the time.

Finding a job in the US where I could use my educational background was not easy. My bachelor's degree was in Biology and Medical Technology. In order to further my career in Medical Technology I was told that I would need to get certification in Virginia. Also, I would have needed an additional 90 semester credit hours plus my education from India, because I was lacking credits in electives. Therefore, I decided to take classes in computer programming and I started working as a computer Programmer. I got a job working with the Fairfax County Government in 1989 and have not left since! Working for Human Services has expanded my understanding about various problems people face in life and how Fairfax County is trying to help them.

The Kori Family in Virginia (Courtesy of Jaya Kori)

Eventually my brother came here for higher education and decided to stay here along with my mother. My mother had problems initially building her social circle because she did not know any senior Indians living here in 1986. Now she has many friends with common interests. She started attending the senior center and participates in their knitting project. Her hobby is writing poetry. She has written a lot of poems in our mother tongue – Marathi. When I asked her to write a poem about her experiences in America and getting her citizenship, she was happy to do so. That was her first attempt to write something in English.

Feeling settled in life with a good husband, young children, and a good job, I decided to focus more on my spiritual well being. My spiritual guru, Baba Muktananda, was already making trips to US and had established an Ashram in Catskill Mountains in New York. As a result, it was easy for me to continue my spiritual practices while in the US. Raj joined me by sharing my spiritual pursuits. Along with the children, every summer we would spend one week in the Ashram.

Eventually we started a Chanting and Meditation center at our home so people in the area could have a local place to chant and meditate. We currently have a regular group of 40-50 people, all of whom come from various cultural, religious, and ethnic backgrounds, though primarily people with a Christian background in the US.

During the spring of 2008, both Raj and I attended a Pranayama (Yogic breathing) workshop offered by Swami Ramdev Maharaj, a Yoga Guru. It was very inspiring and beneficial to maintain our health. Both of us completed Teachers' training and have started teaching people to get healthy by practicing Pranayama. Not only has this helped me spiritually with my other practices, but it also helps with keeping in good health as some of my chronic health problems have all but disappeared. My husband's chronic asthma of over fifteen years has also disappeared due to the practice of Pranayama.

When I was new to this country, I always felt that I will go back to India after some years or after my retirement. Now I feel that this is my home and my roots are here. My two children, Umakant and Sachin, who are in their mid-late 20s, also want to remain in Fairfax County. Though I will visit India from time to time, I know I will retire in the beautiful Fairfax County, where I gave my labor of love and received a lot too! ##

Mrs. Vijaya Ligade, Jaya Kori's 76 – year old mother, wrote the following citizenship poem in honor of the May 29, 2009 first-ever naturalization ceremony in the Fairfax County Government Center initiated by FCAAHP.

Mrs. Vijaya Ligade in center beside Sharon Bulova (Photo by Cora Foley)

My Citizenship Poem
By Mrs. Vijaya Ligade

I was living far away at the other end of the Globe
A lady with torch and book in hand was calling in my
dream all the time

When children of my neighbors went to the US for higher education
I always ran to send them off, wishing them the best from my heart,
Hoping someday my children will too have that opportunity and light

And when my newly married daughter was leaving to the States
With tears in one eye and smile in the other, I gave her send off thinking of my dream

Then, One day I came to US too, to visit my daughter,
I fell in love with this country with smiling people, respecting each other
The Beautiful parks, the libraries and the vast pastures.
I enjoyed these all…

Then when my son came for higher education here,
My dream was fulfilled
And now the third generation is here,

Yes, I respect my India, but I fell in love with this country too
I am teaching eastern values and culture to the next generation
Let us take good things from east to west and west to east
And make the world more beautiful, that world belongs to God

Now I am a World citizen, and we have come closer to each other
Here all the doors are open to those who want to learn and do their best.
And the Lady with torch and book will light their path.
Seventy six years of my life, I found happiness and peace.

Hve you heard the name 'Kalpana Chawla'?
She was my fellow, she achieved her dream!
She made the sky limited and small
She built her home on the star

Like the stars on the America's star spangled Banner
And we are the citizens of this country
God Bless America and Jai Hind!

Note on Mrs. Vijaya Ligade. In 1998, when she was 65 years old, Mrs. Vijaya Ligade got her US citizenship. She wanted to be a US citizen so that she can be part of the process that elects world leaders because US policies affect the global community. She describes her citizenship education as follows: "It was not easy for me to prepare for the citizenship examination as I was not familiar with the US history. My daughter gave me the book published by the Daughters of the American Revolution, to study. I was familiar with English and so I did not have too much problem understanding it. I had very much interest in History and Civics when I was in India also. That helped me prepare for my Citizenship examination and things went easy. I was able to pass the examination in the first attempt only."

Mrs. Ligade was born in 1933 in a small town in India. She considered herself fortunate for having gotten the opportunity to educate herself, since in those days women did not have many educational opportunities. She also participated in India's independence movement.

Mrs. Ligade's American journey began in 1986 when she visited her daughter Jaya Kori. Since Jaya's children were small, she decided to stay and help out – and applied for immigration. She felt welcomed in Fairfax County where neighbors were curious about the Indian saris that she wears. During the early days, the Indian American community was very important for she was able to attend cultural events, celebrate Indian festivals and teach her grandchildren and others about Indian culture. Due to those activities, she did not feel homesick. Not only did she help raise her grandchildren, Mrs. Ligade knits baby hats and donates them to hospitals so they can use them for newborn babies. She also knits blankets that then get donated to the "Warm-up America" project. She also taught Indian culture and languages to the young adults from the local Indian community. She has hosted spiritual gatherings to discus the *Bhagavad Gita* – one of the greatest scriptures of the Hindu religion. She attends chanting and meditation programs in the community. She regularly attends the Herndon Senior Center where she enjoys interacting with her peers. ##

An Indian American Arranged Marriage that Blossomed in Fairfax County
By Swati Damle

It was 2004. I was having a very peculiar conversation with my daughter. Actually, we were having a funny, but nice chat about marriage and finding the right life partner. I kept asking her about several boys I had in mind for her. I must have mentioned at least 20 perspective husbands, but with each candidate came a comical comment. I tried to convince her by making excuses for the boy, but her response was always the same, "We just don't have any chemistry!" I went through the same thing with my son. For all the girls I recommended, there would be "No chemistry".

So, I started thinking, "What is this chemistry? What does 'chemistry' have to do with a girl and boy meeting and getting married? Did I have 'chemistry' with my husband?" I immediately started picturing my youth.

It was 1971 and I had just finished my Bachelor's degree in science. I was beginning my search for the perfect masters program in chemistry. As soon as I started applying to the programs, my aunts and uncles started approaching my parents about marriage. They began bringing various candidates for my consideration. Everyone would tell me to stop studying. "If you get a Masters degree, then the groom needs to at least have a Masters as well. You will never find someone with better qualifications if you continue! You'll be single your whole life!"

Swati and Subhash Damle, Sucheta and Ramesh Rajeswaran, Raj and Jaya Kori at Pohick Library in August 2008 for FCAAHP oral history interviews.
(Photo by Cora Foley)

I disregarded all the warnings, completed my Masters degree in Physical Chemistry, and completed a college teachers training course in 1973.

Upon completion of my studies, my family began their search for a groom. We saw many, many single, eligible bachelors over the next year. I did not like any of them. We had a lot of funny encounters. I actually thought one boy was handsome. He had a nice house and a car, which at the time was quite a plus! The only problem was that he did not know how to conduct a conversation. Any time my father would ask a question, he would give the stupidest answers! So, my father declined the proposal. Was that "chemistry"? I think that was an example of "chemistry". I mean, I liked looking at him and he clearly liked looking at me. It just didn't work out because of my father.

On Dec. 22, 1974, my sister and I were talking about marriage, boys, etc. We thought it had been a long time since we had seen any candidates. So, we decided to go to the community center and check out the database for the available bachelors. These databases used to be filled with thousands of girls and boys with profiles set up for each one. My sister asked me, "Who would your ideal husband be? What are you looking for in a husband?" I didn't care for a doctor or lawyer. I jut knew I didn't want to leave Bombay. So, we narrowed the search to a few boys and took the list to my parents. My father said that none of these boys would work; there was one from the United States and the others were outside of Bombay.

After my father left for work, I decided for fun, we should go see this boy from the US. After all, we did not find anyone within Bombay. Therefore, I decided, let us see how this boy is, coming from America to search a wife in India, what kind of fool will do that. My mother just smiled. So, just for fun, I made a call to the number listed on the profile. The boy's father answered. He asked us to come meet them with my horoscope. Since his father could read horoscopes, he wanted to check if both of our horoscopes matched or not. We immediately called my father. He was out of the office, meeting a client. He did not realize that we wanted him to meet this "important client"! My mother began to panic. A few minutes later we were able to locate my father and we sent him with the horoscope to meet the US fellow. The horoscopes matched!

The next day, we went to see the boy at his place. They had a small living room of about 10 by 12 feet. I still remembered the house. He had all of his relatives there: 9 sisters, 1 brother, multiple cousins, neighbors, parents, etc. There were all of these people, additionally, my parents, bother and off course the boy and me. This was the time where we were going to meet each other and start to get to know one another. It was funny how he was telling us everything sincerely, about himself. He told us about the US, his status and situation, what he wanted to do, what he was expecting from a wife, etc. It was a funny situation. But, somehow, I liked it. We all liked his family. They were very friendly and talkative. His mother was sitting by me and looking at me very lovingly. Something just clicked. I think this is what my children were referring too: "chemistry".

Ramesh and Sucheta Rajeswaran with Swati and Subhash Damle at Pohick in August 2008. (Photo by Cora Foley)

The very next day, my parents and his family were planning the engagement and wedding. The groom had to leave for the US on the 14th of January, so things had to move rather swiftly. With things moving so quickly, my father pulled me aside and asked if I had any last minute thoughts. I just told him "everything is fine as long as they do not ask for a dowry, if they do, the wedding will be off". Within five minutes, the topic came up. Luckily, the groom's family did not want any dowry. The said all they wanted was me. Great.

I was engaged to Subhash on December 25, 1974. Now, my heart was pounding. The wedding date had been set for January 2, 1975. Did I make the right decision? Did I know enough about him to spend the rest of my life with him? Here, as a joke my sister and I went to find some grooms and then went to see this guy for fun. What did I get myself into? Then I started to calm down. One thing, I was sure about that, my parents would not have let me marry him if he was not the right person.

Between the engagement and our wedding, he and I had a chance to meet a few times. However, we were never alone. There was always someone with us. So, we never had a chance to understand each other's needs and expectations. In fact, I ended up spending my wedding night in between my mother-in-law and my sister-in-law. I guess we had to go on thinking about our "chemistry" at that point.

Everything happened so fast. In a matter of 10 days, I met a boy and got married. I had met so many of relatives and friends. There were times where I forgot my own husband's name! Luckily, my sister never left my side and would remind me, "His name is Subhash." Within two weeks, my new husband left for the States. I have to stay behind to obtain my passport, visa etc. I was scheduled to go to the states on March 7th. Though we were apart, we found ways to stay connected. We used to write love letters to one another over the two months apart. As March approached, I was a little worried, "Will I be able to recognize my own husband at the airport?" So, Subhash and I decided that we should decide exactly what to wear so we could recognize each other. I arrived in Fairfax County, Virginia on March 7th 1975. It was very nice. We stayed in Falls Church area. My neighbors were very friendly.

After 34 years of marriage, I feel that the "chemistry" Subhash and I felt was the best thing to gamble with. We have been through many ups and downs, but always know that we have each other to pull us through. We have been blessed with two wonderful children. Our son is now a happily married, father and surgeon. Our daughter is a happily married pianist. We conduct spiritual activities at our home. Our spiritual activity group is called as "Fairfax Sai Center". Our activities include a Sunday school for children where they learn human values such as love, peace, right conduct, non-violence etc. and character building, devotional singing, and several volunteer services (such as working with the Lions Club, Adopt-A-Highway, cooking lunches for the homeless shelters, etc.).

Although we were out of Virginia for ten years (1981-1990), our hearts brought us back home to Fairfax. There is nothing like Fairfax, VA. It is the place where my married life began and continues to grow. I can't imagine living anywhere else. ##

Four Generations of the Damle Family. (Courtesy of Swati Damle)

A Pakistani American Story of Business Success and Community Contributions

(FCAAHP Note: In developing the stories in this book, the Fairfax County Asian American History Project was supported by Pakistani Americans, most notably by M. Siddique Sheikh who shared his personal story of remarkable achievements and generous community contributions that have strengthened America as the land of opportunity.)

TESTING THE "LAND OF OPPORTUNITY"
By M. Siddique Sheikh

I had yet to test my dreamland, the United States, whether it would really prove to be a "land of Opportunity" for me when I stepped into its soil in 1969. As a fresh graduate of High School from Pakistan, my country of origin, my only asset was my determination to change my life for the better. As a teenager, like other immigrants, I, too, was a bit nervous and excited but my ambitions, let me admit, were limited to material pursuits.

One thing I knew from the beginning that whatever I will do for my living, finally I will settle down in business as being born in 1953 in District Gujranwala, Pakistan, in a business-oriented family, my destiny seemed to be written like that. My father, Sheikh Fazal Haq, was a well-known businessman of the area, who was named the "Businessman of the Year" and rewarded by then Prime Minister Bhutto in 1987.

I followed my brother, an accountant in the Embassy of Pakistan, in Washington, D.C. and conveniently found refuge in its metro area. After attending an automotive engineering school and seeking Virginia State automotive certification, I made up my mind to follow this line of business as my career. Having served in various technical capacities in different automobile companies and finally working as a Service Manager at Jerry's Ford, I had enough "on-the-job training" so at this stage I switched over to my own business and found my first service station, the first of many successful enterprises that I established later on in the Washington D.C Metropolitan area. It included ownership of several retail service stations and various other franchise businesses. In addition, I held financial interests in insurance, hotels, real estate and banking companies.

Now when I look back at the past forty years of my struggles and achievements, after being considered a successful businessman and recognized as a leader in the business community in the Washington D.C Metropolitan Area, I bow my head to Almighty God in gratitude. At the same time, I feel obligated to the American free enterprising society which provided me "even ground" of equal opportunity, disregarding color, race and faith, for the "fair play" of my business ventures leading to my personal and professional economic and social advancements.

So having satisfied my material pursuits I mentioned in the beginning, I decided to "invest" my time, energy and money in two areas of education and community service. I felt Pakistani American business community was less organized and integrated as compared to other communities, and, despite their talent, labor and investment, was not progressing as it should be. So in order to create a common platform for joint effort towards progress I founded a not-for-profit organization, Pakistan American Business Association, (PABA) in Virginia in 1986 and currently I am serving as its Chairman.

Whenever need arose in American society, calling for humanitarian assistance to fellow-citizens, I have never stayed behind as I strongly believe in networking through volunteering for good work. I can proudly quote the unfortunate tragedy of Katrina hurricane when I was able to organize fundraisers to help its victims through working with the Salvation Army. For my social work, I have never ignored Pakistan, my country of origin. I helped raise money for cancer patients of Shaukat Khanum Memorial Hospital in Pakistan. I strongly believe our young generation will gain greater participation in the business world in this country, as well as leadership in the political spectrum by getting involved in volunteer work early in their careers.

I have always believed that education provides necessary basis to all kinds of progress and development. So I worked hard to provide support to a prestigious educational institution in my neighborhood like Virginia International University. I served on its Board of Trustees for several years and now in 2009 I have been elected as its Chairman.

For the same purpose, I founded Pakistan American University Group (PAU) to help coordinate opening campuses of American universities in Pakistan. First project under this Group is expected to be launched in 2010.

Today at the time of this writing when I relax and look through the window of my house at the serene beauty of surrounding landscape in the State of Virginia, I recall my distinguished guests who have frequently visited me. I feel honored in hosting political, community and business leaders including a candidate for the office of governor of Virginia. Community values matter more to me than party affiliation. For that reason I have opted for the middle of the road course and so my friendships are across party affiliation lines.

I am the proud father of three sweet daughters and one son, along with six grandchildren. I share my beautiful home with my extended family and have preserved family values and traditions by maintaining close family ties.

I love my motherland but I am equally proud to be an American. The Pakistani community in Virginia and elsewhere has contributed their talent and labor to the development of American nation having gone through the struggles and challenges of culture, religion and language. As a humble representative of this community, I urge them to continue their positive and constructive contribution to the American society and earn a respectable position they rightly deserve. ##

Photo Gallery From the Life of M. Siddique Sheikh

Siddique at Pakistan American Business Association Corporate Head Office

M. Siddique Sheikh with President Alan G. Merten of George Mason University

Virginia International University's soccer team started by Siddique in 2007

Siddique's Indoor Soccer Team, undefeated from 1990 - 1991.

Fundraiser for Shaukat Memorial Cancer Hospital with Pakistan American Business Association (PABA) group

With Redskins Coach Joe Gibbs -- in 1988, Siddque was the top 10 dealer nationwide and won a trip to the Redskins training camp experience

The first station purchased in 1980

An award-winning station

Americans with Blended Asian Heritage in Fairfax County
By Corazon Sandoval Foley

This fascinating chapter is about experiences of American residents of Fairfax County with blended Asian heritage. We begin with the story of Jackie Fong, a second generation Chinese American resident of Fairfax County on her father's side; and on the side of her mother, a Native American, so that she could claim residency from her ancestors for thousands of generations in the area we now call Fairfax County.

Jackie Fong's Long Family History in Fairfax County. Jackie Fong's ancestors on her mother's side, the local Indians of Fairfax County, had been a settled agricultural people for almost two thousand years by the time of Captain John Smith's Potomac River explorations in 1608. At that time, the major tribe living in what is now Fairfax was the Dogue. Their main village, called Tauxenent, was located on or near the Occoquan, and was home to 135 to 170 Indians. They lived in longhouses, arbor-like structures of bent poles covered with bark or reed mats. Three smaller Dogue villages were also in Fairfax: Namassingakent, situated on the north bank of Dogue Run; Assaomeck, on the south side of Hunting Creek, and Namoraughquend, near the present day Roosevelt Island.

Jackie Fong, Rose Powhatan, Jason Fong, Michael Auld at Riverbend Park exhibit on Native Americans.
(Photo by Cora Foley)

On January 23, 2010, Jackie Fong and her husband, Jason, joined many other Fairfax County residents in the opening of the exhibit "Riverbend Park, A Rare and Rugged Refuge" that examined one of the most unique and not often found biological ecosystems on the East Coast, known locally as the Potomac Gorge. The exhibit also explored the lives of Jackie Fong's ancestors -- the first native people who called the shores of Potomac River home.

The most fascinating speaker is one whom Jackie Fong could legitimately call a relative in Fairfax County. Rose Powhatan -- artist, lecturer, and teacher -- is a member of the Tauxenent and Pamunkey Indian tribes. Both are Virginia tribes and the Tauxenent people are indigenous to Fairfax County. Rose Powhatan created a totem pole that is part of the Riverbend Park 2010 exhibit; she has also created totem poles currently on display at the Jamestown settlement.

The Fairfax County Asian American History Project (FCAAHP) has been working since late 2009 with Rose Powhatan in developing the idea of a Multicultural Museum for Fairfax County, beginning with a Virtual Museum. The Multicultural Museum project would involve working with all interested ethnic groups in Fairfax County to develop the story of how Fairfax County grew dramatically from its beginnings with local Indian tribes to 2010 as a very prosperous Multicultural Megalopolis. It would help sustain public interest in the Fairfax County History Museum project that had to be suspended in November 2009 because of budget constraints from the national economic crisis.

Kathy Mathieson and a Chinese American Mother's Perspective. Our next story starts in 1985 with Kathy Mathieson's move to Fairfax County -- and a Chinese American mother's response to her perception of unusual treatment of her children because they were of "mixed race."

Kathy Mathieson wrote that during her family's early years in Burke, their children experienced somewhat unusual treatment because they were of "mixed race." Luckily, the parents participated in school activities, and the children made friends with classmates with similar values and background, so they did not encounter too many hardships.

Kathy is a first generation Chinese American and her husband of over thirty years comes from a Scottish/English heritage. They were told that the education system in Fairfax County was excellent, and that was one of the major factors that enticed them to move to Burke, Virginia in 1985. Since then, the county has undergone dramatic change with traffic getting worse and the international population significantly larger. She noted that the county is like a mini "United Nations," a wonderful place to live in, enjoy diverse cultures, and benefit from rich experiences.

Kathy Mathieson in 1985 photo with her son in Burke. (Courtesy of Kathy Mathieson)

As part of her children's education, she insisted on teaching them Chinese at home. Her family kept family traditions and celebrated special events by sharing customs with their sons' classes. She found that people around them accepted and became tolerant of diverse cultures. Kathy Mathieson's advice to the younger generation is to "bring the best of your culture's strength to society." She would like to see Fairfax County "benefit from our diverse population, rich in multicultural exchange, languages, and activities. Through education and heritage awareness activities, people respect, accept, understand each other's differences, and appreciate and cherish this unique community. Hopefully, we can set a good model for other parts of the country, showing that it is possible to live harmoniously and indeed have a richer lifestyle with a diverse population."

In Fairfax County, Stories of Pride in Multiple Heritages and Civic Activism. Sonia Elmejjad's *"My Confessions"* describes a blended Korean/Arab American teenage struggles and transcendence to a healthy self-knowledge. Kenneth Burnett recounted his family's journey from India and Africa through Jamaica – and his adjustment to life as a Fairfax County resident. Jeanette Rishell was nurtured by a Filipino American father and a European American mother – and she shared lessons from her active participation in the political arena, advising young Asian Americans to become actively engaged in public service to our community.

My Confessions
By Sonia Elmejjad

My name is Sonia Elmejjad, I was born in 1990 and I am an Asian and Arab American; my mother is from Pusan, South Korea and my father is from Marrakech, Morocco.

One thing that I have learned in this life is that there is nothing more valuable and precious than life itself. Never underestimate the extraordinary miracle that we call the human mind; we can make ourselves the way we want us to be depending on our choices we make in this world. Our determination, our passion, and our love and our experiences help us learn and bring us closer to becoming a better someone in this world.

Although I have gone through a lot in my teenage years as being a confused misfit, I never gave up on myself. I went through an identity crisis when I was a child of only eight years old; I was ridiculed for my awkward looks and because of my last name; I grew to be ashamed of myself and I didn't appreciate myself and my heritage at all.

Like many teenagers, I went through phases in my life. I was depressed and engaged in different forms of self-destructive behavior for some time in my life; I have always

Sonia Elmejjad of Fairfax County

doubted my self-worth and felt I couldn't relate to anybody who was like me at all. I was constantly ridiculed, never went to school because of it and I thought to myself that I wasn't good enough for anything because of the things people said to me; as time passed me by, I decided to take charge of my life and change myself for the better.

As a creative outlet, I have always had a passion for music; I played the violin and viola as well as the piano and guitar. I have always enjoyed trying new things and I loved learning as well; I decided that everything that has happened to me happened for a reason. Honestly, I wouldn't do over whatever mistakes I made in my life; if I didn't experience whatever it is that I have gone through I wouldn't be the person that I am today. I know I have made my share of mistakes, but how would we learn if everyone is just undoubtedly perfect in every way?

Perfection to me is something that people want to achieve because it is unattainable; in my opinion, perfection is like beauty. It is relative and whatever maybe perfect to someone else maybe interoperated in a completely different way through the eye of the beholder. Although we may not be perfect as individuals; we are all beautiful as a whole.

Everyone was put on this world with a purpose in this life; we can either try and search for that specific purpose or we create our own purpose and let it come to us at the right time. I believe that people should learn to appreciate themselves as a whole and appreciate our imperfections and look at themselves as something special.

I haven't found my purpose yet, but I have learned to appreciate my well being and my self-worth. I have learned to be proud of being who I am as a person and proud of my heritage as well; I thank God everyday for everything he has given to me. I have control of my own life and my own choices; I do whatever is right for me and I never stop trying even if I fail. Always pick yourself back up whenever you stumble and fall over; never give up on yourself and on life.

I hope that one day I would be a role model for multi-racial children all over the world; they can take after my experiences and accomplishments in a positive way and learn from them as well. I also want to help people; that is why I am planning on studying clinical psychology in college and also hopefully join the Peace Corps in the near future. Until that day comes, I am going to live life happily day to day and appreciate whatever each day brings me.

I love life; no matter how hard it maybe sometimes you always know everything has to get worse before it gets a little bit better. Life needs to be balanced out in this world; we must have bad things happen in order to appreciate the good in life. Balance is one thing that helps this world coexist; it is something that brings on a beautiful meaning to people to help one another. Life itself is beautiful and precious; and I plan on living life and follow my own path to success and greatness. Overtime, I believe everything would fall for into place for everybody in this world and everything would be as it should be… peaceful. ##

Asian American History Project-A Journey to Fairfax County
By Kenneth Burnett

In 1492 Columbus discovered Jamaica and with the discovery, many believed gold was a precious metal could be found in abundance. But after several years of searching, very little of the metal was found. This led to a new a new discovery. The land was fertile and good for planting crops. One such crop was tobacco. When the Spaniards landed they found the natives smoking tobacco and quickly took a liking to it. The natives were driven to plant more and were soon forced in to slavery in order to produce more. Many natives committed suicide and soon they all died. But tobacco was such a success and this led to many leaving Spain to cultivate the crop.

News of the success in the new world spread very quickly throughout Europe. England joined Spain and soon fighting and land grabbing began. By 1655 Jamaica was captured by the English. The English, realizing there was no gold, saw the promise of tobacco and began planting; it was also the time in England when the demand for sugar had intensified. Many plantations sprang up -- and soon tobacco and sugar became the main export to England.

The demand for these crops led to the intensified demand for more labor. Thus began the slave trade to bring labor to the plantations. After many years of uprisings, rebellions, and wars, the government of England was pressured to abolish slavery.

Ken Burnett at AXA tent in 2008 Reston Asian Festival
(Photo by Cora Foley)

The Emancipation Act was enacted in Jamaica in 1838. This ushered in a new era of rule in the colonies. The Act enabled people of African descent to be free from slavery. As these workers became free, they did not want to continue working on the plantations. The plantation owners had for many years depended on these people to perform hard work, such as: planting, harvesting and domestic chores. There was an immediate and chronic shortage of workers. Plantation owners began to feel the effect of the elimination of forced labor when they could not plant or harvest their crops. The shortage of workers had become a statewide problem and a solution was needed quickly to resolve the situation.

With population increasing in both China and India, there was an immediate need on these constituencies to provide work for their people. And in order to boost the labor force on plantations, workers from these constituencies were brought in fill the gap left by freed slaves. Many workers came from all over the world to settle in Jamaica. This began what is known as indentured workers. The groups that stood out the most were the Indians and Chinese as the overpopulation and shortage of jobs in those countries led to many moving west to make a better living—thus spreading their culture in process.

From this situation, we can understand the complexity of the Jamaican people. The integration of these peoples began a cross culture and many blended families were formed. It was through this blended family that my mother was born. Her father was a descendent of an East Indian family blended with an African family.

Mother grew up under two cultures and so too did my father -- and this may have begun my journey to Fairfax. Growing up, I was exposed to education and sport. My father had some success as a cultivator. But his success was soon cut short when he developed an illness that was left undiagnosed. He could no longer manage the farm. I realized that changes to our lifestyle and pertinent structure were needed. It was decision time for me. I had to face the difficult question -- where do I go from here? I knew I did not want to be a farmer, so I had to make a quick decision -- I immediately joined the military.

In joining the military, I studied to be a paramedic. Each day I would assist the doctor by triaging patients. I had the ability to treat those who had minor illnesses while those who were severely ill were sent to the doctor for comprehensive treatment. I was also in charge of the infirmary. As I progressed as a Paramedic, I was chosen in 1987 to attend the American military academy in Fort Sam Brooks Army Medical Center, San Antonio. It was a course to upgrade my Paramedic skills and to become an orthopedic doctor's assistant. While in the military I ran track and was almost considered for the 1988 Olympics. It was from this group of athletes that the Jamaican bobsled team was formed. My visit to America was very intriguing and inspiring. I began to look at how I could develop my medical skills and began to think about moving to America.

In 1992 I resigned from the army and moved to Brooklyn, NY. The journey had begun. In 1996 we heard about Fairfax County, Virginia and began preparing to move to a place called Falls Church. We arrived in Falls Church in early April and settled in a housing establishment called Monticello Gardens off the route 50 corridor. We came with two children and one month's rent, eager to start a new life. We knew no one in the county so we were hard pressed to find jobs. My wife started temping while I stayed home to baby-sit. However, we were not able to make ends meet with one salary, so the need for a second income became extremely urgent. At first, I began looking at jobs that were medical related and was only concentrating in this category. Until it dawned on me that having been an army service personnel, I could do security until other opportunities arise.

And so a renewed effort began. After weeks of looking, one day I was watching television and saw the *Washington Post* ad about the mega job section for the following Sunday. I purchased the paper and began checking the classified ads. After going through the classified job section by section, I finally came to security. And after looking at several agencies, I circled three that I decided I would to call the following Monday.

One company of particular interest was Barton Protective Services. Their office was located in the Fairview Park business complex. I called and the operation director answered the phone; I explained the reason for my call and he scheduled me for an interview the next day. Dressed in a suit-and-tie, I showed up for the interview. The interviewer, the operation director, looked at my resume and told me he could not pay me the same salary I was getting in NY, but he had a position in Washington DC that needed filling immediately. He told me to report to the address in Washington DC. There were no further questions -- I was hired.

My first assignment was at Humana Health Services, a health care insurance provider. For three weeks I showed up on time and when they wanted someone for extra assignments I was always readily available. This gave me an important start with the company; every time they wanted extra help they would call on me. One afternoon after reporting for work I was visited by my supervisor who told me that because of my hard work and the willingness to accept the low wages I was offered, they were planning to send me to a different site, one in which I would get more pay. I was sent to work at the jewel store Tiffany and Company. While working at Tiffany and company, one evening I was getting ready to go home, I asked one of the other personnel if they had any old newspaper. It was my intention to read the paper on the train. He told me to look into the closet and there I saw an old newspaper about three weeks old. I took the paper and after reading a few scores, I decided to take the paper home. Upon reaching home I left the paper on the nightstand. My wife took the paper believing it was the day's paper and began reading the classified ads. And among those ads was an advertised position for Black Child development, a company my wife worked for while we were in NY. After discussing the position, we both decided that my wife should interview for the job. My wife who was temping at the time with a temp agency in Rosslyn worked at The Salvation Army. She did not get the job, but the Salvation Army found out that she wanted a permanent job, and interviewed her. She was hired as a secretary to the second in command at the headquarters in Washington DC.

It was during my wife's brief stay with the Salvation Army that a letter came across her desk; the Salvation Army was opening up a new treatment center in Washington DC and wanted someone to oversee the medical department. Having the experience in the military, I felt this was my opportunity to get back in the medical field. Not only did they want some one with medical experience, but they also wanted someone to train as a lab technician. After discussing the position I decided to interview for the job. Once again, there were no questions asked. The interviewer simply asked me when I could get started. I told him that I only needed two weeks notice, and so I began working for the Salvation Army.

Reporting to the Salvation Army, I quickly realized I would work in many different capacities. They wanted me to head the medical department as well as the Intake department. I soon learned that in working in a treatment center, one of the requirements was to understand the dynamics of counseling and I also needed training in laboratory techniques. I was immediately sent to San Jose, California where I was trained as a laboratory assistant and on my return, I immediately enrolled in NoVA Community College, studying counseling and counseling techniques. It was during this time that I met one of the assistant directors for Fairfax Substance facility. The program wanted someone to assist in the evening with juveniles, and once again I was hired without an interview. This enabled me to get experience from both adult as well as juvenile perspective. I worked for both Salvation Army and Fairfax County until 2006 when I got laid off. For the first time in eight and half years, I was unemployed.

During my final year with the Salvation Army I had planned a reunion for my family. When I got laid off, I decided that if I took a job immediately, I would not be able to take a vacation so quickly, and so I decided to wait until after the reunion to begin my job hunting. After the reunion, I felt rejuvenated and ready to resume my career. On returning to the USA, I began seeking employment and after visiting several employments job fairs, there was still no job forthcoming.

Once again, I resorted to the *Washington Post* for my job hunting. And once again, the Washington Post advertised their mega classified and so I got the paper and began searching. The paper advertised a job fair in Tyson Corner at the Marriott Hotel where they assembled companies from various sectors of the economy. Dressed in a suit and tie, I entered the building and found a line for registering and other information. When I entered the room where all the companies were located, I entered moving from left to right and not noticing who was to my right, I kept on moving until I went around the room. I received some information here and there but I decided to call it quits since nothing had caught my attention.

However, on my way out to leave the job fair, in the last booth on my left there were several people standing and I went over and began a conversation. After talking with them and hearing my situation, they asked me if I have ever done their type of job before and if I was willing to try it, and I said yes. About a week later, I got a call from the recruiting officer who invited me to a seminar at the branch office. To my surprise this was the same building I was interviewed for my first job in the county. Once again, my interview was not complicated, I was hired, and AXA-Advisors had given me the opportunity to work in Fairfax County again.

Working at AXA has been fulfilling, particularly since the company has embraced community development participation as one of its core values... Each year the branch has supported a charity and has been a constant beacon. The civic marketing has been a useful tool that allows Financial Professionals to be out in the community interacting with people.

It was while attending one the many events that I met Cora who had introduced me to the Fairfax County Asian American History Project (FCAAHP). As an employee of AXA-Advisors, I am privileged to be associated with Fairfax County and Falls Church Chambers of Commerce. These organizations have helped foster community spirit and the opportunity to work together for the common good of the citizens.

After thirteen years, Fairfax County is still my home. The county has encouraged literacy as well as entrepreneurial development through its Community College system. This system, I believe, is the best in the country. It also encourages homeownership as a part of the American experience. Fairfax County has not only welcomed immigrants, but has allowed immigrants to integrate and play vital roles in the development of the county. Whether in terms of community building, politics, entrepreneurship, or just being an individual, Fairfax County is the place to be... as the USA Army slogan states: be all you can be…. Fairfax County is the place to be all you can be. ##

A Political Journey in Fairfax County and Prince William County

By Jeanette Rishell

Jeanette Rishell with the 1983 Brownie Scout den meeting in her home. (Courtesy of J. Rishell)

(FCAAHP Note: From October 1978 to December 1994 (16 years), Jeanette Rishell and her husband Ed lived and raised their two daughters in Burke, Fairfax County where her fondest memory was being a Brownie Scout leader. Job considerations made them move to Prince William County where Jeanette Rishell became the first Filipino American Democratic candidate for Delegate 2006, 2007 and 2009. She shared her Filipino American life story and encouraged young Asian Americans to seek political office.)

Jeanette Rishell on her Political Journey. I have always valued outreach, volunteerism and public service. So running for House of Delegates seemed a natural outgrowth of my church and community volunteerism. My family set the example for me early in life. I lived in a Filipino American extended family (mother, grandmother, two uncles, Godfather and stepsister) in which everyone was genuinely concerned for others, particularly those who could not navigate life's challenges as easily as we could.

As a child in the 1950s and 1960s, my family set a strong example of service to others. My family had a small band that played professionally and my mother was the singer. My family volunteered their musical talents whenever and wherever they could, whether it was to help raise money for a good cause or to entertain veterans in the VA hospital. My family also knew widows who had never learned to drive and who needed to go to doctor appointments, to get groceries and other needed shopping trips. They had only to call and someone from my extended family would drive them.

Jeanette Rishell with daughters and uncle in 1978 at their home in Burke. (Courtesy of Jeanette Rishell)

Since my family members were strong Democrats, they also volunteered to drive other Democrats to the polls on Election Day. What we did, we always thought was a natural part of how we should live our lives. So I cannot point to one event or moment when my mind was turned to politics in a committed way, because it was a slow evolution.

I believe my heritage nurtured my expanded view of family and of community, and that good stewardship of these life-giving institutions should be everyone's responsibility. My commitment to volunteerism increased when I saw a need for greater participation, cooperation and progress on public policy issues. I realized outreach alone is not enough, that it needs a political component with it. Volunteerism validates the truth of the slogan: "Democracy is not a spectator sport."

Jeanette Rishell on her American Life Story. I was born and raised in a loving Filipino-American extended family. My Dad, Alex Reyes, and his two brothers Florencio and Quin were born in the Philippines around the turn of the last century. Right before World War I, they joined the U.S. Navy. My father used Florencio's identification in order to sign up since he was too young. They eventually ended up in New York. They were generally either in the Navy or Merchant Marine for several decades. They were also excellent musicians and played in one of the many small bands and orchestras which at that time could afford a person a modest living. My Dad played the guitar, mandolin and Hawaiian steel guitar. My uncle Quin played the guitar and steel guitar. Uncle Florencio did not play any instruments; he remained in the Navy and made it a career. My godfather Max played the bass. Of the three brothers, my Dad was the one who really wanted to attend college. Having no resources of his own, he was able to find a sponsor. He began attending college, but had to drop out. The Great Depression wiped out the assets of his sponsor, who could no longer pay for my Dad's tuition and books.

Jeanette Rishell's mother and father in 1937 (Courtesy of Jeanette Rishell)

I am named after my mother, a European American. She and Dad met when they both played in the same orchestra. My mother played the piano, guitar and was the singer. They were married in 1937. My Mom also attended college briefly, but found the same financial obstacles and did not finish. She had also toured in vaudeville through the south in 1928 and 1929 before she met my Dad. Mom bought a motorcycle from a friend in 1919. She took my grandmother to work in the sidecar of the motorcycle. It's understood in my family that she was the first woman to own and drive a motorcycle in Toronto, which is where she bought it. She also learned how to compete in tub races and did very well. My grandmother made her stop because it was too dangerous.

During the Great Depression, people were getting laid off, the bread lines were forming and some people (many in the Filipino community) had no place to go. They were put out of their apartments and were homeless. My mother fortunately had kept her job and her apartment. She opened her home to friends and the friends of friends until they could get their bearings. At one time she said there were about 25 people sleeping on her living room floor. Although it was a crowded situation, everyone pitched in as best they could to tidy the apartment and cook meals, etc.

My dad was Merchant Marine during WWII, and his ship was sunk off the coast of Greenland by a German torpedo. He had always slept fully dressed and prepared for emergency. Some of his friends would sleep in their underwear, but he never did. That saved his life because when the men poured onto the life rafts in the icy waters of the north Atlantic, some of them froze to death waiting to be picked up. He had many friends who never came home from the war.

My dad loved to cook and my mom said he was always prepared and meticulous about his cooking, too. All ingredients were lined up and ready, kitchen cleaned immaculately and veggies were chopped ahead of time and so on. She said his oyster stuffing at Thanksgiving was the absolute best! Oral history was an important part of our family. We always gathered after dinner, telling stories out of the past in words that could express the vivid reality of the moment. Some of the best times were when aunts and uncles and cousins (many now passed away) came for parties and reunions and shared their stories.

One evening, I was given an idea of what it might have been like to be Asian within weeks of the bombing of Pearl Harbor. Shortly after the bombing, my dad had several friends who were pulled from their car on their way to work by a group of young men, and beaten because they "looked" Japanese. They were lucky to have survived. This happened in New York City. From then on, they drove their car with a small sign taped to their car that read, "We are Filipino, we are not Japanese." When I think of the disrespect that I saw my two uncles and Godfather received, I can't help but remember how patriotic they and my dad really were. When we attended events where the National Anthem was played, I looked around me and no one stood up any straighter or more respectful than my family.

I was the first person in my family to graduate from college when I graduated from Pennsylvania State University. I studied history and was inducted into the Phi Alpha Theta History Honor Society. Together with Ed, my husband of 39 years, I've raised two daughters, Emily and Stacey. I also worked in the financial services industry. Ed and I also have been blessed with three beautiful granddaughters: Miranda, Cora and Vivian.

Jeanette and Ed Rishell in 2008.

Jeanette Rishell on Filipino food and family. My uncle (until his death) would cook tremendous varieties of Filipino dishes and they were wonderful. I still cook adobo (a Philippine stew) despite how hectic our lives have become. I will always remember the gatherings we hosted where many people came, my uncle prepared wonderful meals, and music was central to fun and festivities. These gatherings provided so much togetherness and were definitely a sustaining force in our lives. ##

What Contributions Have Asian Americans Made in Fairfax County?

Patriotism: Military Service and Virginia's Wall of Honor
By Corazon Sandoval Foley

November 1970 OCS class -- Francis Cheng is standing third from right; beside him is another Chinese American; 6th in line is a Vietnamese Americans; 7th is a Japanese American; and 8th is a Korean American. Francis Cheng shared this photo with FCAAHP after the August 14, 2008 interview with him and his wife – and other members of the Chinese American Silver Light Seniors Association of Fairfax County who meet at the Herndon Senior Center. (Courtesy of Francis Cheng)

Asian Americans have a long history of serving this country honorably – and in the case of the Japanese Americans, even when their community has been deprived of constitutional rights by being placed in World War II internment camps. On July 30, 2008, the US House of Representatives passed a resolution recognizing and expressing appreciation for the courageous and local contributions made by soldiers of Asian and Pacific Islander descent during the United States Civil War. The resolution noted that those Asian American soldiers were denied rightful recognition of their service.

This chapter focuses on Fairfax County Asian American military service personnel. Filipino American General (ret.) Antonio Mario Taguba was the keynote speaker at the FCAAHP-initiated first-ever naturalization ceremony in the Fairfax County Government Center on

Captain Ravi Alexander Balaram

May 29, 2009. Fairfax County Vietnamese American Hung Ba Le made history as the first Vietnamese American Commander of a US Navy Destroyer – who also made a unique return on November 7, 2009 to Danang, Vietnam. I also talked to the father of Captain Ravi Alexander Balaram, son of an Indian American father and Filipino American mother, who graduated from Robinson High School in 1997 and the West Point US Military Academy in 2001; he has served in South Korea, Honduras, Germany, Italy, and Afghanistan. And I included in this chapter the moving life stories of the Asian American heroes in Virginia's Wall of Honor who gave their lives to defend America's fight against global terrorism since 2000.

Filipino American General Antonio Taguba at FCAAHP's Naturalization Ceremony. On May 29, 2009, retired General Antonio Taguba, a Filipino American Fairfax County resident, gave an inspirational speech at the FCAAHP-initiated naturalization ceremony for 75 new Americans encouraging them to honor their commitment to defend American values and democratic principles.

He was the 2007 recipient of the Outstanding American By Choice award by the US Citizenship and Immigration Services of the Department of Homeland Security. He authored the 2004 Taguba Report, an internal US Army report on abuse of detainees at Abu Ghraib prison in Iraq.

Major General (ret) Antonio Taguba was the second American citizen of Philippine birth to be promoted to general officer rank in the US Army (the first was Filipino American Lieutenant General Edward Soriano). He was born in Sampaloc, Manila in the Philippines where his family had moved from their home province of Cagayan.

Major General (ret.) Antonio Taguba received the 2007 Outstanding American by Choice Award. (Courtesy of USCIS)

General Taguba's father was a soldier in the 45th Infantry Regiment, Philippine Division (Philippine Scouts) who fought in the Battle of Bataan (January – April 1942) during World War II and after capture by the Japanese, survived the Bataan Death March.

When he was eleven years old, General Taguba and his family moved to Hawaii. At the May 29th FCAAHP naturalization ceremony, he recounted the days (not hours) of air travel then required for new immigrants from the Philippines.

General Antonio Taguba is in left of photo with Sharon Bulova in center during May 29, 2009 naturalization ceremony initiated by FCAAHP.

He also spoke of his deep admiration for his parents, particularly his father who received recognition for his military service many decades after WWII. He saluted his parents' dreams for their children that included becoming citizens of the United States of America. General Taguba also praised his mother for raising seven children – many times alone while his father was honorably performing his military assignments. General Taguba had the honor of presenting the first equity checks for Filipino American WWII veterans, most notably Alberto Bacani, 98 years old in 2009, whose life story is included in the chapter on Filipino Americans.

Fairfax County Chinese American Major General John L. Fugh (Retired) U.S. Army. General John L. Fugh received the Outstanding American By Choice on January 15, 2008. He was the first Chinese American to attain general officer status in the U.S. Army. General Fugh was born in Beijing, China. He was 15 when he migrated to the United States with his family. General Fugh was The Judge Advocate General of the U.S. Army, retiring from that post in July 1993 as a major general. The Judge Advocate General manages the Army's worldwide legal organization, consisting of 4,700 active duty, reserve and civilian lawyers, and over 5,000 paralegal and administrative personnel.

General John Fugh in 2008 received the Outstanding American by Choice Award.

General Fugh in 2008 has been the Chairman of the Committee of 100, a national, non-partisan group of prominent Chinese Americans who brings a bicultural perspective to U.S. relations with China and addresses the concerns of Americans of Chinese/Asian descent. In addition, he has served on the Executive Committee and as a director of the Atlantic Council of the United States. General Fugh graduated from the Georgetown University School of Foreign Service and the George Washington University Law School. He attended the Kennedy School of Government at Harvard University, the U.S. Army War College, and the U.S. Army Command and General Staff College.

Fairfax County Japanese American Captain Robert Nakamoto Jr. who served as an enlisted man in Iraq. On May 5, 2006, former Captain and then Sergeant Robert Nakamoto Jr. gave an interview to discuss his military experience.

"After 10 months of combat duty in Iraq, Sergeant Robert S. Nakamoto, a member of 278th Regimental Combat Team of the Tennessee National Guard, a part of the 4,000 strong unit of Tennessee men and women stationed in southwest Asia, returned in October 2005 to their home state, where he has since been undergoing medical treatment sustained in the line of duty. Sgt. Nakamoto was asked by the Japanese American Veterans' Association (JAVA) to share his Iraq experience. Nakamoto obliged saying,

"During the deployment, I frequently thought about the example of exemplary service that the Nisei had set for our nation. I tried to live up in my own small way to the heritage the *Nisei* gave to our nation. I am a fourth generation Japanese American. My dad served in the Korean War.

"I have been asked, "Why did I rejoin the US Army as an enlisted man," when I left its ranks honorably in 1987 as a Captain. The answer is simple. Like nearly all Americans, the events of September 11, 2001 were a great shock. It was very sad to see such a display of hatred directed against civilians. It was also very sad to think of the number of innocent victims who were killed or injured or had loved ones hurt in that tragedy. As a sense of duty to avenge the indiscriminate killings by international terrorists and to make our country safe from international terrorism, I joined the Tennessee Guard in July 2002. I did this despite the fact that I have five children and, due to a technicality, had to take a cut in rank from Captain to the enlisted ranks. I felt I had to serve and my wife and family supported me.

Sergeant Robert Nakamoto playing with the Charlie Daniels band in Iraq. (Courtesy of Robert Nakamoto)

"One highlight of my Iraq tour was the Charlie Daniels Band visiting us in September 2005 at our remote base in northeast Iraq. A group of us set up the sound system for Charlie Daniels and his band, who journeyed to our base despite risks to their personal safety. Several soldiers in our unit lent their personal music equipment and we were able to patch it together to make a functioning PA system. Charlie's band members said it was the best set-up they had had in Iraq. [Note: Daniels, country music legend, took his band on this tour to Kyrgystan, Uzbekistan, Afghanistan, Kuwait, Iraq and Germany. They traveled more than 16,000 miles, performed three shows per day for American troops deployed in the war on terrorism.]

"I graduated from the United States Military Academy at West Point in 1982 following which I served five years as an infantry officer, primarily with the 82nd Airborne Division and earned the Ranger Tab, Senior Parachutist Wings, and Expert Infantry Badge. I resigned from the Army in 1987. As a result of leaving my name on the reserve rolls while I was in inactive status, I lost my commission in 1995.

"Coming back in the military after being out for 17 years was a bit of a "Rip Van Winkle" experience. The gas mask, radios, vehicles, and weapons had all changed. The military was now using global positioning navigation devices, computers, e-mail, modernized night vision gear, etc. I went to my first two drills in civilian clothes due to not having a uniform anymore, while I waited for my new uniforms. Many of the men I was serving with were young enough to be my son."

Sgt Nakamoto has lived in Nashville, Tennessee since 1992 because of his love for folk music, which some call country music. He also plays Christian music as a hobby. He is the son of Robert Nakamoto, Chairman of Base Technologies, Inc., of McLean, Virginia whose interview with FCAAHP is included in the section on business contributions by Fairfax County Asian Americans.

Fairfax County Vietnamese American Navy Commander Hung Ba Le and his unique return to Vietnam. On Saturday, November 7, 2009, Hung Ba Le, the first Vietnamese American Commander of a U.S. Navy Destroyer, the *USS Lassen,* returned to Danang, Vietnam -- 34 years after he fled at the age of 5 in a fishing trawler crammed with 400 refugees after April 30, 1975 when Saigon was taken by communist troops from North Vietnam. He has shared some memories of his three-day journey on the fishing trawler, which ended just as they were running out of food, water and fuel.

US Navy Commander Hung Ba Le, the first Vietnamese American Commander of a US Navy Destroyer–USS Lassen, and his father Thong Ba Le of Fairfax County, Virginia.

He has often spoken of his great admiration for the example set by his father, Thong Ba Le, who has never returned to Vietnam. After the family settled in northern Virginia, he took a job in a supermarket, where he worked his way up from bag boy to manager.

"I always wanted to be like my dad," Hung Ba Le has stressed. "He persevered and overcame many challenges." He has also been quoted as saying that "My father, he's my hero. He was a South Vietnamese navy commander and his career was cut short because of the war, so I wanted to follow in his footsteps as an officer."

Commander Thong Ba Le of the South Vietnamese Navy began rebuilding his working life in Fairfax County in 1975. He worked at Giant Food Store in Leesburg Pike -- and became general manager before his retirement.

Virginia's Wall of Honor and Asian American Heroes.

By Corazon Sandoval Foley

On May 24, 2007, Virginia's Wall of Honor was set up in Richmond to honor 183 Virginians who died fighting terrorism since January 2000 – and that includes the bombing of the Norfolk-based USS Cole in Yemen. Accompanying the wall is a framed Virginia State Flag, flown in Iraq by Cpl. Jonathan Bowling who was killed in Iraq on January 26, 2005. In front of a Virginia and American flag stand a pair of boots and a rifle with helmet on top in a traditional military tribute to the fallen.

Virginia's Wall of Honor was created to honor those American soldiers who died in the war against global terrorism. The list includes five Asian American heroes – three from Fairfax County and two from Virginia Beach.

On May 25, 2009, Adjutant General of Virginia Major General Robert B. Newman honored the Virginian soldiers. "We gather today not only as Americans, but especially as Virginians, to remember our loved ones and friends who willingly served our nation and paid the ultimate price to secure the freedoms that we enjoy today."

Virginia's Wall of Honor includes five Asian American heroes -- three from Fairfax County, Virginia and two from Virginia Beach. The five life stories are presented in this book to honor the long tradition of Asian American military sacrifices in defense of American democratic values.

Tenzin Dengkhim

Tibetan American Tenzin Choeku Dengkhim of Falls Church, Virginia was 19 years old when he died on April 2, 2005 as a result of hostile action in the city of Hadithah in Al Anbar province, Iraq – less than one month after deploying in Iraq. He was a Lance Corporal in the Marines – 2nd Light Armored Reconnaisance Battalion, 2nd Marine Division, II Marine Expeditionary Force, Camp Lejeune, North Carolina.

He was laid to rest on April 11, 2005 at Arlington National Cemetery, the first Tibetan American to be buried with full military honors at the site reserved for American war heroes. Tibetan monks chanted prayers at his coffin, draped with the Stars and Stripes. When the monks fell silent, seven soldiers fired a 21-gun salute, and a solitary bugler played the anthem "Taps."

His mother, Radio Free Asia Tibetan Service broadcaster Rinzin Choedon Dengkhim, quoted him as saying "Mother, don't worry – we are trained for war. Though Iraq is not our country and it may not directly be our war, the situation is quite similar to the situation in Tibet, where people do not have freedom of speech or enjoy human rights." A devoted follower of the Dalai Lama, his mother said that he hoped he could one day use his military training to help his native Tibet gain independence.

Rinzin Dengkhim had escaped from Tibet as a child to live in exile in India, where Tenzin was born in the Tibetan community of Dharamsala, Himachal Pradesh, base of the Dalai Lama and the Tibetan government in exile. Rinzin, a single mother, was among the first of a group of Tibetan refugees who moved to Utah in 1992, made possible by an Act of Congress that provided 1,000 Tibetans with a chance to immigrate to the US.

Tenzin Dengkhim graduated from George Marshall High School in Fairfax, Virginia, after moving with his mother and brother from Utah. While at school, he collected signatures for an international Campaign For Tibet initiative to support the Tibetan Policy Act later signed into law by President Bush in 2002.

His friends remembered him as a quiet, thoughtful young man devoted to his family and his Buddhist faith. A few days before leaving for Iraq, he went to make offerings at a Buddhist shrine. Friends assumed he was seeking protection for the conflict ahead but he told them later that he had been praying that he would not have to kill any Iraqi people. According to a family friend, "Deep down, he held the great spirit of Tibet. I think his mission is fulfilled and as a Tibetan, he contributed to the American cause."

Vietnamese American Binh N. Le of Alexandria, Virginia was 20 years old when he was killed on December 3, 2004 in the Anbar province of Iraq. He was a Corporal in the Marines -- 5th Battalion, 10th Marine Regiment, 2nd Marine Division and his unit's base was in Camp Lejeune, North Carolina.

Binh Le

On February 10, 2005, Senate Joint Resolution No. 503 was offered celebrating the life of Corporal Binh Le.

WHEREAS, United States Marine Corporal Binh Le, a resident of Fairfax County, was killed in action on December 3, 2004; and

WHEREAS, a 2002 graduate of Edison High School in Fairfax County, where he was active with the Junior ROTC, Binh Le joined the United States Marine Corps shortly after graduation; and

WHEREAS, Binh Le hoped that his service in the Marine Corps would gain him United States citizenship and allow him to bring his birth parents, who gave him up for adoption, from Vietnam to the United States; and

WHEREAS, Corporal Binh Le was assigned to the 5th Battalion, 10th Marine Regiment and was serving his second tour of duty in Iraq, having volunteered to return following his first tour as an artilleryman during the 2003 invasion; and

WHEREAS, Corporal Binh Le, with fellow Marine Corporal Matthew Wyatt of Illinois, was at a forward operating base in Al Anbar Province, Iraq, when a water truck carrying 500 pounds of explosives approached the camp; and

WHEREAS, Corporal Binh Le and Corporal Wyatt were both killed by the suicide bomber while defending the camp and saving the lives of fellow Marines; and

WHEREAS, on January 27, 2005, Corporal Binh Le was posthumously awarded United States citizenship in a ceremony at the Navy Annex in Arlington;

The Senate, with the House of Delegates concurring, then resolved that the General Assembly note with great sadness the loss of a courageous and patriotic Virginian, Corporal Binh Le – and that the resolution should be presented to his family as an expression of the high regard for his memory by the citizens of Virginia.

On January 27, 2005, a citizenship ceremony was held for Binh Le in which a letter from his commanding officer, Captain Christopher J. Curtain, was read. "His final act of bravery saved the lives of others. I will be forever grateful for his heroism." Binh Le grabbed his rifle when the truck packed with explosives attacked his military post on December 3, 2004. He had run to a position to fire on the driver and hold back the vehicle when it exploded. His commanding officer recommended him for a Silver Star.

Binh Ngoc Le was 4 when he was adopted by Hau Luu and Thanh Le, his aunt and uncle. They immigrated to America in 1991 when he was seven years old and he was raised in the Alexandria section of Fairfax County. He visited his birth parents twice, once after he graduated from Fairfax's Edison High School in 2002. Binh Le grew up a typical American teenager, a member of the Junior ROTC and active in Lorton's Gunston Bible Church. He played in a series of bands with young

members of his church. Drums were his passion, but he also had a talent for the keyboards and trumpet.

Laotian American Krisna Nachampassak of Burke, Virginia was 27 years old when he died on July 10, 2004 in a vehicle accident in Al Anbar province in Iraq. He was a Sergeant in the Marines -- 3rd Battalion, 1st Marine Regiment, 1st Marine Division, I Marine Expedition and his unit's base was in Camp Pendleton, California.

On February 15, 2005, House Joint Resolution No. 945 was offered in the Virginia State Legislature celebrating the life of Sergeant Krisna Nachampassak.

Krisna Nachampassak

WHEREAS, United States Marine Corps Sergeant Krisna Nachampassak, a resident of Burke and a graduate of Lake Braddock Secondary School, died in Iraq while in support of Operation Iraqi Freedom on July 10, 2004; and

WHEREAS, Krisna Nachampassak was a native of Fairfax County, and his parents came to the United States in 1976 after making their way out of Laos and into a refugee camp; and

WHEREAS, shortly after his 1995 graduation from Lake Braddock Secondary School, Krisna Nachampassak joined the Marine Corps; and

WHEREAS, following basic training at Parris Island, South Carolina, Sergeant Nachampassak attended the Marine Corps' School of Infantry, Motor Transport School, and Service Support School at Camp Lejeune, North Carolina; and

WHEREAS, during his career in the Marine Corps, Sergeant Nachampassak earned the Navy and Marine Corps Achievement Medal, the Marine Corps Good Conduct Medal, and the Sea Service Deployment Ribbon; and

WHEREAS, Sergeant Nachampassak was killed with three other members of the 1st Marine Regiment, 1st Marine Division in a Humvee accident in Al Anbar Province, Iraq, on July 10, 2004;

The House of Delegates, with the Senate concurring, then resolved that the General Assembly note with great sadness the loss of a courageous and patriotic Virginian, Sergeant Krisna Nachampassak – and that the resolution should be presented to his family as an expression of the high regard for his memory by the citizens of Virginia.

Krisna Nachampassak's parents said that he often told his two sons about their struggle in Laos which they left in 1976. His wife said that he thought of other people not himself – worried about who would take care of his family if anything were to happen to him. In his early years Krisna Johnny Nachampassak was remembered serving his community at the Lao Buddhavong Temple. Wearing an orange safety jacket, he helped others find parking during events and even picked up the trash after the events were over. Many a time he was seen carrying the alms bowls for the monks, or helping elders carry things to their cars – with nary a complaint, greeting everyone with a reverent bow and a smile.

Filipino American Keith Casica of Virginia Beach, Virginia was 32 years old when he was killed on December 10, 2005 in Baghdad. He was a Sergeant in the Army - 1st Battalion, 502nd Infantry Regiment, 2nd Brigade Combat Team, 101st Airborne Division and his unit's base was in Fort Campbell, Kentucky.

On February 9, 2006, the House Joint Resolution No. 293 was offered celebrating the life of Sergeant Kenith Casica.

WHEREAS, Kenith Casica was born in the Philippines and, from the age of two, grew up in Virginia Beach; and

Kenith Casica

WHEREAS, as a teenager, Kenith Casica held part-time jobs delivering The Virginian-Pilot and working at the McDonalds on Bonney Road; and he graduated from Green Run High School in 1994; and

WHEREAS, Sergeant Casica enlisted in the Army in 1996 and was assigned to the 1st Battalion, 502nd Infantry Regiment, 2nd Brigade Combat Team, 101st Airborne Division based at Fort Campbell, Kentucky; and

WHEREAS, Sergeant Casica was injured by shrapnel from a rocket-propelled grenade during his first deployment to Iraq; and

WHEREAS, serving his second tour of duty in Iraq with the 101st Airborne, Sergeant Casica's platoon was patrolling in a neighborhood near Baghdad when he and a fellow soldier were killed by small-arms fire; and

WHEREAS, Sergeant Casica was a dedicated soldier, who believed in his mission; the day before his death, he told an Army journalist that he wanted the Iraqi citizens "to realize that we are here to help them"; and

WHEREAS, Sergeant Casica always wanted to be granted his American citizenship, which he will receive posthumously; and

WHEREAS, Sergeant Casica loved to joke around and have fun, enjoyed the ocean and fishing, and was ardently devoted to his wife and three children, his mother, father, and step-father, all of Hampton Roads, as well as his beloved sister and brother;

The House of Delegates, with the Senate concurring, then resolved that the General Assembly note with great sadness the loss of a courageous and patriotic Virginian, Sergeant Kenith Casica – and that the resolution should be presented to his family as an expression of the high regard for his memory by the citizens of Virginia.

In death, Kenith Casica got something he had long hoped for: U.S. citizenship. "He wanted it more than anything, because this is his country," said his wife. Kenith Casica married his girlfriend, who lived down the street, when she was 16 and he was 19. He had her name tattooed on his arm and gave both his daughters the same middle name: his wife's name, Renee. "My husband was a man that when he smiled, he lit up a room.I'm thankful for the time God gave me with him, and that's what I'm going to hold on to."

Filipino American Jeremy M. Dimaranan of Virginia Beach, Virginia was 29 years old when he died on June 16, 2004 in Balad, Iraq. He was a Specialist in the Army - 302nd Transportation Company, 172nd Combat Support Group Army Reserve and his unit's base was Fort Eustis, Virginia.

On February 18, 2005, Senate Joint Resolution No. 530 was offered celebrating the life of Specialist Jeremy M. Dimaranan.

Jeremy Dimaranan

WHEREAS, United States Army Reserve Specialist Jeremy M. Dimaranan, a resident of Virginia Beach, was killed in a mortar attack on a former Iraqi air base on June 16, 2004; and

WHEREAS, Jeremy Dimaranan grew up in California's Bay Area and resided with his wife and three young children in Virginia Beach; and

WHEREAS, Specialist Dimaranan was assigned to the 302nd Transportation Company, 172nd Combat Support Group, stationed in Fort Eustis, Virginia; and

WHEREAS, the 302nd Transportation Company was mobilized in December 2003 and deployed to Iraq in February 2004; and

WHEREAS, Specialist Dimaranan died during a June 16, 2004 mortar attack on Camp Anaconda, near the former Iraqi air base at Balad, about 50 miles north of Baghdad;

The Senate, with the House of Delegates concurring, then resolved that the General Assembly note with great sadness the loss of a courageous and patriotic Virginian, Specialist Jeremy M. Dimaranan – and that the resolution should be presented to his family as an expression of the high regard for his memory by the citizens of Virginia.

Jeremy M. Dimaranan's shyness hid a romantic side. He wrote poetry to his wife, professing his devotion. "From the first time I saw you, I knew you were the one," he wrote in a poem titled "Miracle." The Filipino-American called his wife "mahal," the Tagalog word for love. He belted out karaoke to her at their wedding in 1995.

Through a grainy Web camera in Iraq, the 29-year-old Reservist from Virginia Beach, Va., tried to calm his wife's fears, saying all he needed was sleep. He died the next day, killed June 16 in a mortar attack in Balad.

A computer technician, Dimaranan had a new job with Canon Computer Systems in Chesapeake, Va., and was scheduled to leave the Reserves in August. Then he was activated and deployed to the war. He tried to put it in a good light. "He thought, it's tax-free over there," his wife said, "so we could save for

a house," Other survivors include his children Celynna, 6, Jeriah, 4, and Jerico, 17 months. ##

Hall of Fame tributes are made by Defense Department not only for military service but also for civilian public servants. In the photo is the Defense Department civilian hall of fame in the Pentagon that, among others, honors Judith Gilliom with whom I worked in developing the Asian American Federal Foreign Affairs Council and other interagency civil rights groups.

Volunteerism: Asian American Lord and Lady Fairfax.
By Corazon Sandoval Foley

The tradition of honoring Lords and Ladies Fairfax began in 1984 as a unique way to recognize outstanding citizens of Fairfax County. Each year, the Fairfax County Board of Supervisors selects two people from each district who have demonstrated exceptional volunteer service, heroism, or other special accomplishments to receive the award. The Lords and Ladies are presented by the Board of Supervisors during a June Monday meeting at the Fairfax County Government Center prior to the opening of Celebrate Fairfax. Later that evening, the Lords and Ladies are honored at a special dinner hosted by Great American Restaurants, Celebrate Fairfax, Inc., and the Fairfax County Board of Supervisors. In 2009, more than 470 individuals have been named a Lord or Lady Fairfax by their respective member of the Fairfax County Board of Supervisors.

On May 28, 2009, Mason District Supervisor Penny Gross wrote this about the award: "In Fairfax County's long history (the county was created in 1742), a few names stand out. George Washington may have been Fairfax County's most illustrious and significant resident, but England's Fairfax family played a significant role in the early history of our now-burgeoning locality. According to *Fairfax County, Virginia, A History,* the Fairfax family "exercised powerful influence on the affairs of Fairfax County. Until the time of the Revolution, they were, even before the Washington family, the first family of Fairfax County." Thomas, fifth Lord Fairfax, and his son Thomas, sixth Lord Fairfax, controlled the proprietary patent, or land grant from the king, and Lord Fairfax arrived in 1735 to ensure the boundaries were properly surveyed. So it is not surprising that the Board of Supervisors, in the mid-1980s, when seeking an appropriate title to honor outstanding citizens, chose to call these honored volunteers "Lord and Lady Fairfax." The designation carries with it no special duties or responsibilities, and definitely not any land, but it does provide an opportunity to say "thanks" for service to the community. Every year since 1984, each Supervisor selects appropriate recipients who are honored at a Board of Supervisors meeting and at a dinner prior to the Celebrate Fairfax! weekend."

Celebrate Fairfax! has been Northern Virginia's largest community-wide celebration, with the annual festival hosting tens of thousands of visitors during the three-day run. In 2009, the 25-acre site in the Fairfax County Government Center was filed with more than 400 exhibitors, food vendors, crafters, and interactive activities. Celebrate Fairfax! has showcased live concerts on five stages, an interactive SciTech Center and ExxonMobil Children's Avenue, a petting zoo, karaoke contest, carnival rides, and great festival foods. Nightly fireworks have been a highlight of the festival. A recipient of one of the International Festivals and Events Association's top honors, Celebrate Fairfax was named a Bronze Pinnacle Award winner in 2005 for its long-time quality and success. It was named a 2006 honoree as one of the Top 20 events in the Southeastern United States.

The First Asian American Lord Fairfax in 1993 Vilay Chaleunrath. The Fairfax County Board of Supervisors in 1993 recognized Vilay Chaleunrath as the first Asian American Lord Fairfax (Mason District). A Laotian American, Vilay Chaleunrath was a leader of the Newcomer Community Service Center (NCSC). The center's offices in Washington, DC and Falls Church, Virginia reported serving approximately 4,000 refugees and immigrants from more than 50 countries each year.

According to the NCSC website (www.newcomerservice.org), the Newcomer Community Service Center is a minority-based non-profit organization that helps refugees and immigrants from all countries achieve self-sufficiency and become participating members of American society. Founded as the Indochinese Community Center by Cambodian, Lao and Vietnamese refugees, NCSC has served the metropolitan Washington area community since its inception in 1978.

1997 Lord Fairfax (At Large) Vietnamese American Toa Quang Do. For his numerous contributions to the Fairfax County communities, Toa Do was honored as the first Vietnamese American Lord Fairfax in 1997. He has also been honored for many other contributions. In 2004, he received the inaugural Barbara Varon Volunteer Award from the Fairfax County Board of Supervisors. The award was established to recognize a Fairfax County resident's dedication to improving the community through volunteer service and to honor the memory of Barbara Varon, former chairman of the Fairfax County Electoral Board.

Toa Do was one of the first to assist FCAAHP. He introduced me to many Asian American small business owners when I attended the BDAG conference on August 2, 2007 at Ernst Community Cultural Center of Northern Virginia Community College in Annandale, Virginia. The conference was aimed at helping small and women owned businesses to learn to navigate the State of Virginia's procurement system.

Toa Quang Do, a resident of Fairfax County, Virginia founded Business Development Assistance Group, Inc. (BDAG) which is a not-for-profit, 501(c)(3) organization. Incorporated in the State of Virginia in 1992, the mission of BDAG is to help small and minority-owned businesses become more viable in American economic life through educational programs, workshops and training seminars.

On May 15, 2004, Toa Do testified to the Virginia Asian Advisory Board Public Forum on the challenges facing Asian Pacific Americans (APAs) who wish to start, stay in or expand a business in the Commonwealth of Virginia. He noted that according to the 1997 census, there were more than ten thousand Asian-owned businesses in Fairfax County with total sales of nearly 2 billion dollars. However, APAs face

1997 Lord Fairfax (At Large) Toa Quang Do in 1986 enjoying his first Christmas in Fairfax County, Virginia with his family. (Courtesy of Toa Do)

many challenges, including: "cultural and language barriers, lack of American business techniques and tools, and limited or no access to capital." He recommended that the state of Virginia should create specific business assistance programs to assist APAs; conduct disparity study and collect data on APA owned business in Virginia to determine if they have a level playing field with mainstream businesses in terms of securing state contracts; and increase access to capital for business start up or expansion for APAs through state financing programs through training in business financing and partnership with banks.

2002 Lord Fairfax (Springfield) Kenneth G. Feng.

Kenneth G. Feng

According to the Fairfax County Park Authority website, Kenneth G. Feng served as the Springfield District representative to the Fairfax County Park Authority Board from October 1995 to 2007. He came to the Board with more than 25 years of public service at all levels and branches of government. His experience includes local government, state universities, and the U.S. Congress. His career started with 7 years of service with Los Angeles County – then over 20 years of service with the US General Accounting Office (GAO).

In addition to the Park Authority, Kenneth Feng served Fairfax County as a member of the Civil Service Commission. During his tenure on the Park Authority Board, he served as Board Treasurer and Chairman of the Resource Management Committee – as well chairman of Administration, Management and Budget, and service on Membership, Diversity and Succession and the Elly Doyle Park Service Awards.

2003 Lord Fairfax (Dranesville) Sudhakar Shenoy.

The Fairfax County Economic Development Authority Commission website notes that "Sudhakar Shenoy is founder, chairman and CEO of Information Management Consultants, Inc. (IMC) located in McLean. Founded in 1981, IMC is an internationally recognized systems and software development firm serving both governmental and commercial sectors. In addition to the Fairfax County Economic Development Authority Commission, Sudhakar Shenoy has served on the State of Virginia Technology Commission, the Virginia Innovative Technology Authority, and the Northern Virginia Technology Council.

Sudhakar V. Shenoy

The IMC website provided the following information about Sudhakar Shenoy's biography: In 2003, Sudhakar Shenoy was the recipient of the Lord Fairfax distinction for Fairfax County's Dranesville District for outstanding community involvement and volunteerism. In 2002, Bio-IT World recognized Mr. Shenoy as a Bio-IT Champion for IMC's innovative work in bringing together information technology and the life sciences. In 1999, Mr. Shenoy was recognized as Citizen of the Year in the local area while a year earlier he received the 1988 Greater Washington High Technology Entrepreneur of the Year award, sponsored by Ernst & Young, NASDAQ and the *Washington Post.* Mr. Shenoy was also selected by the US Small Business Administration as the Washington Area Minority and Small Business Person of the Year in 1995. In 1996, Mr. Shenoy was inducted into the University of Connecticut's School of

Business Alumni Hall of Fame and was recognized as a Distinguished Alumnus of the Indian Institute of Technology (IIT) in Bombay, India in 1997.

Sudhakar V. Shenoy was awarded the 2004 Executive of the Year by the Northern Virginia GovCon Council, the Professional Services Council, and Washington Technology. He is a frequent lecturer and radio personality, often discussing impacts and directions of various technology trends – and was singled out by Business Forward as one of the 40 most influential Global Players in the Washington region.

The First Asian American Lady Fairfax in 2004 -- Korean American Heisung Lee. Heisung Lee is a registered dietitian (RD) with the American Dietetic Association and worked as a clinical dietitian at hospitals for 30 years. She received her M.S. in gerontology from George Mason University in 1996 and earned her PhD in Public Health from the University of Maryland at College Park. Heisung Lee wrote the following about her reaction to receiving the award as Lady Fairfax 2004.

Heisung Lee, 2004 Lady Fairfax (At Large)
(Courtesy of Heisung Lee)

"When Chairman of the BOS, Connolly, and now Congressman appointed me as Lady of Fairfax at large, I was not grasping what it meant to me at all because I even did not know of the honor. After I received the honor, I decided to be a liaison person advocating for both parties, Korean American elderly who have difficulty to access the local government services/programs and the Fairfax County that has difficulty to outreach the Korean communities for disseminating information and news. I am doing this job as volunteering for different organizations, providing educations for the Korean Americans, and participating in advocacy events and rallies with seniors and governmental employees.

"I immigrated to the US in 1971 in search of higher education and better opportunity. I first lived in Detroit where I completed an internship in dietetics. It was not easy--I had no family, little money, and limited English. After internship, I moved to Richmond, VA where I held my first job in hospital food services. After my husband and I got married, we moved to northern Virginia in 1980. There were very few Asians that lived in this area at the time. For 16 years, I worked as a clinical dietitian at INOVA Fairfax Hospital and Alexandria Hospital, then I went back to school to earn my masters in gerontology and doctoral degree in public health. We also raised my two wonderful daughters.

"As time passed, northern Virginia changed dramatically. The Asian population boomed, and with it the numbers of Asian seniors increased. There became a great need for senior services that could reach this vulnerable population. I retired from dietetics and began working as the volunteer director of the Korean Senior Center in Vienna. Over the last 10 years, through the hard work of our volunteers and our partnerships with Fairfax County, area hospitals, and community colleges we have been able to achieve a great deal. Ours is the largest senior center by number of participants in Fairfax County.

"Among many of our services, we provide English language and citizenship classes, health education and exercise, and operate Korean Meals and Wheels to frail seniors who miss their native food. We also began a training program to train personal care aides who understand the culture and language of our ethnic seniors. This program is now a model for other communities.

"In 2004, I was very surprised and honored to be named Lady-of-Fairfax at large by Chairman (now Congressman) Gerry Connolly. This award is meaningful in that it represents the hard work of many individuals who strive to keep our communities connected and care for those who cannot care for themselves. I hope to continue advocating for our Asian seniors as long as I can, and would like to work with others to develop new programs and facilities that will promote a better quality of life for our frail ethnic elders. It has been an incredible journey so far and I feel very fortunate for God's many blessings in my life."

Congressional Record

Proceedings and Debates of the 111th Congress, First Session

WASHINGTON, D.C. Monday, June 01, 2009

House of Representatives

Recognizing Lords and Ladies of Fairfax

HON. GERALD E. CONNOLLY
OF VIRGINIA

MR. CONNOLLY: Madam Speaker, it is my great honor to rise today to recognize a dedicated group of men and women in Northern Virginia. For the past twenty five years, each member of the Fairfax County Board of Supervisors has selected two people from their district who have demonstrated an exceptional commitment to our community. Since the program's inception in 1984, over 470 individuals have been recognized as a Lord or Lady Fairfax by their representative on the Board of Supervisors. Individuals recognized as Lords and Ladies of Fairfax have dramatic impacts on their communities in a range of endeavors.

This year, the Fairfax County Board of Supervisors was able to recognize outstanding individuals who have made significant contributions in areas such as the public school system, support for parks, recreation, and youth sports, the advancement of the arts, providing assistance to those serve the county as firefighters, and support for human services. It is nearly impossible to fully describe the diversity of accomplishments by the honorees. The efforts of these individuals contribute greatly to the quality of life for residents of Fairfax County and should be commended.

The following individuals were recognized as Lord and Lady Fairfax Honorees for 2009. Each of these individuals was selected as a result of his or her outstanding volunteer service, heroism, or other special achievements. These individuals have earned our praise and appreciation.

The 2009 Lord and Lady Fairfax Honorees and the nominating Districts are:

Chairman of the Board – At Large: Lady Corazon Sandoval Foley and Lord William "Bill" Hanks
Braddock District: Lady Pamela K. Barrett and Lord Thomas Frenzinger
Dranesville District: Lady Lisa Lombardozzi and Lord Vance Zavela
Hunter Mill District: Lady Joan Dempsey and Lord Howard Springsteen
Lee District: Lady Michele Menapace and Lord Doug Koelemay
Mason District: Lady Suzanne Holland and Lord Kevin Holland
Mt. Vernon District: Lady Christine Morin and Lord Gilbert McCutcheon
Providence District: Lady Lola Quintela and Lord G. Ray Worley
Springfield District: Lady Leslie Carlin and Lord Erik Hawkins
Sully District: Lady Patrica "Trish" Strat and Lord David L. Lacey

Madam Speaker, in closing, I ask my colleagues to join me in expressing gratitude for these men and women who volunteer their time and energy on behalf of our community. The selfless commitment of these individuals provides enumerable benefits to Northern Virginia and serves to strengthen and enrich our communities.

2009 Lady Fairfax (At Large) Corazon Sandoval Foley. The June 1st citation reads:

"Cora Foley was born in the Philippines and made Fairfax County her home 29 years ago. Cora is an accomplished writer and a founding member of the Friends of the Virginia Room Library group. She served as former Chairman Connolly's appointee to the Fairfax County Jamestown 400 Committee and the Fairfax County History Museum Subcommittee. Cora also initiated and co-chaired the Fairfax County Asian American History Project (FCAAHP) to document the history of Asian Americans who have made Fairfax County their home. Cora and FCAAHP volunteers have recorded dozens of oral history interviews, created an FCAAHP website and are working on a book to be published in May of 2010 during Asian/Pacific American Heritage Month. In addition to her work in the historical arena, Cora has also been an advocate for senior citizens. She is pursuing the development of Fairfax County's "Burke/Springfield District Senior Center Without Walls" project to provide wellness programs for seniors." The Burke Connection in June 2009 published an article entitled "Building Bridges Not Walls" about Cora Foley's innovative project for a Burke/Springfield Senior Center Without Walls. (BSSCWoW).

Education: Remarkable Students, Teachers and School Board Leaders

By Corazon Sandoval Foley

The Fairfax County Public School system was created when Virginia adopted a Reconstruction-era state constitution after the Civil War. For the first time in its history Virginia guaranteed free public education in 1870 -- the very same year that the Census recorded the first Asian resident in Fairfax County, a Chinese student named Suvoong.

The role of Asian American students in Fairfax County has certainly changed dramatically since 1870 with that solitary student. In their 1992 book *"Fairfax County: A Contemporary History,"* Nan and Ross Netherton noted that "suddenly in the 1970s and 1980s it became noticeable that the lists of high school valedictorians and honor students regularly contained large numbers of Asian and Hispanic names." The Nethertons would have been impressed as Asian American students continued their remarkable achievements in the Fairfax County school system through the 1990s until 2010. The attached photo shows the Fairfax County Times of June 17, 2009 with pictures of high school graduates, including a Fairfax Asian American valedictorian from West Springfield High School.

Wednesday, June 17, 2009   FAIRFAX COUNTY TIMES

Graduation 2009

(Above) One of the 39 valedictorians from West Springfield High School, Gloria Myong-chi Kim gets a hug after picking up her 2009 high school diploma June 15. (Above, right) Stella Ta Mach gives a thumbs-up to the crowd as the students stand to receive their diplomas at the Fairfax High School's 2009 Commencement Ceremony, also June 15. (Below, right) Graduating senior Sara Johnson performs "America the Beautiful" with the Fairfax High School Band during the school's 2009 commencement ceremony.

Photos by Shamus Ian Fatzinger/Fairfax County Times

Asian Americans have also made major contributions in the leadership of the Fairfax County School Board and as dedicated teachers. The educational arena is one in which Fairfax County Asian Americans have engaged intensely in PTAs and other activities to promote good education and a better future for their children. The Fairfax County School Board was also the earliest venue for civic and political leadership for the Asian American community -- most notably with Korean American Ilryong Moon who from 1995 to 2009 was the first and only elected official in Fairfax County.

Fairfax County School Board: Asian American Pioneer Leaders

The Fairfax County School Board first met on September 6, 1922. Over seventy years later on July 1, 1993, the first Asian American was appointed to the School Board by Fairfax County Board of Supervisors Chairman Tom Davis.

Le Chi Thao was 49 years old when he was appointed to the Fairfax County School Board. He came to the United States in 1973 as a diplomat and stayed after South Vietnam fell to the Communists. He was nominated in 1993 by Fairfax County Board of Supervisors Chairman Thomas M. Davis III as part of his promise to share political power with immigrant groups in a county where demographics have been changing dramatically.

Le Chi Thao, Vietnamese American lawyer with Le Chi Thao and Associates, served on the Fairfax County School Board from June 1, 1993 through June 30, 1995. He received his law degree from George Washington University, attended schools in Vietnam and the Johns Hopkins University School of Advanced International Studies. He served in the Ministry of Foreign Affairs for South Vietnam. He volunteered as the minority achievement representative and was past chairman of the Legislative Liaison Committee for the Mosby Woods Elementary Parent Teacher Association.

Ilryong Moon followed in Le Chi Thao's footsteps by being appointed by then-Braddock District Supervisor Sharon Bulova as School Board Member from Braddock District in 1995. That same year, Fairfax County decided to elect rather than appoint School Board Members. Ilryong Moon won the right to represent Braddock District from 1996 – 1999 in the first elected Fairfax County School Board.

Ilryong Moon (fifth from left) in 1996 with the first elected School Board in Fairfax County

Ilryong Moon was elected again in 2004 as an at-large representative, served as Vice-Chairman in 2005, Chairman in 2006, and won another term in the 2007 election for School Board. In 2009, he won the Democratic primary to become the first Asian American Democratic Party candidate for Braddock District Supervisor. Moon's campaign brought out many Asian voters, particularly Korean Americans, who probably would not have participated in a Democratic party "firehouse" primary normally; nearly four times the anticipated 700 voters participated in the primary. However, Ilryong Moon lost the election to Republican candidate John Cook by a heartbreakingly slim margin of 89 votes -- with Cook garnering 6,292 votes and Moon 6,203 votes. More details about Ilryong Moon could be found in the chapter on Fairfax County Korean American History.

Students: Growing Asian American Presence & Remarkable Contributions

The story of the Asian American student experiences in the Fairfax County school system is not a simple straight road to success. Many have stumbled and failed, some have joined gangs, and Seung-Hui Cho, a graduate of Westfield High School was the shooter of several students and faculty members in the tragic Virginia Tech massacre of April 16, 2007. Those are very serious problems that need to be recognized even as we dedicate this book to honoring those Asian American students whose hard work resulted in positive contributions to the prosperity and robust future of Fairfax County.

The excellent educational system in Fairfax County has been the major pull factor for many county residents, including Asian Americans. Since the early 1990s, the fastest growing segment in the Fairfax Public School system has been its Asian American student population. The Asian American student population in the Fairfax County Public School System has grown from 4.1% from 1979-1980 up to 18.3% in 2008.

SAT I

**Average Scores for Fairfax County Public Schools, Virginia, and the Nation
by Ethnicity
2005-2007**

Ethnic Group	Year	Critical Reading			Math		
		FCPS	VIRGINIA	NATION	FCPS	VIRGINIA	NATION
ASIAN	2005	523	509	511	590	562	580
	2006	529	512	510	593	566	578
	2007	536	518	514	594	566	578
BLACK	2005	459	436	433	464	429	431
	2006	468	438	434	467	429	429
	2007	470	435	433	464	428	429
HISPANIC	2005	497	488	458	505	486	464
	2006	496	489	456	503	488	463
	2007	494	489	458	503	476	463
WHITE	2005	572	538	532	577	532	536
	2006	568	533	527	576	532	536
	2007	565	534	527	570	531	534

Ethnic Group	Year	Writing		
		FCPS	VIRGINIA	NATION
ASIAN	2006	529	510	512
	2007	533	512	513
BLACK	2006	454	429	428
	2007	458	424	425
HISPANIC	2006	485	475	451
	2007	481	475	450
WHITE	2006	555	521	519
	2007	554	520	518

Date	Asian/Pacific Islander		Hispanic No.	%	Black No.	%	White No.	%	Total No.
1979-1980	5,239	4.1%	2,297	1.8%	8,085	6.3%	112,287	87.7%	128,030
1984-1985	9,822	7.9 %	3,890	3.1%	10,385	8.4%	99,913	80.5%	124,184
1989-1990	14,000	11.0%	7,310	5.7%	12,292	9.6%	93,863	73.4%	127,822
1994-1995	18,156	13.1%	12,273	8.8%	15,499	11.1%	92,406	66.4%	139,103
1999-2000	22,720	14.7%	18,202	11.8%	17,188	11.1%	91,570	59.3%	154,368
2008	30,879	18.3%	28,855	17.1%	17,887	10.6%	80,490	47.7%	168,742

Fairfax County Public School System (FCPS)
Ethnic Membership 1979 – 2008

Source: Fairfax County Public Schools Website - Statistics Report

The Asian American performance in the public school system has been remarkable as young students demonstrate achievements in all fields from music to sports and most notably, in academic performance in the math and sciences. The FCPS report of SAT scores show continued improvement as Asian American students work hard and improve the learning environment of their schools.

The academic achievements of Asian American students reflect the strong desire and commitment for their children to have a good education that are often found in many immigrant communities. This situation is particularly true for second-generation Asian Americans already fluent in English and encouraged by immigrant parents who came to the United States in search of a better life, higher education or professional positions.

Many Asian American students in Fairfax County have strong, early academic encouragement from families and communities, particularly in math and science. Many pursue extracurricular academic activities, receive private tutoring, and pay for preparation courses for the entrance exam to the prestigious Thomas Jefferson High School for Science and Technology (TJHSST).

Established in 1985, Thomas Jefferson High School for Science and Technology (TJHSST) is the result of a partnership of businesses and schools created to improve education in science, mathematics, and technology. Representatives from business and industry and staff of the Fairfax County Public Schools worked together in curriculum and facilities development for the school. In recent years, local business leaders and Jefferson parents have formed the Jefferson Partnership Fund to help raise money to maintain and equip labs and classrooms in the school.

TJHSST has ranked among the nation's top public schools with its average combined score in 2007 at

2155, compared with 1639 countrywide. In December 2009, for the third consecutive year, Thomas Jefferson High School for Science and Technology of Fairfax County topped US News & World Report's list of America's Best High Schools – besting more than 21, 000 other public schools in 48 states for the honor. TJHSST has fielded more National Merit Semifinalists than any other high school in America for most of the 1990s and 2000s. In 2007, TJHSST had more Intel Science Talent Search Semifinalists (14) than any other school. In 2009, TJHSST repeated this feat with 15 semifinalists.

TJHSST Admissions Statistics for Class of 2012

	Applicants	Percent	Admitted	Percent
Gender				
Male	1358	52.70%	261	53.81%
Female	1219	47.30%	224	46.19%
Total	2577	100.00%	485	100.00%
Ethnic				
White	1159	44.97%	205	42.27%
African American	139	5.39%	9	1.86%
Hispanic	149	5.78%	10	2.06%
Native American	6	0.23%	3	0.62%
Asian	975	37.83%	219	45.15%
Other*	133	5.16%	35	7.22%
Multiracial	16	0.62%	4	0.82%
Total	2577	100.00%	485	100.00%

In 2008, Asian American students made history when they became the largest group in the freshman class (class of 2012) of the prestigious Thomas Jefferson High School for Science and Technology (TJHSST). More than 2,500 applicants vied for 485 slots in TJHSST -- Asian Americans got 219 or 45% of the total while white students got 205 or 42%. In the preceding school year, Asian Americans accounted for some 38% of the total student population.

The remarkable trend of academic achievement has continued during the FCAAHP research period. In September 2009, for the first time ever, Asian students were awarded more than half of the freshman slots for Thomas Jefferson High School for Science and Technology (TJHSST) -- or 54.2% of the class of 2013.

Making History with the Intel Talent Science Search

On March 11, 2009, Fairfax County Public Schools announced that two TJHSST Students finished in the top ten in Intel Science Talent Search – and they were both Asian Americans. Naren Tallapragada and Alexander Kim placed in the top 10 at fourth and seventh, respectively, marking the first time in competition history that two students from the same school were winners in the same year. An Intel STS spokesperson stated "it's pretty unusual that a school would have more than one finalist."

The fourth place finisher was Narendra Tallapragada of Burke, who received a $25,000 scholarship for his project to find ways to simplify complex models of atomic and molecular interactions. His goal is to one day create minicomputers that could be used, for example, to create automatic insulin pumps that can be placed inside diabetic patients or intelligent clothing that responds to temperature.

Seventh place went to Alexander Kim of Fairfax, who received a $20,000 scholarship for researching the variation and diversification in populations of the giant American river prawn, the largest freshwater invertebrate in North America. His research furthers understanding of how species evolve and has implications for the future of ecosystems.

The 2009 Intel Science Talent Search finalists came from 17 states and represented 35 schools. Of the more than 1,600 high school seniors who entered the 2009 Intel Science Talent Search, 300 were announced as semifinalists in January. Of those, 40 were chosen as finalists.

Both Kim and Tallapragada look forward to continuing their research work. Tallapragada already has his own

Congressman Gerry Connolly congratulates Intel Science Talent Search winners Narendra Tallapragada of Burke and Alexander Kim of Fairfax. Both are seniors at Northern Virginia's Thomas Jefferson High School for Science and Technology, and were chosen as top winners among 1,600 entries in the prestigious national science competition.

bionanotechnology business aspirations while Kim plans to study ecological sciences and organisms. Congressman Gerry Connolly congratulated the pair of Fairfax County Asian American students by saying "This is a remarkable triumph for Narendra and Alexander... These honors are a testament to their hard work and their academic achievement. It also bears testimony to the quality of Thomas Jefferson High School for Science and Technology and the entire Fairfax County Public School system."

Narendra "Naren" Tallapragada, 17 years of age in 2009, of Edgewater in Burke was selected for his project, *"Determining the Dielectric Function for Crystalline Solids from the "Bottom Up," Using Atomic, Ionic and Molecular Properties."* Naren is the son of Ravi and Jyotsna Tallapragada. His mother is a neonatologist and his father is an engineering management consultant. At Thomas Jefferson, Naren is a National Merit Semifinalist, Secretary General of the Model UN Team, member of the AAA Travel High School Challenge and Captain of the Quiz Bowl team, *"It's Academic."* He also ran cross-country for three years and helped tutor minority students in the Diversity Committee Test Prep program. He's a member of the National Honor Society, French Honor Society, and on the Jeopardy Team tournament. He also competed in the National Geographic Bee.

Narendra Tallapragada has credited his parents' willingness to help him pursue his many interests, which include cross-country track, nanotechnology research and Model UN. His parents drove him from a Model UN tournament in Charlottesville, Virginia to his "Jeopardy!" callback in New York the next day. In a 2007 press interview, Narendra's father, Ravi Tallapragada, said that his son chooses his activities, and that it is a pleasure for them to devote whatever time they have to his endeavors. His mother, Jyotsna Tallapragada, said that she is a little disappointed that piano lessons had to go by the wayside to devote more time to high school academics. She added that Naren has agreed to learn an Indian instrument in the future.

Alexander "Alex" Kim, 17 years old in 2009, of Fairfax Ridge was selected for his project, *"Morphological and Molecular Phylogeography of a Giant American River Prawn, Macrobrachium carcinus."* He is the son of Duckju Kim, an artist, and John Kim, a computer networking engineer. For his project, he looked at the variations of the largest freshwater shrimp in the Western hemisphere – the Giant American River Prawn.

For Alex Kim, it all started with a book. He was 13 years old when he picked up Thomas H. Huxley's *"The Crayfish"* and his interest was sparked by a brief line: "No crayfish has yet been discovered in the whole continent of Africa." A few basement experiments, a research expedition in Puerto Rico and almost five years later, Kim's project was chosen for Intel STS finals. Kim's project proposed that genetic and physical differences in a specific series of river shrimp are a result of them living in separate regions.

At Thomas Jefferson, Alexander Kim was co-captain of the Debate Team, on the Ocean Bowl – a quiz bowl for ocean science, and regional winner for two years. He's on the school's Environmental Impact Club, is a regional finalist in the Siemens Science Competition, a semifinalist in the Biology Olympiad, and a fourth-place winner in the 2008 National Vocabulary Championship. For two years, he went to the Intel Science and Engineering Fair, and was the student representative to the Fairfax County Environmental Quality Advisory Council. For college, he hopes to pursue his PhD at Yale in ecological sciences and to study how organisms are distributed in the planet.

Fairfax County Asian American Student Contributions Beyond Math and Science

A review of local press reports underscored for me how much Fairfax County Asian American student performance go way beyond just the math and science arena where they have demonstrated excellent performance. Listed below are a few of the notable accomplishments in art, sports, and charity work by Fairfax County Asian American students.

It is perhaps fitting that an Asian American student Bobby Koo designed the outdoor sculpture for the prestigious magnet school Thomas Jefferson High School for Science and Technology (TJHSST). He was the winner in the 1985 design competition sponsored by the Northern Virginia Building Industries Association. It is titled *"Today is Tomorrow."*

In April of 2009, the Fairfax County Board of Supervisors honored Jamie Chang for her artistic achievement. Her father was Director of Transportation in the Fairfax County Government. She was one of eleven Fairfax County students who were recognized on March 9, 2009 at the state level of the PTA Reflections Contest. The winners included: Pierre Quan for music composition; Kaitlin Phan for Visual Arts; Jamie Chang of Union Mill Elementary School for Visual Arts, intermediate division; Noah Shin for music composition; Ji Whae Choi for Visual Arts.

The March 20-26, 2008 edition of the Burke Connection reported that Jason and Creson Lee, brother and sister, of Burke in Fairfax County, brought home two national art competition titles in GEICO's 21st annual Safety Belt Poster Contest. Jason Lee won in the 6-8 age group and Creson Lee won in the 9-11 age group. Both students won cash awards for earning the grand-prize title in their age group. Their school, Cherry Run Elementary, will receive $1,000 toward the art program. The contest drew more than 2,400 entries from students age 6-18 illustrating the importance of seat belt safety. This was the first time in the contest's history that a family has won two national grand-prize titles in the same year.

Asian American students also have a way with words, winning prestigious debate competitions. On February 12, 2009, the Fairfax County Times featured the Potomac School forensics team that won its second-straight state championship at the University of Virginia in Charlottesville. Included in the team is Madhu Rhamankutty who was also selected by National Geographic's JASON Project as one nine student 2008 National Energy Argonauts. In her application for the JASON Project, she wrote essays on global warming and on her fear of public speaking that she overcame by cultivating her advocacy skills as a member of Potomac School's varsity debate team.

Comedy has its Asian American student participants as well. On March 12, 2009, the Potomac Almanac reported on the Mr. Churchill event that benefits students and Leukemia & Lymphoma. Brian Sun, a junior from Winston Churchill High School, became the first non-senior in the three-year competition to earn the title of Mr. Churchill – and he had his biology homework to thank. Knowing that he needed to come up with a humorous pickup line to wow the crowd at the competition, academia and amorous pursuits converged in his head, and "You're more curved than my biology exam" was born. He said: "It was a nerdy pickup line that I thought the teachers in the crowd might like." Sun's victory was credited to a sense of humor that caught the student body off guard. Winning Mr. Churchill is mostly an achievement of pride and notoriety and Sun said that he would use his new title to represent the school in any capacity needed. And he will bask in the glow of newfound notoriety. The annual event raised roughly $1,000 for future Student Government events an ad additional $100 for the Leukemia and Lymphoma Society.

In a 2008 video report, Ami Patel of Thomas Jefferson High School (TJHSST) focused on the *Bhangra* Bash -- the story of how Indian American students have fun and raise money for a good cause in dance competitions. Teams from five area high schools came together to participate in a *Bhangra* competition. They were able to enjoy an evening of clean fun and raised $3,200 for India Literacy Project. Indian students make up a significant portion of TJHSST population. *Namaste*, the Indian culture club, is one of the school's largest organizations. One of the participants in the *Bhangra* Bash was Vishaka Ravishankar who was Miss American Junior Teen in 2008.

In the sports arena, the TJHSS student sports achievements were reported by Nikki Pangilinan, Filipino American student who was Sports editor for the school newspaper, member of the Gymnastics team, cheerleader for *"It's Academic"* team at TJHHS and a volunteer for St. Bernadette's Catholic Church.

In June 2008, the Burke Connection reported on the remarkable legacy of four-time state championship swimmer Derek Bui. The legacy Derek Bui leaves at Robinson High School is staggering. His senior class won district, regional, and state titles every year, continuing the streak that started when he was in seventh grade. He also holds two state records: the 100-yard breaststroke, which he originally broke during his sophomore year, and the 100-meter breaststroke, which he set last year with a 1:04.03 time. "Where are we going to find the next Derek Bui?" wondered swim coach Gordon, when asked about his star swimmer's impact on the program. "There's nobody else like him." Derek Bui is just as proud, though, of his accomplishments away from the pool. He coaches swimmers of all ages at the International Country Club in Fairfax, something he describes as "giving back to the sport" that has taught him so much. He took six classes in the difficult International Baccalaureate program this year and was a member of the National Honor Society.

In April 2009, the Burke Connection reported that Ian Huang, the Lake Braddock boys' tennis team's No. 1 singles player and, along with partner David Kim, half of its top doubles pairing, is the perfect example of what makes Lake Braddock Bruins tick. Lake Braddock's boys' tennis team has spent a hefty potion of the spring dictating play, with the seven other Patriot District teams chasing after the Bruins.

In April 2009, Burke Connection reported the honorees of the Springfield-Annandale Branch of the American Association of University Women for the 2009 Student Diversity Awards Program. Aleena Inhthaly of Robert E. Lee High School, who is of Laotian descent, was recognized for her work with Invisible Children, among other things. Inthaly co-founded and is the current president of the Invisible Children program, a group that raises awareness of child soldiers and other abused children around the world. At her school, she organized a book drive to donate books to children in Africa, where she offered free Chipotle food as a prize for the homeroom that donated the most books. Modest in her expectations, she assumed she would collect 2,000 books at most. On the final day, she walked into a room in the school to find 4,000 stacked against the wall. Aleena Inthaly said "I didn't have to be perfect academically or be a model, I just wanted to help. When I saw all of those books stacked up, I knew that is what we were here for."

Some Dedicated Asian American Teachers.

Charles dela Cuesta of JHSST. The March 2008 student newspaper of Thomas Jefferson High School for Science and Technology (TJHSST) profiled Filipino American science and technology teacher and robotics lab director Charles dela Cuesta. Some schools – notably science and technology magnets with selective admissions – use big-name contests as goals to guide and motivate students to do independent research projects, which are developed into contest entries. Charles dela Cuesta ran the robot competition in fall 2007 for schools belonging to the National Consortium of Specialized Secondary Schools for Mathematics, Science, and Technology. He said that he uses contests regularly at the school to sharpen students' focus and to gauge the level of their learning. Winning is secondary, says Dela Cuesta, who teaches a 9th grade design and technology course.

Charles dela Cuesta, robotics lab director, said, "We're working on some pretty crazy projects." If you walk into the Automation and Robotics Lab, you might think you are in just another freshmen tech classroom. If you turn off the lights, however, you will see lasers bending around objects, stereoscopic vision systems, and two cars that will drive themselves as they evolve from plans to reality. In 2008, there are only 15 seniors in the robotics lab.

Unlike other senior tech labs, those students are all working on one project – The Grand Challenge. They will be building two autonomous vehicles, cars that will drive themselves. The robotics lab has been collaborating with the Prototyping and Engineering Materials Lab and the Energy Systems Lab; the prototyping lab is constructing the frames of the robots, and the Energy Systems Lab is developing the engines. The robotics lab allows students to apply courses that they've taken at TJHSST to real world challenges. Some students are developing complex algorithms that will be used by the vehicles to find efficient routes, while others are tweaking lasers and cameras that will provide the cars with vision. Robotics lab assembles vehicles and new perspectives on future careers.

Mamiya Sahara Worland at Great Falls Elementary School. In October 25, 2007, the Sun Gazette reported on Mamiya Sahara Worland, a teacher since 1991 at Great Falls Elementary School, who was honored as 2007 Teacher of the Year for grades kindergarten through 12 by the National Council of Japanese Language Teachers. The group based its award on Worland's teaching skills and style, leadership, community contributions and her ability to inspire students. Worland helped establish a 10-year sister-school relationship between Great Falls Elementary and the Kake Educational Institute in Fukuyama, Japan. The relationship has brought students from both schools to each other's country, encouraging the sharing between the cultures and building new friendships around the world. Worland also forged a close relationship with the Japanese government that, during the past three years has let visiting Great Falls Elementary students meet two former prime ministers and given the students private tours of the Japanese Diet and the prime minister's residence.

Thu H. Bui, Teacher and Assistant Principal. Thu H. Bui started life in Fairfax County as JEB Stuart High School ESL teacher from 1976 – 1980 and then rose to be Assistant Principal from 1982 – 1989. In 1992, he became Assistant Principal at George C. Marshall High School from where he retired in 2000. He was a TV host for a talk show named *"The Vietnamese Hour with Dr. Bui"* for Channel 24 Apple for Fairfax County Public Schools (FCPS) for nine years from 1991-2000."

On experience with Fairfax County Public Schools (FCPS): "I helped to fight racism in FCPS. Many times while teaching at Stuart HS, I was called upon to go to other schools, such as Herndon and Falls Church to help with gang wars. Channel 7 did a report about "How JEB Stuart HS Combats Racism." When I first started at Stuart, the Vietnamese students were harassed by other students. I was in the middle of 50 kids fighting in the cafeteria with num-chucks, baseball bats, chains and chairs. I was able to stop the fight."

"I established a club called SAVE (Students Against a Violent Environment) for kids who had been involved in any conflicts. I organized field trips to DC and Philadelphia inner city schools. I taught the kids conflict resolution and how to become mediators. They built a Japanese Garden in the courtyard of the school. I organized Friday afternoon dances, and helped kids to mingle. I also organized international weeks each year. The students were so proud of their performances on stage. They stopped to be just a foreigner. Kids paraded in the hallways in their national costumes and shared their exotic food and talents during the week."

Dr. Bui at dedication of the Vietnamese Catholic Church. (Courtesy of Dr. Bui)

On coming to America: Dr. Bui was Deputy Chief of Staff for Naval Training, Vietnamese Navy Headquarters in Saigon from 1969 – 1973 where he was in charge of training of 27,000 officers and men. In 1974, he received his Masters degree in educational administration and supervision from the American University in Washington, DC. In 1975, a Navy officer who used to be his advisor in Vietnam took his family into his home in Falls Church. Dr. Bui's family learned how to shop and cook from this friend.

After getting his first job in DC, Dr. Bui moved to Fairfax County in 1975 and first settled in the Pimmit Hills neighborhood. As the first Asian family in the area, he had a neighbor who was hostile at first, even using a BB gun to shoot at his bay window. But after several months, the neighbor softened and shared with Dr. Bui's family whatever he picked from his garden. "I guessed he had learned more about our family and changed his mind. Two of my friends later moved into this neighborhood and did not get unwelcome treatment."

On the Asian American community: "We are Asian at home and American outside the home. My children still speak Vietnamese to me. My wife and I speak English with our grandchildren. We maintain our traditions and celebrate Vietnamese New Year and other Vietnamese feasts. I helped to establish the Vietnamese Catholic Community in Northern Virginia in 1976; the Holy Martyrs of

Vietnam Parish in Arlington Diocese in 1979 (First Vietnamese parish in the nation); the Vietnamese Knight of Columbus Council 9655 in 1979 (first in the nation); the Northern Virginia Vietnamese Senior Citizens in 2000; the *Le Thi Thanh* Choir Group in 2001. I established the Vietnamese Language School at Holy Martyrs of Vietnam Church in 2003. We now have 32 teachers and 250 students from grade 1 to 7. I established the ESL classes at Holy Martyrs of Vietnam Church in 2004, we now have two classes: Beginners and Intermediate. I am the principal. The parish has expanded from 25 families in 1976 to over 2,000 families and 9,000 parishioners – and I am helping with the multi-million dollar renovation project which started in the spring of 2009."

And in College, a Filipino American Summa Cum Laude in 2009. As I researched this book, I was presented with a wonderful graduation celebration. Melanie Sandoval, a daughter of my younger brother Rafael, graduated in May 2009 at the top of her class, *Summa Cum Laude* with a 4.0 average from Marymount College with a degree in Psychology. She had been working as a summer intern with the National Institute of Health and two days after graduation, she was hired for a professional civil service job at NIH. Her graduation and that of many other Asian Americans in Fairfax County are good signs for the future of Fairfax County for they bring fresh perspective and good education to the search for solutions to economic recessions and many other social issues. Melanie and her siblings, Mike and Rosemary, are products of St. Michael's elementary school and Bishop Ireton High School in Fairfax County. Her Filipino American family members are active in the Catholic Church community in Fairfax County. Photo shows Melanie with her parents, Vicky and Rafael Sandoval on graduation day in May 2009.

Melinda Sandoval with her proud and happy parents Vicky and Rafael Sandoval at college graduation in 2009 as *summa cum laude* graduate in psychology.

I conclude this section with two wonderful stories of Fairfax County Asian Americans and George Mason University. On November 13, 2009, George Mason University (GMU) officially named its new state-of the-art engineering building the "Long and Kimmy Nguyen Engineering Building," the largest academic building on Mason's Fairfax campus and Mason's first LEED-certified green building. The Nguyens donated $5 million to the university as a result of the success of Pragmatics, an information technology company established in 1985 by Long Nguyen in McLean, Virginia.

And on October 22, 2008, the Outstanding American By Choice Award was presented to Dr. Abul Hussam, Professor and Director of the Center for Clean Water and Sustainable Technologies of George Mason University in Fairfax County, Virginia where he directs a research team to work on sustainable methods for water. Born in Bangladesh, Professor Abul Hussam received his Ph.D. in Chemistry from the University of Pittsburgh. He completed his postdoctoral training from the University of Minnesota and Georgetown University. Professor Hussam joined George Mason University in 1985 where he is a Professor in the Department of Chemistry and Biochemistry.

In 2007, Time Magazine named Dr. Abul Hussam as one of the "Heroes of the Environment." Professor Hussam was awarded the 2007 Grainger Challenge Prize Gold Award from the National Academy of Engineering for his SONO filter, a household water treatment system that removes arsenic from contaminated groundwater. This was the highest prize given to an individual by the National Academy of Engineering that comprises a citation, a gold medal, and one million dollars. Professor Hussam has given away most of his prize money for the cause. As of December 2009, over 100,000 SONO filters have been distributed in Bangladesh, India, and Nepal, which are saving millions of people from drinking arsenic contaminated water and suffering its health effects.

Professor Abul Hussam on October 22, 2008 received the Outstanding American By Choice Award at George Mason University from USCIS Acting Director Jock Scharfen.

Business: Entrepreneurship and Sheer Hard Work
By Corazon Sandoval Foley

The commercial landscape of Fairfax County has been a particularly active arena for Asian American contributions. Fairfax County has more Asian-owned firms than any other locality in the Washington area and Virginia, and more of these businesses than 37 states. Fairfax County in 2007 accounted for about 47% of all the Asian-owned businesses in Virginia, and 35.6% of the Asian-owned businesses in the Washington area.

On May 16, 2006, the US Census Bureau reported that 14,313 Asian-owned businesses operated in Fairfax County in 2002, a 34.7 percent increase since 1997 when the last count was taken. The Fairfax County increase is larger than the 24 percent national increase noted by the Census Bureau. The 2002 Economic Census found that Asian-owned firms in Fairfax County employed 25,075 people in 2002, up 49 percent since 1997; had $2.7 billion in sales and receipts; and had payrolls totaling more than $922 million. Such business growth helps Fairfax County fund public services such as a top-ranked public school system and library, public safety, social services, and park systems.

Researching Fairfax County Asian American Business Entrepreneurs. I interviewed several Asian American business entrepreneurs and managers in Fairfax County and several life stories are provided in this book, including: Robert Nakamoto of BASE, Roger Saplan of Manila Café, and several female Asian American small business owners.

Robert Nakamoto's Biographic Profile. Robert Nakamoto is founder, Chairman and principal owner of Base Technologies, Inc., McLean, VA, an information technology company founded in 1987. Prior to that, he was Director of Corporate System, MCI, Deputy Commissioner for Planning in Texas (Honorary Texas Citizen), and Director for Planning over Medicare and Medicaid Programs in the Federal Government. Previously, he was a manager of Data Processing for the State of California and Sacramento County. He has served on Presidential Task Forces for both parties.

Bob Nakamoto was born in California and graduated from California State University and is a Veteran of the Korean War. At the age of ten, he and his family were interned in a WWII internment camp for Japanese Americans. As head of the Japanese American Veterans' Association, he was a speaker in the July and August 2008 programs by the National Japanese American Memorial Foundation that marked the 20th anniversary of the Civil Liberties Act of 1988. The Act mandated a historic national apology and reparations to Japanese Americans unjustly interned by the US government during World War II.

Robert Nakamoto is a life member of the Japanese American Veterans' Association (JAVA) (and in 2010 has been serving as JAVA President), American Legion, Veterans of Foreign Wars, and Armed Forces Electronic Association. He is also a member of Business Executives for National Security, Intelligent Transportation Society, Health Finance Management, Japanese American Citizen League, British American Business Association and the Chamber of Commerce.

I interviewed Robert Nakamoto in May 2009 at the BASE headquarters in McLean, Virginia. He spoke of the years when he was detained in an internment camp in WWII as teaching him to be more conservative in his political thinking. He shared with FCAAHP the following snippet of his life story.

A _Sansei_ in America by Robert Nakamoto. "My Washington D.C. career started in 1967 when I was recruited by the Federal Government. My broad responsibilities included introducing computer technology to state and local governments. I traveled to 36 states and conducted studies in cities of Boston, New York and Minneapolis.

"After working 5 years in county government in Sacramento, 4 years for the State of California and 4 years for the State of Texas and two assignments with the Federal Government, I joined MCI Communications Corporation. I got interested in business at MCI so I decided to start my own business, Base Technologies, Inc. in 1987.

"When I first came to Washington, I was a member of the JACL (Japanese American Citizen League) Board. I was a member of several local organizations. I got elected as President of the Japanese American Veterans' Association (JAVA) in 2007. I have participated

Robert Nakamoto with Veterans Affairs Secretary Retired U. S. Army General Eric Shinseki at an event of the Japanese American Veterans' Association (JAVA) on January 16, 2010. (Courtesy of JAVA)

in task forces for President Carter's Economic Stimulus Program, President Nixon's Welfare Reform Initiative, President Reagan's Telecommunications Policy on Spectrum Allocation for International Satellites, and President Bush's panel on Medicare. Being from the silent generation of 1950s, I kept a very low profile.

"To improve Japan/Japanese American and/or society, I suggest a more proactive role of Japanese business with Japanese Americans here. Some of that has started to happen with a friendly Ambassador now and before, as well as corporate support of Japanese American activities such as Toyota's support of the Japanese American Museum in Los Angeles. From a business standpoint, we have an alliance with Fujitsu to provide integration services and they funded our staff to travel to Japan from the West Coast. Other countries support their immigrants to this country in a variety of ways and I look forward to seeing Japanese companies continue their efforts to bring US and Japan closer."

Gary Nakamoto at podium in 2006 during a Fairfax Chamber of Commerce event with then-Chairman Gerald Connolly standing second from right.

Gary Nakamoto, Robert Nakamoto's second son, became the 2006-2007 Chairman of the Fairfax County Chamber of Commerce -- the first and only

Asian American Chairman of the Chamber since its 1925 founding. The May 29, 1925 edition of the Fairfax Herald published a report entitled: "The Fairfax County Chamber of Commerce has been launched." It all began when a group of local business leaders gathered at a Fairfax County Courthouse on a Saturday afternoon to create an organization to promote the interests of business in a county that was beginning to outgrow its agrarian roots.

Fairfax County Asian American Business Development Groups. In July 2007, I participated in a very successful seminar for small business development sponsored by the Business Development Assistance Group (BDAG) led by Vietnamese American Toa Quang Do whom we met in the chapter on Lord and Lady Fairfax and who stands second from left in the photograph.

Toa Quang Do, founder of BDAG, and second from left at August 2, 2007 conference. (Courtesy of Cora Foley)

Other Asian American groups have also formed business assistance and networking associations. For example, the Philippine American Chamber of Commerce was founded in 1992 by Rogelio Saplan who was a Filipino American restaurant owner in Fairfax County and whose story is told in the chapter on Food and Festivals.

Note on Fairfax County Female Asian American Small Business Entrepreneurs: During the October 2008 Women's Expo at Springfield's Waterford Hotel, I met Maria Ana R. Cerezo who was manning her exhibit of specialty jewelry from the Philippines for sale by her company "*Paruparu* (Butterfly) Gifts." Shown in photo is another Filipino American entrepreneur Cora Arca who was also at the Women's Expo. A Burke resident, Cora Arca has managed a day care business in her home for many years. Her family has operated a catering business and since 2008, a home-based assisted living for the elderly.

And in November 2008, I spoke at the Fairfax County History Commission conference with Brigitte Le, a Vietnamese American gallery owner. She talked of her family's escape from Vietnam in 1975 to Fairfax County where they worked hard and have managed to build prosperous lives. After working in the computer field, Brigitte Le decided to open a gallery focusing on Vietnamese cultural traditions and artists. Her gallery was featured in a *Washington Post* magazine article in January 2009 with her amusing flying pig figurines that she cleverly used to celebrate the historic election of the first African American President Barack Obama.

Cora Arca at Women's Entrepreneur Expo at Waterford on October 2008 in Springfield. (Photo by Cora Foley)

Political Arena: Partisan and Non-Partisan Political Activists
By Corazon Sandoval Foley

Some Asian American Political Candidates. In 2007 and 2009, several Asian Americans who were Fairfax County residents or former longtime residents were official Democratic or Republican candidates for political office:

- In 2007, Korean American Ilryong Moon won reelection for Fairfax County School Board (but lost the 2009 special election for Braddock District Supervisor), while Filipino American Vellie Dietrich-Hall lost the 2007 election for Mason District Supervisor to Penny Gross.
- In 2009, Korean American Mark Keam and Chinese American Sasha Wong ran for Delegate seats in Fairfax County, while former longtime Fairfax County resident Filipino American Jeanette Rishell ran for the third time (2006, 2007 and 2009) for Delegate in Prince William County.

In November 2009, Mark Keam made history by winning election as the first Fairfax County Asian American Delegate (D-35) in the Virginia House of Delegates – along with Ron Villanueva, Filipino American Delegate from Virginia Beach.

The stories of Ilryong Moon and Jeanette Rishell are included in other sections in this book. In this section, we will discuss the biographic profile of Vellie Dietrich Hall and Mark Keam who have provided some information to FCAAHP.

Vellie Dietrich Hall invited FCAAHP to participate in the Census 2010 programs. She has committed herself to getting accurate count of minorities, particularly Filipino Americans in Fairfax County.

Vellie Dietrich Hall in 1990 with daughter and mother visiting from the Philippines. (Courtesy of Vellie Dietrich Hall)

In 2007, Vellie Dietrich-Hall became the first Filipino American to be the official candidate of the Republican Party for Supervisor in the Mason District. She ran against incumbent Penny Gross, raised a large amount of campaign funds but in the end did not succeed in her political quest in 2007. She remains very active in the Republican Party and is expected to run again as a candidate in Fairfax County.

Tony Yeh, a Chinese American Fairfax County resident and active in developing the Chinese American Republican group, participated in the 2008 FCAAHP oral history interview training with Mary Lipsey and Dzung Nguyen in photo.

Tony Yeh, a leader of Virginia Chinese American Republicans participated in the 2008 FCAAHP interview training. (Photo by Cora Foley)

Korean American Mark Keam in 2009 was elected as the first Fairfax County Asian American member of the Virginia House of Delegates. He was born in Korea and moved with his family to Vietnam where his father, a Presbyterian Minister, established a church. In 1975 the family moved to Australia and then to the US. He moved to Virginia in 1998 while serving as a political appointee for the Federal Communications Commission. In 2001 he joined the staff of US Senator Dick Durbin on the Senate Judiciary Committee. In 2007 he joined Verizon as a legal counsel. In 2009, he has been married to Alex Seong Keam for over ten years. They have two children, Tyler Jefferson (7) and Brenna Nicole (5) who were born at Inova Fairfax Hospital.

Mark Keam and his two children in 2008

Asian American Political Activists.

Some Fairfax County Asian American political activists supported FCAAHP work. Tania Hossain, shown in photo beside Congressman Gerry Connolly, is a Bangladeshi American resident of Fairfax County who has been a longtime political campaign activist. In 2009 Tania Hossain joined Congressman Connolly's Fairfax County office staff and has worked on resolving issues involving local constituents in the 11th Congressional District.

Rose Chu, shown in photo with Dranesville Supervisor John Foust at the 2008 Reston Asian Festival, has been a recognized leader in the Fairfax County Democratic party, organizing the Asian American Democrats in Northern Virginia.

Rose Chu (Photo by Terry Sam)

Joe Montano (shown sitting front center in photo) is a Filipino American political activist who has worked for the National Democratic Committee, for President Obama's campaign, & many other Democratic candidates in Northern Virginia.

Political Arena: Non-Partisan Political Activists
By Corazon Sandoval Foley

This section describes two Fairfax County civic groups that supported FCAAHP: The Vietnamese American Voters' Association and the League of Women Voters in the Fairfax Area (LWVFx). The LWVFx story is told by Tin Yin Tai, Chinese American.

The Vietnamese American Voters Association. The Vietnamese American Voters Association (VAVA), a non-profit tax-exempt organization, was established in 1999. Its mission has been to educate Vietnamese Americans in the areas of education, health care, and civic responsibilities and to support their efforts to participate fully in mainstream American democratic society.

Besides its primary goal of registering Vietnamese Americans to vote, VAVA has partnered with the League of Women Voters, youth associations, and various ethnic organizations, including Asian Pacific American, Hispanic, and Middle Eastern groups, to hold six annual Candidates' Forums. The purpose is to inform constituents of the candidates' political platforms and to help them make educated choices among the candidates. VAVA was also one of 12 community-based organizations that sponsored a Rock and Vote Concert in 2002.

In 2000, VAVA registered over 2,000 citizens to vote and in 2004, nearly 4,000, prompting the Washingtonian Magazine to name its President & CEO, Jackie Bong-Wright, a 2003 Washingtonian of the Year. In 2005 and 2006, the Virginia General Assembly passed a House Joint Resolution commending Jackie Bong-Wright for her "outstanding services on behalf of the nation's immigrants and refugees." Jackie's life story is included in the section on Vietnamese Americans in this book.

The work of VAVA was made possible by hundreds of volunteers donating thousands of hours registering and training voters. VAVA's staff also volunteered and cooperated with various community-based organizations to provide citizenship classes that prepared legal residents to take their exams – 80% of the students passed the citizenship tests.

Tin Yin Tai on The League of Women Voters. Tin Yin Tai, a Fairfax County Chinese American, has been very active with the League of Women Voters in Fairfax County and shared his perspective on the importance of civic participation.

"I did not originally intend to become a member of The League of Women Voters of the Fairfax Area. I decided to learn more of the League because I had felt that the individual had become more of an afterthought in the 1990s American political system. Individual voices and ideas had become background music, a massed choir to support the main political performers on the American and World stage. To me, everything centered on polls and the big picture as far as the political agenda schedulers were concerned.

"I remembered the League per my childhood and student memories, nice ladies that held debates and wanted citizens to exercise our voting rights and privileges. Joining the League made me see that this organization reflects the diversity of opinions and beliefs of the American people of which we are a part. Being a nonpartisan organization is an important part of staying objective enough to be of value to the public, as well as making it more likely to speak and print the truth.

"Education comes slowly, methodically and many times dearly for me. My experience with the League has made it clear to me that education is a fundamental key to being a productive, supportive and free citizen. Discerning relevant information in order to learn truth and make decisions for my continued progress as an individual citizen is what ultimately the League has taught me. Progress lies in making decisions that provide for some measure of self-determination. In American politics and society in general, I am both a spectator and participant, so I must be aware of what matters to me and be ready to act when I should. The League of Women Voters of the Fairfax Area has helped me to clarify and be more certain that being a citizen of this nation involves willingness to always learn and be a part of the community I live in."

Tin Yin Tai's Life Notes: "My grandfather (father's side) arrived in the United States of America on March 8, 1946 from Singapore (he had served with the United Kingdom during World War II) and settled first in New York City, then Washington DC. My grandmother arrived sometime in the 1950s (as best as I can recall). My father arrived in 1962 and my mother and I arrived in 1966 from Hong Kong. I was born in Hong Kong in 1963. Except for me, both families of my mother and my father can trace their lineage to Shanghai, China up through my great, great grandparents. Father's side as farmers, mother's side as educated professionals.

"Between myself and my parents, there is a culture gap. First in Hong Kong then here, I was always under the influence of Western Culture, especially with the English language as the primary language. In Hong Kong, my mother had to bring me up herself, but a lot of her friends that helped spoke English frequently or even were British. Any Chinese customs mean more to my parents than to me. I do regret that my parents would not make me learn Chinese, but they felt it wouldn't be of much use in the USA.

"My parents say I am too Western, especially too American. What The Declaration of Independence states as the inalienable rights of life, liberty and the

Tin Yin Tai during FCAAHP 2008 interview.
(Photo by Cora Foley)

pursuit of happiness, I take as the most basic premise of this nation's credo. A lot of my civic activities involve some aspect of these three declarations, one a time or in any combination. Therefore church (freedom of religion), helping nonprofit arts organizations (freedom of expression), shelters and food banks (life), League of Women Voters (liberty). I generally work through three organizations for my civic/charity devotions: The Church of Jesus Christ of Latter-day Saints, The League of Women Voters of the Fairfax Area and the public affairs/community outreach arms of Exxon Mobil Corporation." ##

Public Safety: Courageous Firefighters and Police Officers.

By Corazon Sandoval Foley

Fairfax County Firefighters. The photos of the 109th and 110th Recruits of the Fairfax Fire Departments show the changing face of the Fairfax County Fire Department.

In 2004, the Fairfax County Fire Department 109th Recruit School included two Filipino Americans: Patrick S. DeVera of Station 14, B-Shift and Isagani M. Matias II of Station 31, B-Shift.

The Fairfax County Fire Department 100th Recruit School 2004 included two Korean Americans: Hyun J. Lee, of Station 1, A-Shift and the first female Asian American Fairfax County firefighter; and Tae K. Pak of Station 35, B-Shift.

Filipino American Sam De Vera in 2009 was the highest-ranking Asian American Fairfax County Firefighter – and a founding member of the Asian American Firefighters Association in Fairfax County. He, along with his brother Patrick DeVera, a firefighter in Burke, Isagani Matias, and Mark Baban participated in FCAAHP interviews.

All four Filipino American firefighters were born in the Philippines and came to the US with their families. They recounted memorable service that they performed for Fairfax County, including participation in emergency firefighter responses to the tragic Pentagon bombing on September 11, 2001.

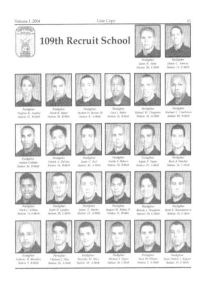

Sam De Vera with Sharon Bulova in 2008.
(Photo by Cora Foley)

Patrick De Vera discussed how participating in the Public Safety Honor Guard has been very moving for him, reminding him of the solemn duty that he and other firefighters have dedicated themselves.

The varied talents of Fairfax County firefighters were also discussed at the interview. The Filipino Americans found that the best way to encourage friendships and teamwork has been to share Filipino cuisine with their fellow firefighters. Mark Baban and Patrick De Vera laughingly described how sharing *pancit* (Philippine noodles) and *adobo* (a Philippine stew) have facilitated improved relationships with their colleagues, particularly during their early days as recruits.

Mark Baban submitted the photo gallery below with him and other Asian American firefighters – as well as a photo of him playing the bagpipe for he participates in national bagpipe competitions, demonstrating the versatility of Fairfax public safety officers.

Hyun Lee driving the Fairfax County Fire Station antique fire truck (Courtesy of Hyun Lee)

In August 2008, Hyun Lee, the first female Asian American firefighter in the Fairfax County Fire Department joined Police Lieutenant Gun Lee in an FCAAHP-sponsored mentoring session with Korean American high school students. The goal was to encourage more Asian American young students to consider careers as public safety officers for Fairfax County.

Fairfax County Asian American Police Officers.   In 2004, a group of officers formed the Washington area Asian Law Enforcement Society. On June 14, 2008, the group of Asian American police officers sponsored the first outreach to the Fairfax County Asian American community in an attempt to build important bridges with Asian communities across the region.   The first-ever Asian Forum and community engagement covered a series of safety and crime issues -- including gang prevention and internet crime -- as well as a facilitated feedback dialogue with community members and police. Members from local, state and federal agencies were present to discuss potential careers in law enforcement with attendees and their families.   The forum was held at the Fairfax County Criminal Justice Academy in Chantilly, Virginia.

Fairfax County Asian American officers have helped improve effective policing for the county by communicating with Asian residents, not just linguistically but culturally.   Fairfax County Lt. Gun M. Lee recounted how in the mid-1990s, he was summoned to a fender-bender. One of the drivers, an elderly Korean grandmother, was practically hysterical because she spoke limited English, could not give her side of the story, and was fearful of the police. His presence calmed her down. Because of such situations, Northern Virginia police recruiters believe that their cities and counties with growing Asian American populations would be better served by more Asian American officers.

Fairfax Asian American Law Enforcement Officers at June 2008 Forum. (Photo by Terry Sam)

Fairfax County, with 40 Asian American officers, has one of the biggest such contingents of area departments. However, those officers are only about 3 percent of the county's force of 1,400 county police officers while over 16 percent of Fairfax County residents are of Asian background.

Gun Lee said that Fairfax County has the largest Korean community in the Washington area. Some Korean immigrants are hesitant to report crimes or work in law enforcement because of lingering distrust of the police in their native land. In addition, some Asians encounter cultural pressure to hide problems among themselves and to keep everything within the family. The Fairfax County Asian American police officers have been working to ensure that the system could work for the Asian American community and that the community could contribute to the public safety requirements of the county.

Lt. Gun M. Lee of Fairfax County Police Department. As Assistant Commander of the Major Crimes Division of the Criminal Investigations Bureau, Gun Lee in 2009 was serving as the highest-ranking Asian American in the Fairfax County Police Department. The middle-level management job entails major responsibilities, including supervising the work of 100 detectives and support staff, preparing the budget, including identifying resources/funding to conduct investigations, and at times working with the Human Resources department on outreach programs.

Gun Lee is the founder and President in 2008 of the Washington-area Asian Law Enforcement Society (ALES). The society is composed of local, state and federal law enforcement groups; in 2008, it had 35 members. ALES aims to increase representation of Asian American officers who come from varied backgrounds.

On August 2008, Gun Lee led a mentoring discussion with Korean American high school students organized by FCAAHP leader Soo Yee. An accounting major in college, Gun Lee told the students that he got bored doing cash flow spreadsheet calculations and saw a recruitment ad for the police department. His father was not happy with his shift in careers for he did not trust the police in Korea and did not trust them in Fairfax County either – plus he did not think Gun Lee will make a lot of money in this career.

Gun Lee advised the students to choose careers in which they could make a difference in society –not to think simply of making money. He noted the increasing numbers of Asian Americans in Fairfax County and the growing need to have more Asian police officers to assist Asian residents who may have language problems and thus ensure improved public safety for the county. He shared stories of how he was able to help elderly Korean grandmothers who get into automobile accidents and could not communicate in English in their excitement. And how he was able to explain complicated cultural cues in the Asian community to his American-born colleagues in the Fairfax County Police Department.

He described to the high school students how he began as a police officer by doing patrol duty in Annandale, Virginia for five years – and shared stories of learning from his mistakes as a young rookie. Gun Lee was promoted to sergeant in 1988 and was assigned in Reston. Later, he became second lieutenant assigned in West Springfield. He worked in the fingerprint section for over two years, went back to Reston and three years later, in 2006, he was promoted to first lieutenant.

Detective Lam Nguyen of Fairfax County Police Department. Detective Lam Nguyen in 1991 became the first Vietnamese-speaking police officer in the Fairfax County police department. He applied to the Fairfax County Deputy Sheriff's office and got hired in 1989. While he was going through training at the academy, he was recruited by the Fairfax County Police Department in 1991.

On Asian police: "There was a time around the early 90s when Asian gangs, especially Vietnamese gangs, were rampant in Fairfax County and I worked with the community to educate them about the problem to help bring down gang activity. I think it helps to have Asian police officers in the force, because when citizens are in trouble and they don't speak English well, they can at least feel relieved to see a face that they feel they can relate to their cultural needs. Even though I don't speak other Asian languages, I can at least try to help the person by contacting someone who does speak his or her language."

On the Asian American community: "The Asian American community has not really been supportive of me in my life in Fairfax County, primarily because of the cultural traditions of distrust of the government, and in particular, the police. While my passion is to help members of the community live a better life, I don't think that the Asian community really respected law enforcement officers. However, I understand and respect their perspective; that's why I've tried to help Asian families understand how law in America works. It's been tough being the minority in the force and not getting the support I need from my community members. On the other hand, it's also been hard over the years to get more colleagues to understand Asian cultures, but I see that changing as the Asian population grows...what 16% now in Fairfax County? That's more than the Hispanic population."

On escaping Vietnam: "On April 29, 1975, my dad came home and took us kids down to the pier where my mom was waiting. There were seven of us so my dad put five of us on a scooter with him and my two older sisters took their bikes and followed behind. We lived in a military base at the time because my dad was in the South Vietnamese military, working in the motor pool as a mechanic. We met our mom at the pier. One by one, my dad threw us up on the boat to my mom. They didn't tell us anything; we didn't know where we were going. We just knew we were going somewhere far. I was 11 years old at that time. We were picked up by a battleship that took us to the Philippines where we stayed at a refugee camp."

On coming to America and Fairfax County: "It was about a six-month trip from Vietnam to Annapolis, Maryland where we lived from 1975 – 1980. My family moved to Fairfax County when I was sixteen years old. We moved to Falls Church because my parents wanted to be closer to the growing Vietnamese community and wanted me to attend a good school. The Vietnamese businesses started to build into a community. There was not an Eden Center when I moved here. Nha Trang on Route 50 (by Loehman's Plaza) was developing, but there was a lot more Vietnamese business firms in Clarendon (Arlington)." ##

Health Care Workers: Healing Support and Compassion
By Corazon Sandoval Foley

The health care arena is one in which Fairfax County Asian Americans have made many contributions, from doctors to nurses and numerous other health care workers. Stories of Asian American medical doctors are spread out in several chapters of this book starting with the story of Dr. V.P. Suvoong, the first Asian resident of Fairfax County. In this section, we feature two FCAAHP team leaders – Masako Huibregtse and Soo Yee – along with ExpressCare, Eppie dela Cuesta and Sue Lee.

The Japanese American Care Fund and Notes from Masako and Liz Huibregtse. The Japanese Americans' Care Fund (JACF) was founded in October 1999 and approved as a 501(c)(3) non-profit organization in the year 2000, according to Yoshie Rozali and Masako Huibregtse. Their office is located in Annandale, Virginia. The history of JACF goes back to the time when founding members were helping a Japanese woman who was suffering from terminal cancer. When she passed away, she left the group with a gift of appreciation. It was this gift that

JACF Flower Arrangement Class. (Courtesy of JACF)

inspired them to set up the JACF. They realized that there was a great need to create an organization that provides support and services for such individuals in our community.

JACF services have included: telephone help line; referral to doctors, nurses, lawyers, counselors, and other professionals; information on legal/financial matters; transportation; language assistance; visitations; home meal services; annual senior luncheons; educational programs including computers, calligraphy, crafts; exercise classes; fundraising with annual bazaar and concerts. The services and programs are conducted primarily in Japanese.

Masako Huibregtse's Japanese American Journey. Masako Huibregtse works with the Japanese Americans' Care Fund and has served as the Japanese American Team Leader for the Fairfax County Asian American History Project.

She came to the US on August 17, 1968 because she had a scholarship to study cytology at the University of Wisconsin; she was sponsored by Helen Huibregtse, the mother of John

Masako arrived on August 17, 1968. (Courtesy of M. Huibregtse)

Huibregtse who became her husband.

Masako and her family have lived in Fairfax County since 1971. Her work involves screening cell samples, such as Pap smear, for any cellular changes and organisms. Masako got involved with JACF because a friend told her about it.

Notes from Liz Huibregtse. Masako's daughter Liz Huibregtse also responded to the FCAAHP oral history interview questions and she focused on intergenerational issues.

Liz Huibregtse is in the middle of photo beside Masako. (Courtesy of M. Huibregtse)

Liz Huibregtse stated that not only is there a generation gap but also a cultural difference because her mother grew up in Japanese culture and she grew up in American culture with Japanese influence. Her father's ancestors came from Holland.

She enjoyed the Fairfax County public schools, the diversity of people and of activities in which one can participate. She noted that it is a great place to get a good job. There were times when she felt different from her peers but for the most part, Fairfax County is a very diverse area and most people enjoy and embrace the university.

She noted that at one point in time, as a teenage thing to do, she did not embrace her Japanese heritage. But as she grew older, she grew closer and closer to her Japanese heritage and took Japanese classes in George Mason University (GMU), as well as Japanese cooking class with the Japanese American Citizens League. In an interesting aside, she noted that at GMU, she was a member of the Filipino Cultural Association (even though she is not Filipino).

Liz Huibregtse's thesis project for her Masters degree is increasing Long Term Care Services of Ethnic Older Adults and she hopes to form a coalition in Fairfax County to continue working on these issues. She said that she likes to help older people – that she thinks she learned this from her mother, as well as the importance of education. She noted that she did not think she was largely influenced to choose her career of social work but that it was something she chose on her own.

Masako with Sharon Bulova in 2008. (Photo by Cora Foley)

Her advice to elders (including her mom) is to keep an active mind, body, and spirit in order to stay healthy. "Share your experiences and wisdom with others. You can always contribute and participate no matter what stage you are in life." ##

<u>Soo Yee, Fairfax County Outreach Official on Pandemic Flu.</u> The FCAAHP Korean American team leader, Soo Yee, has been at the forefront of one of the most dangerous epidemics that Fairfax County and the world have faced in 2009 and 2010 – avian flu. Soo Yee has managed table exhibits at numerous public meetings in order to provide information to Fairfax County residents about ways of avoiding avian flu. I took the two photos showing Soo Yee with her husband, Jung, and Soo Yee at her table exhibit on health issues at the 2008 Lunar New Year in Fair Oaks Mall.

The photo (courtesy of Naila Alam) shows Herndon-based Express Care officials Naila Alam and Yasmeen Durrani receiving the White House Honor of Hope Award through the White House Faith-Based and Community Initiative on June 26, 2008. Express Care was founded in 2003 as a humanitarian organization and support network.

Chinese American Sue Li Lee showed pioneering leadership in working for a Bone Marrow Bank for Asian Americans suffering from cancer. She was a longtime Fairfax County resident and is shown in the photo at the State Department library that she served for 27 years. Her death in 2007 from cancer was mourned by many of us who admired her kindness. I was fortunate in working with Sue Li Lee in developing the State Department's Asian Pacific American Federal Foreign Affairs Council (APAFFAC) and the interagency Federal Asian Pacific American Council.

Sue Li Lee

Senior Centers: Aging Gracefully Among Friends
By Corazon Sandoval Foley

The Fairfax County Office of Senior Services has worked closely with many Asian American senior centers in developing wellness programs for their members. In the photo is FCAAHP member, Chinese American Phyllis Lau of Fairfax County, who has devoted many hours as a Fairfax County employee to help seniors.

FCAAHP work with senior centers has expanded beyond oral history interviews of members to joint development of a grant proposal for citizenship education that we submitted to the US Citizenship and Immigration Services. We proposed citizenship education for senior Asian

Phyllis Lau and Cheryl Laferty work to help seniors. (Photo by Cora Foley)

American citizens and legal permanent residents. The partner organizations for grant submission with FCAAHP were the Chinese American Silver Light Seniors Association (SLSA), the Korean American Central Senior Center, and the Vietnamese American Voters' Association.

The Chinese American Silver Light Seniors Association. The Silver Light Seniors Association was established in October 2004 in Northern Virginia. It is a non-profit, non-political and non-religious organization with more than 800 members, senior Chinese Americans and senior Chinese in America. In 2008 the Fairfax County Office of Senior Services recognized the outstanding work of SLSA in promoting the welfare of senior citizens, particularly Chinese Americans – it highly commended the volunteer spirit of SLSA members. Ms. Linying Gong in 2008 was the President of the Silver Light Senior Association; she has been SLSA President since 2004.

The rich and colorful activities sponsored by the Silver Light Seniors Association have greatly

2008 Fairfax Recognition of SLSA. (Courtesy of SLSA)

improved the quality of life of Chinese seniors in Fairfax County, turning their dull and lonely life abroad into a rich and colorful life with many companions. SLSA has enabled senior members to take part in social activities and get acquainted with new friends. Its website is www.silver-light.org.

The association mainly carries out its activities in the Herndon Senior Center, several branches of the Hope Chinese School and other places. The seniors can join activities near their homes.

The SLSA activities include:
1. Learning: Oral English and dialogue with basic and advanced two courses, according to the seniors' own respective English speaking ability. Learning how to use a computer, practicing calligraphy, drawing, violin and others;

2. Information exchange: Information about the seniors' welfare and medical care and news of the community, the country and the world.

SLSA co-founder Lingying Gong (2nd from left) during the 10/24/2009 5th anniversary.

3. Recreation and body building exercise: Song or opera singing, chess and cards playing, dancing, traveling, Tai chi (including Tai chi boxing and Tai chi playing with a sword or a folding fan), body building exercises, and others.

SLSA has also sponsored numerous celebrations of Chinese traditional festivals, such as Spring Festival, and *Chongyang* Festival (the seniors' day). It has taken part in performances at multicultural festivals to share Chinese culture with all neighbors in Fairfax County.

The Silver Light Seniors Association has actively served the local community. It has often helped the Herndon Senior Center to sponsor various activities such as ping-pong games, art and talent exhibitions. SLSA participated in the Northern Virginia Senior Olympics and won 4 gold medals, 3 silver medals, and 2 bronze medals in the 2007 table tennis tournaments.

Dr. Nathan Yining Wang discussing Medicare with President George W. Bush. (Courtesy of SLSA)

SLSA has assisted the US Department of Health and Human Services in explaining the new Medicare policy in many forums in Fairfax County. On April 12, 2006, SLSA participated in a conversation with Asian Americans on Medicare Prescription Drug Program that was attended by President Bush and Secretary of Labor Elaine Chao. Dr. Nathan Yining Wang, the SLSA Executive Director, led that discussion. Dr. Wang has also been active in the Fairfax County Asian American History Project.

Dr. Nathan Yining Wang, the Executive Director of SLSA, was a professor and a cardiac surgeon in China before he immigrated to the US in 1988. His career included service as Director of Experimental Surgery in the Department of Surgery of the Georgetown University Medical Center from 1989 to 1999; Director of Surgical Research Laboratories in the Department of Surgery in the University of Rochester, NY from 1999 to 2004. After he retired in 2005, he was elected as Executive Director of SLSA in 2006.

Below are photos of the 2008 FCAAHP interviews with SLSA members (Francis and Theresa Cheng in top left photo; with Shaw and Lily Zee in top right photo), plus a set of family photos from the co-founders of SLSA, Zhongying Chen and Xianyi Sun.

Korean Central Senior Center Experience: In 2009, the Korean Central Senior Center became the lead organization in the Fairfax County Asian American Citizenship Education (FAACE) that FCAAHP helped to organize in order to apply for the FY 2009 Citizenship Grant Program by the US Citizenship and Immigration Services.

The Korean Central Senior Center was created to support Korean Americans and immigrants who are 55 years old and over. Programs are provided by the Korean Central Senior Center to assist Fairfax County in developing well-informed citizens and lessening the need for translation/ language services for Korean immigrants and Korean Americans.

Korean Americans face multiple barriers in their life in the US, including language difficulties, cultural differences, inadequate transportation, low level of education, and low socioeconomic status. According to a recent Fairfax County Senior Trends Report, the Korean senior

Korean Central Senior Center Choir in 2008. (Photo by Cora Foley)

population is the second highest of all ethnic groups after the Hispanic senior population – its number is estimated at over 5,400 from the 2000 census in Fairfax County.

The Korean Central Senior Center began operations in 1994 and some 15 years later, it had about 1,000 registered members in 2009. The center was born out of a ministry for the elderly by the Korean Central Presbyterian Church (KCPC). Since 2001 it has been separate as a non-profit organization to deliver culturally and linguistically appropriate senior services at very low cost to the Korean elderly in the Northern Virginia area.

Heisung Lee, Director of the Korean Central Senior Center, has been honored with numerous awards for her distinguished service to the community. In 2004, Heisung Lee received the Lady

Heisung Lee at InterFaith Summit 2008. (Photo by Cora Foley)

Fairfax Award from the Fairfax County Board of Supervisors for her outstanding contributions to Fairfax County. In 2008, Heisung Lee received the Virginia Commonwealth Council on Aging Best Practices Award. Heisung Lee has also won and successfully implemented grant programs from federal and county sources, including the $103,655 award in 2007 for expanding the Personal Care Aide program.

__How have Asian Americans shared their Heritage with County Neighbors?__

Asian Pacific American Heritage Month in Fairfax County
By Corazon Sandoval Foley

Since 1994 Fairfax County has officially joined the national celebration of the month of May as Asian Pacific American Heritage Month. The creation of the Fairfax County Asian American History Project (FCAAHP) in 2008 has boosted the sharing of Asian American heritage and contributions during the annual May proclamations by the county.

The official proclamation of May 2008 as Asian Pacific American Heritage Month by the Fairfax County Board of Supervisors included the following key rationale for the month's celebrations: "Whereas a project began in January 2008 to focus on the experiences of Asian/Pacific Americans in Fairfax County will capture oral history interviews and develop community projects that may include articles, a video, a website and publication of a book."

For the May 2008 proclamation, Filipino American Arnedo Valera, Executive Director of the nonprofit Migrant Heritage Commission made the official response on behalf of the Asian American community to the Fairfax County Board of Supervisors then chaired by Gerald Connolly who in 2008 won election as Congressman from Virginia's 11th District.

The Fairfax County Asian American History Project (FCAAHP) oral history interviews became the focal point for discussion by the Asian American representatives during the official proclamation of May 2009 as Asian Pacific American Heritage Month. Vietnamese American Amy Trang, a member of the history project and a Fairfax County employee, made the official response to the Fairfax County Board of Supervisors on behalf of the Asian American community.

Mount Vernon Supervisor Hyland expressed his pleasant surprise at the group members' willingness to come forward and share the stories of how they came to Fairfax County and the contributions that the Asian American communities have made to the county.

May 2009 - First-ever Naturalization Ceremony in Fairfax Government Center. In its programs to commemorate Asian Pacific American Heritage Month, the Fairfax County Asian American History Project (FCAAHP) began making history. It initiated the first-ever naturalization ceremony in the Fairfax County Government Center for 75 new Americans of all races and ethnicities on May 29, 2009.

The program was co-sponsored by the Fairfax County Asian American History Project (FCAAHP), the Fairfax County Government, the United States Citizenship and Immigration Services (USCIS), with Cox Communications as the sole corporate sponsor of the event. The Daughters of the American Revolution supported the event and provided American flags as mementos for the new Americans.

USCIS Asian American officers headed by Ted Kim, Korean American Field Manager, led the management of the naturalization ceremony. The program was so moving and so successful that Chairman Sharon Bulova of the Fairfax County Board of Supervisors stated that the 2009 naturalization ceremony would be the first of many more naturalization ceremonies to be held yearly in Fairfax County to honor Asian Pacific American Heritage Month.

Congressman Gerald Connolly led pledge of allegiance at FCAAHP-initiated naturalization ceremony on May 29, 2009 at Fairfax County Government Center. (Courtesy of Congressman Connolly's office)

On June 22, 2009, the Fairfax County Asian American History Project Task Force was recognized by the Fairfax County Board of Supervisors for its work in the first-ever naturalization ceremony that also resulted in the registration of 200 new American voters.

In addition, the Fairfax County Board of Supervisors honored the outstanding contributions of FCAAHP official photographer, Terry Sam who made the following official response:

"I was born in Detroit, Michigan, so I gained American citizenship as a birthright. My father immigrated to the United States in 1921 and was barred from citizenship by the 1882 Chinese Exclusion Act. He was not eligible for citizenship until the Act was repealed in 1943. On May 29, I was reminded of him.

COUNTY OF FAIRFAX, VIRGINIA

Resolution

WHEREAS, the Asian American History Project Task Force suggested that U.S. Citizenship and Immigration Services hold a naturalization ceremony in the Fairfax County Government Center where the Oath of Allegiance would be conferred upon those who have fulfilled all requirements for citizenship; and

WHEREAS, the Asian American History Project Task Force organized numerous people, organizations, businesses and government agencies to have the first ever naturalization ceremony on May 29, 2009, in the Fairfax County Government Center; and

WHEREAS, 75 people took the Oath of Allegiance to become a citizen of the United States and more than 200 new voters were registered by the Office of Elections at the Government Center on that day; and

WHEREAS, this event was a noteworthy success made possible through the initiative, dedication and excellent work of all who were involved; NOW THEREFORE

BE IT RESOLVED, that the Fairfax County Board of Supervisors, on behalf of all residents of Fairfax County, does congratulate and thank the Asian American History Project Task Force for its initiative in suggesting and organizing this event.

Sharon Bulova, Chairman
Fairfax County Board of Supervisors

June 22, 2009
Date

"During the reception in the Forum after the Naturalization Ceremony, a new citizen asked me to take a photo of him and his family. As he held his citizenship certificate in front of him for the photo, I noted the details of it...his certificate is nearly identical to the one my father was granted in 1947. The major difference is my father's photo is black and white while his photo is in color....

"One of the joys of witnessing a Naturalization ceremony is seeing the smiles on the faces of the new citizens... I was 10 when my father became a US citizen. I wish I could talk to him now about his citizenship. He was a thoughtful man. I believe he had strong feelings about becoming an American."

FCAAHP has also sponsored several library programs to honor Asian Pacific American Heritage Month and has created a Literary Group and a Genealogical Group to sponsor even more programs in the coming years.

Terry Sam's Recognition Certificate 2009.
(Photo by Cora Foley)

What is the history of the Asian Pacific American Heritage Month celebrations?
A longtime Fairfax County resident and a fourth-generation Chinese American Roberta Chew (who also heads the FCAAHP Genealogical Club) was present at the creation of this national proclamation when she served as a congressional staffer in the late 1970s.

My Perspective on Asian Pacific American Heritage Month
By Roberta Chew

It was 1975 when I left San Francisco for Washington, D.C., freshly minted with a master's degree in East Asian Studies. At that time, if you had a higher degree, you simply dropped your resume off at the Congressional staff office and waited for the calls to come. In no time I had 10 job interviews lined up. My first was with Ruby G. Moy, then deputy administrative assistant to Rep. Frank Horton (R-NY). It was encouraging to find a professional Asian American woman in a position of authority in our nation's capital. I accepted an offer from another office, but I soon learned how pivotal Congressional staffers are in getting legislation passed.

In 1976, former Congressional staffer (who also became a Fairfax County resident) Jeanie Jew realized that Asian Pacific Americans had been left out of stories celebrating the Bicentennial. Black History Month had been a reality for

Roberta Chew seated second from left in front of the exhibit on
***"Remembering 1882"* (Fighting for Civil Rights in the Shadow of the Chinese Exclusion Act of 1882) that was displayed in 2008 and 2009 in the Pohick Library of Fairfax.** (Courtesy of Cora Foley)

years and a movement had begun to proclaim a Women's History Week. Jeanie worked with her friend, Ruby G. Moy, to develop a proclamation to recognize the contributions of Asian Pacific Americans to this country. The legislative effort began in earnest in June 1977 when Reps. Frank Horton and Norman Mineta (D-CA) introduced a House resolution calling upon the President to proclaim the first ten days of May as Asian/Pacific American Heritage Week. The following month, Senators Daniel Inouye and Spark Matsunaga, both of Hawaii, introduced a similar bill in the Senate.

Early May was chosen to commemorate the first Japanese national to immigrate to the United States on May 7, 1843, and also to mark the anniversary of the completion of the transcontinental railroad on May 10, 1869, a success made possible by the labor of thousands of Chinese workers. Ruby G. Moy was key in lining up co-sponsors for the House bill. She contacted me and I got my Congressman on board, although there were few Asians in his district. (Note here the power of the staffer.) I remember my excitement at reading the text of the proposed bill and thinking that we could actually get this bill passed.

Ruby G. Moy and other staffers eventually got the 218 votes needed to pass the bill in the House. The Senate bill also passed and a joint Congressional Resolution was passed in 1978. On October 5, 1978, President Jimmy Carter signed the resolution into law, proclaiming the ten-day celebration. The legislation had to be renewed every two years, so community groups continued to press their representatives to support the bill. Finally, in May 1990, President George H.W. Bush expanded the commemoration by designating May as Asian Pacific American Heritage Month.

It was a very significant victory. For many years, Asian Pacific American Heritage Month has been an annual observance for federal, state and local governments across the nation. They promote and engage in educational activities to celebrate the contributions of Asian Pacific Americans every May. Fairfax County, with its own significant Asian Pacific American population, has done much over the years since 1994.

For 2009, Fairfax County celebrated Asian Pacific American Heritage Month by hosting at its Government Center its first-ever U.S. naturalization ceremony for 75 new Americans, including new Asian Americans. The event was made possible by the efforts of the Fairfax County Asian American History Project.

Roberta Chew on Life as a California Transplant to Northern Virginia. I was initially reluctant to write an essay about my family history in Fairfax County, because – hey! – I have no history here. Like many thousands of citizens who work for the federal government, it was an accident of geography that led me to live in the county. I first came east from San Francisco in the 1970s to be a summer intern at the Library of Congress. Along with three other female interns from the University of California at Berkeley, we rented a townhouse in Alexandria, Virginia. I liked the name Alexandria because it evoked for me an exotic, distant place in Egypt. When I decided to buy a house in the 1980s, I again ended up by chance in Alexandria, although not in the city proper. We have an Alexandria street address, but we actually live in southern Fairfax County.

For the 30 years I worked off and on in the District and in foreign countries, it didn't much matter where my house was located. I scarcely thought about Fairfax County nor did I feel any attachment to it. I was a commuter to D.C. for many years and absentee landlord during other years. But since I retired 4 years ago and made the tentative decision to live here in retirement rather than return to my home state of California, my husband, Jay, and I have become more aware of and interested in D.C. and county matters.

There's a lot to be said for the virtues of Fairfax County. I'm an avid user of the county libraries; I'm close to Sherwood Regional, Martha Washington and Kingstowne libraries. In retirement, I decided I needed to get fit. For the past few years, I've been taking yoga, Pilates, and water exercise classes at both Mt. Vernon and Lee District Recreation Centers. Recent highway improvements around I-495 have eased our driving in the region considerably and we're very happy about that. I brag that every place I need or want to go to – museums, restaurants, theatres, stores, malls – are all reachable within half an hour. We're an 8-minute drive to the Huntington Metro station. We vote in every election, even primaries (we don't understand why everyone doesn't). We're part of the tide of Northern Virginia voters that have turned this part of the state into trending Democratic and we're proud of it.

I don't notice too many Asian Americans in our part of the county. We seem to skew more Hispanic hereabouts. For this reason, I'm quite glad that enterprising fellow Asian Americans have developed the Fairfax County Asian American History Project. It has provided a vital focus and helpful mechanism for Asian Americans from different parts of this vast county to meet and share their interests and common concerns.

We expect to live in Fairfax County for the foreseeable future. We love it here. ##

Jay and Roberta stand in the center flanked by Cora and Mike Foley in a Fairfax Chinese restaurant. (Courtesy of Cora Foley)

FCAAHP and the Chinese American Heritage Tour
By Corazon Sandoval Foley

Not only does the Fairfax County Asian American History Project (FCAAHP) organize programs to celebrate May as Asian American Heritage Month in Fairfax County, FCAAHP also has promoted other programs, like the Chinese American Heritage Tour. During the August 3, 2008 FCAAHP meeting at Pohick Library, we displayed the exhibit on the 1882 Chinese Exclusion Act and a discussion of the Chinese American Heritage Tour was led by Dale Hom and John Kusano.

In 2008, Dale Hom published a report on *"Asian Immigrant History in the National Forests"* that summarized the vision behind the Chinese American Heritage Tour. He discussed the parallel challenges facing the United States National Forest Service and museums, as both struggle to incorporate and serve diverse communities across generational, cultural, and ethnic lines. As a solution to the issues of cross-cultural communication that often prevent the forest service and museums from fully connecting with minority audiences, Hom pointed to efforts on the part of the US Forest Service (USFS) and Seattle's Wing Luke Asian Museum (WLAM) to fill gaps in public programs on frontier history.

Together, the USFS and WLAM organized two conferences, and the *"Chinese Heritage of the American West Tour,"* that illustrate the effectiveness of community collaboration. The conception and implementation of these events centered on contributions from Asian Pacific American community leaders and elders that have enabled the APA community to be served in a legitimate and inclusive fashion. The success of these programs has provided insight and infrastructure that may be used by other institutions to better serve the community, particularly minority groups.

Sometimes called the Dale (Hom) and Ron (Chew) Chinese American Heritage Tour in some circles, the program has flourished with the support of John Kusano, a longtime Fairfax County resident and public service employee of the US Forest Service of the US Department of Agriculture. In promoting an "outdoors classroom" approach. Dale Hom worked through John Kusano, American Indian and Asian Program Manager for the USDA Forest Service to get co-sponsorship by the Wing Luke Museum and USDA Forest Service. John Kusano very kindly shared his life story with FCAAHP.

Stranger from a Different Shore
By John Kusano

Although the title of my story comes from Ron Takaki's overview of the Asian American experience, my move in 1993 to Fairfax County, Virginia from my beloved California in some small way seem to me a kind of "immigrants' story" with plenty of highs and lows and triumphs along with trials and tribulations.

I was born in 1953, the middle child of Toshi and Jim Hagimori's three children. I am a third-generation Japanese American, the grandson of immigrants who arrived in the United States in the 1920s. I was raised in the San Francisco Bay area where my father owned a restaurant and my mother was a hospital worker. I am also a third-generation San Franciscan. The Bay Area is a place of great natural beauty, where I have always had a strong connection to nature and the outdoors. That bond prompted me to study forestry at the University of California at Santa Cruz and the University of California at Berkeley, and in 1979 to join the US Forest Service where I continue to work today.

My opportunity to work in Washington, DC and live in Fairfax County came in 1993 when I was selected for a position in the Forest Service Headquarters. The position, I thought, was unique and exciting—helping the Forest Service to increase the participation of the Asian Pacific American (APA) communities in the agency's programs. And on a personal level, my two sons were starting elementary school and I looked forward to the opportunity to have them a part of the nationally renowned Fairfax County School District—something that, looking back, was beneficial to my family.

Living on the east coast took some getting use to. I particularly found the climate difficult, especially the heat and humidity of the summers. In my native San Francisco, we had nothing like this, where summers, like all seasons, were relatively pleasant. Although at times I struggled with my new east coast environment and culture, I found great satisfaction in my professional life. I was able to initiate several exciting new programs. I helped to form an Asian Pacific American Employee Association in the Forest Service that helped to mentor and promote the many skilled APA employees within the agency. I started an APA student recruitment initiative in partnership with UC Davis. This recruitment initiative continues to this day and has provided hundreds of APA students with scholarships and employment opportunities with the Forest Service.

In addition to the more common employment programs aimed at the APA community, I was also able to get involved in outreach to engage the APA community in programs that are the core mission of the Forest Service. One example of this was related to the agencies recreation program. In 1995, in a partnership with the Wing Luke Asian American Museum in Seattle, the Forest Service offered what was called *"The Chinese Heritage Tour of the American West."* This was a 6-day bus tour of historic sites mostly on Forest Service land in Washington, Oregon, and Idaho. It was a great way of introducing members of the APA community to some of the historic resources that the Forest Service preserves and interprets. It was also an opportunity for Forest Service managers to discuss these historic resources with Asian Americans who often bring a unique and valuable perspective of these resources.

As an offshoot of the success of this tour, I was involved in establishing an APA community outreach position in Pacific Northwest Region of the Forest Service. This position over several years worked on various projects that improved the involvement of and service to the APA community -- projects such as translation services for the Southeast Asian Community involved in mushroom harvesting in the forests of the Pacific Northwest, and providing the Hmong community youth in California with outdoor recreation opportunities. Needless to say I found the opportunity to work with the Asian Pacific American communities across the country rewarding and worthwhile. I was also appreciative of the US Forest Service for providing me the chance to come to the Washington, DC area and work in this unique area of my profession. Just as importantly, my family very much enjoyed our life in Fairfax County (after we got used to the climate), and my two sons benefited from their education in the Fairfax County schools. They are both now attending Virginia Tech, another great benefit of life here. ##

Cultural Landmark: The Bell Pavilion Garden in Meadowlark Park

By Corazon Sandoval Foley

Meadowlark Botanical Gardens Park Planning

Korean Garden Site
건립 부지

Direa- the Newsletter of
Meadowlark Botanical Gardens
Volume 10, Number 1, Spring 2008

On December 19, 2007, I attended a press conference held by the Korean American Cultural Committee (KACC) at the Meadowlark Botanical Gardens to discuss the progress of the Korean American Bell Pavilion Garden project based on a memorandum of agreement on April 18, 2007 between KACC and the Northern Virginia Regional Park Authority (NVRPA). The design approved on November 15, 2007 was by David Chung, Art Professor at the University of Michigan and formerly at George Mason University. The first phase of the Korean Bell Pavilion Garden is scheduled to open in 2010.

In Korea, bell pavilions are used to mark places of great significance. The KACC has been developing the first Korean Bell Pavilion Garden in an American public park – and this will mark Meadowlark Botanical Gardens as a place of cultural identity for Korean Americans in Northern Virginia.

KACC is funding the project that it describes on its website as follows.

"The pavilion has no religious or scriptural function. The Bell is the size of a small car and is rung with a suspended log. It is rung about five times a year – 4t[h] July, 9-11, the date of the end of the Korean War and other dates of remembrance. The Bell has a very low tone. Korean Bell Pavilions have been built for hundreds of years as a focal point for gatherings that celebrate the meditative quality of nature. The finished pavilion will not be highly ornate but finished simply in natural wood tones. The Bell itself has many etchings or carvings on it that depict the natural world. Water is an important feature in a Bell Pavilion. Thus, there will be a flowing creek in the design. One of the most important aspect is the landscape, providing Meadowlark the opportunity to create a collection of Northeast Asian plants as part of a cultural landmark. The

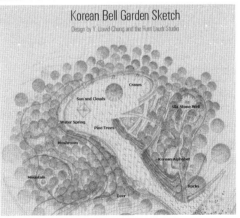

Korean Bell Garden Sketch
Design by Y. David Chung and the Hunt Laudi Studio

climate of the Korean Peninsula is similar to Northern Virginia so there are many plants that are well adapted to the climate."

We in FCAAHP deeply appreciate the support from JeungHwa Elmejjad-Yi, Founder of the Korean American Cultural Committee (KACC) that is spearheading creation of the Korean Bell Pavilion Garden at Meadowlark Park. She shared the following insights.

The Korean Bell Garden: A Goodwill Landmark
By JeungHwa Elmejjad-Yi
Founder of the Korean American Cultural Committee

The Korean American Cultural Committee (KACC) is a non-profit, non-partisan organization with mailing address at P.O. Box 198 in Annandale, Virginia. Its website address is www.kacc.us. KACC has four key goals:

     (1) To bring awareness to the issues affecting Korean Americans;
     (2) To encourage the participation of Korean Americans in all aspects of American life;
     (3) To educate our children about their Korean heritage and culture; and
     (4) To reach out to the American community.

As its first major undertaking, KACC is building a goodwill landmark that recognizes the history and development of Korean Americans in the greater Washington DC area – and also celebrates the importance of the great diversity represented in this area."

The Korea Bell Pavilion: "A symbol of goodwill towards all"

Korean Bell Pavilions have been built for hundreds of years as a focal point for gatherings that celebrate the meditate quality of nature. According to an old Korean saying, bells instill a righteous spirit in those who hear its ring, and gives rise to hope, a sense of cherishing life, alarm against disaster, and sense of unity that brings people together, in order to bring prosperity, happiness, friendship, freedom, and peace for all people.

During the Chosun Dynasty, King KoJong sent an initial diplomatic mission to the United States in 1903 aboard the S.S. *Gaelic,* with the first group of Korean immigrants, who arrived in Hawaii to work on the pineapple and sugar plantations. They endured hardships with hopes of a better future. Even under financial constraints they supported the country that gave them life by donating more than half of their earnings for the Korean Independent Movement, while emphasizing the need to cultivate and educate their next generation. It is this undying spirit of our first Korean ancestors that represents the essence of our Korean American heritage today. The Korean Bell Garden is a goodwill landmark, gifted to NVRPA and the great diversity of people residing in Fairfax County and the Washington DC metropolitan area. This landmark is especially meaningful as it is a historic symbol being passed on to our 2nd and 3rd generation Korean American descendants, as well as to the general public.

The pavilion that houses the bell is approximately 21 feet high and 21 feet wide, and the bell is approximately 7 feet high, and will be rung five times a year – 4th of July, September 11, June 25

---

commemorating the Korean War, and other important dates of remembrance. The groundbreaking ceremony for the construction of the Bell Pavilion is scheduled for June 2010."

The Korean Bell Garden

The Korean Bell Pavilion will be the centerpiece of the surrounding Korean Bell Garden. The Garden will also display the beauty and nobility of Korean history and culture by showcasing the history of the Korean alphabet, Shilla Stones, a Turtle Garden, the Ten Elements, a pond, study area, etc. Furthermore, flowers, plants, and trees that are dear to Koreans will also surround the garden. The Garden will surely become a popular destination for those seeking rest and relaxation, beautiful scenery, and a perfect outdoor setting for weddings.

JeungHwa Elmejjad-Yi in Seoul in 2009 studying traditional Korean Bell Garden Pavilion structures with Northern Virginia Park Authority officials. (Courtesy of JeungHwa Elmejjad-Yi)

Photo Gallery of the Bell Pavilion Garden at Meadowlark Park
(Photos courtesy of JeungHwa Elmejjad-Yi)

Food and Festivals Facilitate Friendships
By Corazon Sandoval Foley

Proliferating Asian Restaurants. Asian restaurants have become familiar landmarks in Fairfax County and have become more popular, even as their offerings go up in quality and price for a more cosmopolitan county clientele. In April 2009, a Fairfax County Thai restaurant owner managed to beat well-known TV chef Bobby Flay in a TV competition to cook the best Pad Thai.

FCAAHP has interviewed two Filipino American restaurant and food storeowners, as well as a Chinese American restaurateur – their full stories are in the FCAAHP website and are excerpted here in the book.

Manila Café and Fiesta Oriental. I took the photo in 2008 showing Roger Saplan and his granddaughter, fourth generation Filipino American Alyssa Ybanez (whose Filipino American grandmother was born in California). They were standing in front of the Manila Café buffet counters. The other 2008 photo shows Lando Sunga of Fiesta Oriental in Rolling Road in Springfield, selling traditional Filipino food items.

Rogelio Saplan and granddaughter Alyssa Ibanez at Manila Café. (Photo by Cora Foley)

Most Filipino food stores operate like Fiesta Oriental, aiming primarily at take-out customers and catering for Filipino family parties.

Rogelio Saplan opened Manila Café in as the first
sit-down restaurant offering Filipino food that served as a pleasant venue for business meals with his real estate clients.

Fiesta Filipino Food Store – another eatery in Springfield. (Photo by Cora Foley)

Rogelio Saplan started as a Navy recruit from the Philippines. His Navy career included stints in the White House as a chef. He noted that his son-in-law is an Annapolis graduate and a military officer – a career track that was denied to him and other Filipino naval recruits.

After retiring from the Navy, he moved with his second wife, a medical doctor, to live in Fairfax County where he began a successful career as a real estate broker and restaurant owner. He was the founder in 1992 of the Philippine American Chamber of Commerce in Washington, DC aimed at developing opportunities for Filipino American entrepreneurs and managers.

It was with great pride that Rogelio Saplan informed me during the FCAAHP interview that Congressman Tom Davis passed legislation for a "Rogelio Saplan Day" honoring his contributions to the community as a longtime resident since 1978 of Fairfax County. After his wife died, Rogelio Saplan sold Manila Café and has gone into retirement that involves spending half a year in the Philippines and the rest back in Fairfax County.

A Chinese American Restaurateur's Story.
Ching-Jung Lee and her husband opened a Chinese restaurant in Burke in 1994. She recounted some unwelcome treatment over the years. She noted that running a Chinese restaurant is hard. The hours are long and the physical work is hard. The survival rate of small business is low, and one must deal with cultural differences.

"We have tried to introduce Chinese cuisine to customers while adjusting the taste of food to meet the acceptance of local society. We try to provide healthy and nutritious elements of Chinese cuisine. At the same time, we want customers to experience Chinese hospitality, culture and values."

The Lee family in 1990 at the Fortune restaurant in Fairfax County, Virginia. (Courtesy of Lee family)

Ching-Jung Lee also noted that the children of Chinese business owners are generally hard working, diligent and well behaved, but because of their parents' need for economic survival and language barriers, they are often ignored in some families. She suggested that teachers must be more patient and understanding of such difficult family situations.

Their children graduated from Thomas Jefferson High School for Science and Technology as well as from Robinson High School. They have enjoyed living in Fairfax County and as of 2009, have no plan to move away. They sent their children to local weekend Chinese schools and tried to contribute to celebrations of Asian traditions. The family has experienced generation gap issues and even had to seek a counselor's help to face the son's period of rebellion, like many other parents. ##

Notable Thai American Chef. Photo shows Thai Basil chef/owner Nongkran Daks who in March 2009 won a Pad Thai competition against Bobby Flay on the Food Network's *"Throwdown with Bobby Flay."* Thai Basil restaurant opened in 1999 in Chantilly, Fairfax County.

Nongkran Daks of Thai Basil
(Courtesy of Thai Basil)

Fairfax County Festivals
By Corazon Sandoval Foley

Asian festivals in Fairfax County are often sponsored by cultural groups and faith-based communities. The latter celebrations will be covered in this book's discussion of Faith Communities. We focus in this section on two well-known festivals in Fairfax County – the Lunar New Year and the summer Asian Festival in Reston.

Lunar New Year Cultural Program in Fair Oaks Mall. Hank Chao, the video team leader of the Fairfax County Asian American History Project, has been the head for several years of the Hai Hua cultural group that sponsors annual Lunar New Year celebrations at Fair Oaks Mall in Fairfax County. Hank Chao's life story is discussed in more detail in the chapter on mass media and television shows.

Fair Oaks Shopping Mall opened in 1980 and is located at the major interchange of I-66 and Route 50, roughly in the center of Fairfax County. It includes regional and local retail, offices, a hotel, and multi-family residential facilities, including housing for the elderly.

Chinese Lunar New Year at Fair Oaks Mall 2008

The Reston Asian Festival sponsored by the Thai Tennis Association.

I took the two photos above during the 2007 and 2008 Asian festivals that featured Asian cultural dances and other performances. In 2008, the Philippine exhibit won the competition for the best presentation in the festival – and in 2009, for the second time in a row, the Philippine exhibit won the same award. In the left photo, the Filipino American performer in 2007 was dancing the Philippine bamboo dance called *"tinikling."*

In 2008, the Reston Asian program included the fife and drum corps presenting the winners of the Chinese American beauty contest – a combination that seems so appropriate to the changing dynamics in Fairfax County demography.

Fife and Drum and Chinese American beauty contestants at the 2008 Reston Asian Festival. (Photo by Terry Sam)

Chairman Sharon Bulova was the keynote speaker at the 2008 Reston Asian Festival (Photo by Terry Sam)

Robert E. Simon and Supervisor Cathy Hudgins at the 2008 Reston Asian Festival. (Photo by Terry Sam)

The Asian Festival was held in Reston, a "new town" in the Old Dominion that was first designed in 1962. The concept and the initial funding for the 7,000 acres of land were provided by Robert E. Simon Jr. (shown in photo) whose initials plus the English suffix for town form its name. The land on which the concept was developed was once part of Thomas, Sixth Lord Fairfax's Great Falls Manor.

Faith Communities: Spiritual Comfort and Cultural Traditions

By Corazon Sandoval Foley

Korean American Churches in Fairfax County. As of 2003, there were more than 300 Korean American churches in the metropolitan DC area, with many having membership of less than 500.

One of the largest is the Korean Central Presbyterian Church whose history was shared with FCAAHP by Heisung Lee, recipient of the Lady Fairfax award in 2004 and shown in photo with a church deacon Se-Woong Ro. FCAAHP in 2008 conducted interviews with members of the Korean Central Senior Center housed in the church. The Korean Central Presbyterian Church (KCPC, the name changed in 1974 from the original Korean Central Church) was founded on November 4, 1973 by Rev. Myung Ho Yoon with 20 Korean American Christian families. The first service was in his residence at 313 Park Street, N.E., Vienna, Virginia.

Even with some difficulties in the early years, the KCPC has grown to become one of the largest Korean American churches in the metropolitan DC area. The church statistics of 2003 showed that the adult attendance in five Sunday worship service was some 2,800 with the youth program attendance of 900 and the English ministry attendance of 500.

The history of the Korean Central Presbyterian Church could be seen in the photo gallery starting with Reverend Myung Ho Yoon's home in the top right corner growing to the church in which members worshipped in 2009. The next chapter for the church will be in Centreville, Virginia where a new building has been constructed for planned occupancy in 2010.

두번째 예배 처소였던
알링턴 트리니티교회

첫 예배를 드린 윤명호 목사 자택
313 Park St. NE, Vienna

세번째 예배 처소로 사용했던
워싱턴 DC 6가에 있는 필그림장로교회

비엔나 성전을 건축할 때까지
마지막으로 빌려쓰던
맥클린의 투인스힐 장로교회

The Ekoji Buddhist Temple. FCAAHP has benefited tremendously from the support of the Ekoji Buddhist Temple that started in 1978 with five Japanese American families, including Ken and Nori Nakamura, organizing their first services at the Nakamura home. The community has grown dramatically and in 1998, it dedicated a beautiful building located in Lakehaven road in Burke, Virginia. Ken Nakamura discussed the Ekoji story in the section on his life story as part of the Japanese American History chapter.

The photo collage shows left to right: the Ekoji Buddhist Temple congregation; Ken Nakamura at the Ekoji garden; Ekoji Nen Daiko Taiko Drum Group; *Obon* Festival.

The Ekoji Buddhist temple supports the practice of Shin Buddhists throughout the area. Its activities include study groups (such as an August 2008 workshop on Naikan self-reflection) and a taiko drum ensemble. The Dharma school offers Buddhist education for children and related social activities. The taiko drum group was founded in 1994 and named by Reverend Kenryu Tsuji as Nen Daiko: Nen is a name for Amida Buddha, and Daiko is Japanese for "fat drum."

On July 11, 2009, the Ekoji Buddhist temple hosted its 27th *Obon* celebration with a diverse group of some 700 Fairfax County residents enjoying the taiko drumming, folk dancing, wonderful cuisine with sushi and other delicious Japanese food – and participating in the evening ceremony to honor the memory of dead ancestors. FCAAHP shared wonderful moments of the Ekoji *obon* celebrations of 2008 and 2009 via youtube.

The Durga Temple in Fairfax County. On July 22, 2009, the *Fairfax County Times* published an article entitled "Celebrating their Hindu Culture." Photos were taken at the Durga Temple with the lighting of the wick lamp at the Forum for Hindu Awakening. The lamp burnt purified butter to attract a pure divine Hindu god. Participants said the forum helps to teach traditional Hindu culture to future generations.

Photos show Durga Temple and Neal Aggerwal in a Hindu ceremony.

The Durga Temple was constructed in 1994 and the goddess Durga was installed in 1999. It is less common in Hindu tradition to dedicate

an independent temple to the goddess, making the Durga temple the first of its kind in Northern Virginia.

The temple is a community project and since its inception, has been completely funded and run by the community – although it has acquired corporate sponsors such as Ascend Healthcare systems, iLOKA Inc., netGraphics and Wachovia Bank.

Apart from the regular rituals and ceremonies that are performed according to the Hindu calendar year, the temple every Sunday holds a discourse on the *Bhagavad Gita,* the holy book of the Hindus, along with cultural activities for children and tours for people from other faiths. The temple's philosophy extends to include everybody in the community, with the hope that the *Shikars* (spiraled

domes of the building) will inspire everyone who passes by to aspire to the right path. The Hindu domes are a public representation of the 3,000-year-old culture of Hindu India among the many religions and cultures that enrich the ethnic landscape of Northern Virginia.

Another Hindu temple in Fairfax County is the Rajdhani Mandir inaugurated in March 2000 and located on a wooded 8-acre site in Chantilly, Virginia.

Notes from Sant D. Gupta. FCAAHP interviewed Sant D. Gupta, President of the Durga Temple who moved to Fairfax County in 1999. He said that "my wife and I have been active in a variety of activities in Hindu places of worship such as the Durga Temple, neighborhood activities, and political forums, social, humanitarian and cultural events – mostly in Fairfax County." For him, the Asian American community was not particularly important for he had been in the US for over 30 years when he moved to Fairfax County and therefore needed no special assistance.

Fairfax Filipino American Catholics. Most Fairfax County Filipino Americans celebrate cultural traditions in the Catholic Churches. Weddings, baptisms and other church rites involve celebrations that feature Philippine food and cultural performances.

Filipino Americans in Fairfax County often observe traditional customs and rites during weddings as shown in the Philippine veil ceremony during Josh and Clare Foley's wedding in September 2007 at St. Raymond of Peñafort Catholic Church . (Courtesy of Cora Foley)

Weddings usually involve the veil, cord and coin ceremony as shown in the photos from the wedding of my son Joshua and Clare Foley on September 1, 2007 in St. Raymond of Peñafort Church (the newest Catholic Church in Fairfax County that officially opened in December 2006). I was so happy that the new church was to be the site of my son's wedding that I wrote the front-page article for the *Fairfax Chronicle* about the official church opening. The wedding reception for Joshua and Clare was held at the Officers' Club in Fort Belvoir where the first Filipino residents of Fairfax County (Ramon Rojo and Benjamin Trillanes) lived in 1930.

During the Christmas season, Fairfax County Filipino Americans have celebrated the *"Simbang Gabi"* -- a very popular Filipino tradition sponsored since 2000 by the Filipino American Catholic Ministry of Northern Virginia. It involves nine consecutive evening masses usually officiated by Filipino priests who celebrate mass in the *Pilipino* language. The Filipino Catholic Church celebrations have become special occasions for Filipino Americans to wear traditional costumes and to share delicious Philippine cuisine.

Throughout the year, a monthly Filipino mass has been celebrated in St. Bernadette's Catholic Church in Springfield, Virginia since May of 2006. In 2009, at the 50th anniversary celebration of the founding of St. Bernadette's Church, the mass included prayers and songs in Pilipino by a choir made up of Filipino American residents of Fairfax County dressed in traditional Philippine costumes.

Note on other Faith Communities in Fairfax County. We featured in this book those houses of worship for Fairfax County Asian Americans that participated in the FCAAHP oral history interviews.

There are hundreds of houses of worship for Fairfax County Asian Americans and we in FCAAHP hope to continue our research, visit more faith communities and include them in our website, including:

- The Sikh Foundation that was built in the late 80s with a golden dome in Ox Road in Fairfax Station. It has grown in importance with some 1,000 families worshiping regularly. *The Fairfax Chronicle* published a story about it entitled "Golden Dome Marks Sikh Temple."
- Muslim mosques are also in our "to visit" list. We have requested assistance from our Pakistani American interviewees and plan to include information on their houses of worship in Fairfax County in the website.
- The Tzu Chi Buddhist Temple in Reston, Virginia was inaugurated on October 25, 2008. It purchased the Good Shepherd Lutheran Church for $4.2 million in 2007. One of the largest Buddhist congregations in the US, it has 50 chapters in the US and more than 5 million followers worldwide.

And there are many other Catholic and Christian churches attended by Fairfax County Asian Americans that we plan to do more research for FCAAHP website inclusion.

Sikh Foundation. (Photo by Cora Foley)

Tzu Chi Temple in Reston October 2008. (Courtesy of Hank Chao)

Mass Media: Sharing Heritage & Contributions of Fairfax County Asian Americans
By Corazon Sandoval Foley

In this section, I have profiled some of the Fairfax County media outlets – television, newspapers, and books – that have served to share the history, heritage, and contributions of Fairfax County Asian Americans. Many thanks go to Maryam Shah who discussed Fairfax Public Access (Channel 10) and Asian Americans in an FCAAHP youtube video.

TV: Washington My Home TV Station (WMHTV).
In 2007, FCAAHP video team leader Hank Chao led a group to create an hourly Chinese American Community TV program *"Washington My Home"* (WMHTV) at Fairfax County Public Access Channel 30. In June 2008, it expanded to Maryland – the Montgomery County Channel 21.

Hank Chao's American Dream. Hank Chao, Executive Producer of Washington My Home Chinese Community TV, came to America from Taiwan in 1984 when he was 25 years old. He arrived without a college degree and did not speak much English. By 2009, Hank and Liling Chao both work at the IT/IS function in a large corporation, and they have become the owners of a Chinese historical building in Chinatown, Washington, DC. He is the Executive Partner for 618 H Partnership and President of Chinatown Garden Restaurant Inc. In 2009 their two daughters, Melody and Krystal, were enrolled in Fairfax County Public Schools. Photo below shows Liling, Krystal, Melody and Hank Chao during their Bahamas vacation in July 2009.

Hank Chao believes that Asian Americans need to help build the bridge to the mainstream society. He joined in 2003 one of the largest Chinese organizations, "Hai Hua Community Center", and has held the titles of CEO and President of HHCC through 2009. During his five years in office, Hank has initiated and organized yearly cultural celebrations of Chinese Lunar New Year at Fair Oaks Mall in Fairfax County.

Hank gave an interview with the *Springfield Connection* on February 14, 2007 on the Lunar New Year celebrations. He said that the event "not only educates area residents about cultures in Asia, but also plays an important role in reconnecting those removed from the geographic area to the culture of their ancestors. Attendees have continued to enjoy this celebration over the past few years. People who went through the Cultural Revolution miss the old traditions of celebrating Chinese New Year. The celebration helps second-generation Asian children who grew up here in America connect with Asian culture. We are also educating children of the next generation."

Because of Hank's contributions to the Asian American community, he was appointed to several important county and state boards. They include the Tysons Corner Urban Development and Transportation Committee, as well as the State Board of Community College to serve a total of 23 community colleges in the Commonwealth of Virginia.

Newspapers: The Asian Fortune. As the number of Asian residents has grown, more newspapers in Fairfax County have been publishing stories about the contributions and heritage of the more than 160,000 Asian residents, particularly in the field of educational achievements. They include popular local papers like the *Connection Newspapers*, the *Fairfax County Times,* and the *Fairfax Chronicle.* For example, the March 2008 edition of the *South County Chronicle* featured a front-page article about the Fairfax County Asian American History Project.

In addition, newspapers based in Asian American communities – some published in different ethnic languages – have been increasing in Fairfax County. The most widely distributed newspaper in the county is the Asian Fortune with copies available free-of-charge in Fairfax County Public Libraries.

The *Asian Fortune* Newspaper was founded in January 1993 as an independent newspaper serving all Asian Pacific Americans – and it has proudly reported awards that it has received, including the 2000 Small Business Journalist of the Year Award and the 1998 National Minority Media Cornerstone Award. Photo shows June 2008 *Asian Fortune* article written by Fairfax County resident Jackie Bong-Wright about the Fairfax County Asian American History Project.

The *Asian Fortune* has published numerous stories about Fairfax County Asian Americans – and the following examples of relevant articles were included in its May 2009 Asian Pacific American Heritage Month edition:

- Fairfax County Filipino American resident Major General (ret.) Antonio M. Taguba representing US Veterans Administration Secretary General Eric Shinseki in presenting the first batch of compensation benefit checks to Filipino American veterans – and in particular, to Filipino American WWII veteran Alberto Bacani who was then 98 years old
- Fairfax County Vietnamese American resident Jackie Bong-Wright and Huyen Phan performed the Vietnamese "Conical Hat Dance" and the "Drums Dance" at the Northern Virginia Community College in Annandale, Virginia.
- Fairfax County's George Mason University sponsored a Chinese American zither ensemble for Asian Pacific American Heritage Month performances.
- The Federal Asian Pacific American Council (FAPAC) that was once chaired and was co-founded in 1984 by Fairfax County Filipino American Corazon Sandoval Foley held a successful 24th

annual conference in May 2009. FAPAC provides professional training conferences for federal Asian American employees.

• Fairfax County Japanese American resident William Marumoto who died in early 2009 was honored for his 50 years of public service during the May 2009 gala by APAICS (Asian Pacific American Institute for Congressional Studies). In June 2008, Marumoto was given the Lifetime President's Volunteer Service Award with estimates showing that he had contributed over 40,000 volunteer hours to 35 local, regional, and national non-profit organizations over his lifetime.

Ruth Baja Williams, Filipino American Journalist for Fairfax Chronicle.

Ruth Baja Williams at FCAAHP interview.
(Photo by Cora Foley)

In August 2008, Ruth Baja Williams interviewed me for an article about the Fairfax County Asian American History Project. In the process, she shared her own perspective as a Filipino American who has traveled widely with her African American husband. She has written a book entitled "Detour Berlin" published in January 2009 and read during FCAAHP's potluck lunch meeting on October 24, 2009. Ruth Baja Williams shared with FCAAHP the following essay on her life story.

Several Tries
By Ruth Baja Williams

It took several tries before I could immigrate to the United States for good. My father was a student at the University of the Philippines when he was awarded a scholarship to study International Relations at the University of Southern California. He seized the opportunity not only to travel to Los Angeles but also to bring his wife, two children and sister-in-law with him. I was two-and-a-half. It was October 1941. Six weeks later, Japanese bombs destroyed the American fleet anchored at Pearl Harbor and the war in the Pacific began.

My family left the U.S. in 1948. By then the war had ended. The Philippines had gained independence from the United States and organized a fledgling foreign service. My father was one of the first five Philippine diplomats, trained by the U.S. State Department in Washington DC. Thus, began my life as a global nomad. Dad was stationed in San Francisco, Hong Kong, and Sydney and Djakarta. On graduating from high school in Sydney, I returned to Los Angeles for college. I fell in love with Charles my college sweetheart, but our romance was interrupted by the U.S. draft board that sent him to West Germany. I finished my undergraduate studies and joined him in Augsburg where we were married. Once more world events intervened. In 1961 President Kennedy sent U.S. Army battle groups, one by one, to a city called West Berlin. Soviet tanks and U.S. tanks faced each other at a line that divided the city, and symbolically Germany and the world. It situation was called The Berlin Crisis.

By the time his tour of duty was over, Charles had fallen in love with Berlin and suggested a one-year adventure in the city. For me, Berlin was just another metropolis in the list of big cities that spelled my life. But the planned year stretched to twenty. Two children were born to us and Charles's music career was established. We were middle aged when we re-located to Alexandria, Virginia. For the children, it was a chance to examine their roots. For Charles, it was a homecoming. For me, the way was open to apply at last for U.S. citizenship, but it was a special kind of homecoming as well.

Life in the U.S. has been rewarding, but challenging. I had worked diligently to rid my speech of an Australian accent, but my plain English reveals nothing of my travels. I have written a memoir "Detour Berlin" about the two decades my family and I lived in Berlin when the Wall still stood. I am now a freelance writer and I teach English to adult speakers of other languages. ##

Ruth Baja Williams also kindly shared with FCAAHP her wonderful story about a Fairfax County Filipino American that was published by the Fairfax Chronicle.

Dreams Really Do Come True
By Ruth Baja Williams
The Fairfax Chronicle October 2006

Whenever Ellie Torres Garcia enters the Lorton Senior Center, she is greeted with smiles, waves and many hugs. The diminutive, silver-haired Filipina is known for her warmth, friendliness--and her roses. Throughout the spring, summer, and into early fall, Ellie supplies the center with fragrant roses, which she cultivates in her Crosspointe garden. The center is like a second home to her. "We are like a family here," says Garcia. "I come here every Tuesday and Thursday."

It has been a long journey from the 89-year-old birthplace of Abra, a northern province of the Philippines, to Lorton, Virginia. Her Filipino name is Eluteria, and she was born into a family of wealth. "My grandfather was Spanish, my father half-Spanish, but my mother was pure Filipino, and she was not accepted by the family. We were cast out." Garcia's parents, and therefore she and her siblings, became poor. She has painful memories, particularly from third grade when her classmates looked down on her and made her feel ashamed. Ellie and her eight siblings worked hard to obtain an education.

Ellie had two important dreams. She wanted to become a nurse and she wanted to come to the United States. To earn money to complete her high school education, Ellie worked as a maid in the homes of uncles. She did all the hard work maids do and she took care of the small children, her cousins. She went straight from high school to St. Paul's Hospital in Manila where she received nurse training under American Catholic sisters. In 1940 she graduated. War was imminent. "I was on duty when the first bombs dropped. We had to put the patients on the ground floor," recalls Garcia. "We Filipino nurses were inducted into the American Army."

Garcia clearly remembers a certain Captain Berry before whom she and her fellow Filipino nurses took an oath. "We considered ourselves American because we had been inducted," says Garcia. "We worked 24 hours a day to take care of the war injured, but we received no payment at all." A bigger disappointment came later. When the Americans returned to the Untied States, Ellie and her fellow nurses could not come to the United States because, they were told, there was no room on the ship. "Even after the Americans went home, Manila was full of makeshift hospital tents. I worked there to care for the injured," explains Garcia.

Nurse Eluteria Torres married Rosario Garcia in 1942. Rosario was unable to find a job as an auditor in Manila, so he went to work for the government in the provinces. Ellie followed him. "I cared for patients wherever he was needed. I took care of people and at times stayed with them until they died. But I never charged a single cent. But God has compensated me ten times over. The people I cared for and their relatives gave us food: rice, fish and meat. When I gave birth to my nine children, my doctor never charged me, even though I was not a relative."

U.S. immigration laws toward Filipinos are restrictive. Ellie's son, a doctor, was the first to come to the United States. He petitioned for his parents. In 1979 Garcia's childhood dream of coming to the United States was fulfilled. In 1985, Garcia became a U.S. citizen, and the Filipina named Eluteria became known as Ellie. One by one, eight of Garcia's children have joined the family in the United States. One daughter is still in the Philippines.

Three years ago in 2003, Rosario was diagnosed with Alzheimer's disease, so Ellie's days of caring for an ill person continue, but family members are near. She says she has two dozen grandchildren and seven great grandchildren. They are her greatest joy but she admits to not being able to remember all their names. Today, Ellie and Rosario live with their son in a house much bigger than any Ellie knew in the Philippines. The living room is enhanced by crocheted doilies made by Ellie, who also contribute her crocheted pieces to the handicraft projects at the senior center. With loving care, she tends her garden of roses in front of and behind her house.

Despite a difficult journey, we can safely say that her fondest dreams have come true. ##

Fairfax County Author Veronica Li on her book "Journey Across the Four Seas." (FCAAHP Note: On December 12, 2009, Veronica Li shared with FCAAHP members the story of her book. She submitted the following essay for the FCAAHP book.)

My parents moved into my home in Vienna, VA, ten years ago (1989). They had brought the family to California in 1967 and slaved away to put their children through college. As they entered their eighties, their wish, like that of other Asian parents, was to live with one of their children. I invited them, and they left sunny California for the swamps of the capital area.

My mother was a fantastic storyteller and loved to tell stories of her life. I decided to tape them for posterity. Being a writer, I took it a step further. I wrote them down and wove them into a memoir, her memoir. The book was published at the end of 2006. The title *Journey across the Four Seas: A Chinese Woman's Search for Home* speaks for itself. The Chinese woman is my mother, and the book is about her search for a better life for her children. Having lived through poverty and wars in Asia, she wanted to spare her children such hardships. She also wanted them to have the opportunity of a good college education. The U.S. met all her specifications.

Veronica Li with her mother at the book launch in a Vienna library in 2009. (Courtesy of Veronia Li)

My mother has accomplished her American goals. My siblings and I got the education we needed to fulfill our potential. I received my Bachelor's in English from the University of California at Berkeley and a Master's in International Affairs at Johns Hopkins. I went on to work for the World Bank in D.C., which explains why I've been living in Fairfax County for the last 25 years. I had always thought that my achievements were the result of my own hard work. It wasn't until I wrote my mom's life that I realized that my mother had done most of the work for me, even before I was born.

The project has led me to great discoveries about my parents and grandparents, but the greatest discovery was myself. I've come to believe that a person can't really know himself unless he's connected with his roots. We inherit legacies passed on from generation to generation. Even if we were born in the New World and don't know our forefathers from the Old, their legacies still affect us. Our heritage is alive in us, no matter where we are.

Since the book was released, the interest from readers of diverse ethnicity has taken me by surprise. Part of it, I think, is due to the widespread interest in Chinese culture. The other part is the universal appeal of the human spirit. My mother's strength is the foundation of every immigrant's pursuit of a better life. I've given talks at libraries and universities and to book clubs, women's clubs, senior groups and other organizations. My message to my audience is always: pass on your stories; your children will thank you for it. For more information about my book, please visit http://veronicali.com.

Note on another FCAAHP Book Author Catherine Gong: FCAAHP member Catherine Gong published in 2008 her book on "George's Kaddish: For Kovno and the Six Million."

The review from Harvard Professor John Felstine: "A welcome fresh presence in the realm of Holocaust history and remembrance. Catherine Gong has created one of the most compelling accounts I've seen in three decades. The photos George Kaddish made constitute on their own a limitless gift. Yet the story of the story, Gong's venture of understanding, illuminates even more this honest and courageous book."

Another Harvard professor Richard Breitman wrote "Catherine Gong's moving account of her encounters with George Kaddish's photo of the Kovno ghetto and with the photographer himself help us understand why he did what he did. She also played an important role, described in detail here, in the preservation and exhibition of the collection." ##

GEORGE'S KADDISH
FOR KOVNO AND THE SIX MILLION
CATHERINE GONG
EDITED BY MICHAEL BERENBAUM

Suzanne Levy of the Virginia Room is on the left of the photo standing beside Roberta Chew and Ken Burnett. Suzanne has been most helpful in the library research on census data and historical information about Asian residents in Fairfax County. Suzanne has also helped launch the FCAAHP Genealogy Club.

Useful resource books on Fairfax County for the 2010 FCAAHP book.

APPENDICES

Fairfax County Asian Arrivals:
Report by Fairfax County Demographer Anne Cahill.
By Corazon Sandoval Foley

On February 17, 2008, the *Fairfax County Chronicle* published the following article that I wrote about the kick-off meeting of the Fairfax County Asian American History Project on January 23, 2008 that focused on the report on Asian American population trends by the Fairfax County Demographer Anne Cahill. I also included in this book the charts and tables that accompanied the Cahill presentation to FCAAHP members in January but were not included in my report that was published by the Fairfax Chronicle.

Fairfax County Launches Asian American History Project
By Corazon Sandoval Foley

On February 11, 2008, Braddock District Supervisor Sharon Bulova presented to the Fairfax County Board of Supervisors an update on her project to document the history and contributions of Fairfax County Asian Americans – the largest minority group in the county since 1990.

In 2006, Asian Americans accounted for some 16% of the county population or about 160,000 residents. Supervisor Bulova noted that the project was initially suggested by Cora Foley of the Filipino American National Historical Society of Northern Virginia. It has the support of the Fairfax County History Commission and members of Supervisor Bulova's "A Look Back at Braddock History Committee" will be assisting in an advisory capacity.

Supervisor Bulova hosted a kick-off meeting of the project Task Force on Wednesday, January 23, 2008. The group will be working to capture and tell the history of Asian Americans who have chosen Fairfax County as their home. Terry Sam, a Fairfax County Chinese American resident, generously volunteered to be the Task Force photographer.

Through oral history interviews and community projects, the Task Force will tell the stories of how, why and when different Asian American groups came to the U.S. and to Fairfax County, where they have settled – and what their experiences and contributions have been to the Fairfax County community. Products of the project may include articles, a book, a video and a web presence. The target date for publication of a book is May of 2010 to coincide with Asian American Heritage Month in Fairfax County.

At the January 23, 2008 meeting, Fairfax County Chief Demographer Anne Cahill set the stage for the meeting with an educational presentation about Asian immigration to Fairfax County. She began by describing Fairfax County foreign-born residents who accounted for 73% of the net increase in county population between 1990 and 2000. In 2006, more than one out of every four County residents had been foreign-born. Fairfax County has benefited from the high education of its foreign-born citizens – nearly 48% have a four-year college degree or higher.

Ms. Cahill provided a glimpse of the potential demographic future of Fairfax County by noting that among county residents, today's children are more racially and ethnically diverse. She noted that 45% of persons under age 20 are racial or ethnic minorities compared to 38% of all Fairfax County residents. In addition, 38% of children have at least one parent who is foreign-born. Of these children with a foreign-born parent, four out of five are US citizens.

Ms. Cahill underscored the growing role of Fairfax County Asian Americans by comparing the county's demographic profile with the nation as a whole. She emphasized the fact that the foreign-born population from Asia accounted in 2006 for some 27% of the total foreign-born population in the whole of the United States – while in Fairfax County, Asians accounted for 51% of the total foreign-born population.

Fairfax County Asian Americans in 2006 included some 139,828 persons who were born in Asia. Of the foreign-born population from Asia, Korean Americans accounted for 20.2%, Vietnamese Americans 15%, Asian Indian Americans 14.8%, Chinese Americans 14%, and Filipino Americans 8%. This population distribution is also reflected in the most frequently spoken languages other than English in Fairfax County. Ms. Cahill concluded with maps showing where Fairfax County Asian Americans reside that also indicated the growing presence of Asian American landmarks, including churches, temples, and the Eden Center – the largest Vietnamese American commercial center on the East Coast of North America.

Supervisor Bulova then discussed the lessons learned from her "A Look Back at Braddock" History Project. She was assisted by Mary Lipsey, co-author of the book *"Braddock's True Gold"* and by John Browne, author of Braddock History Map and Project Manager of the Braddock Heritage Website (www.braddockheritage.org). The Task Force members agreed to adopt the mission statement and meeting schedules. The February 27, 2008 meeting was the second orientation program for volunteers. The Task Force plans include a video outreach program for a May 14, 2008 celebration of Asian American Heritage Month in Fairfax County… ##

Asian Immigration to Fairfax County

Presentation for Braddock District, January 2008

Anne Pickford Cahill, Demographer
Fairfax County Department of Systems
Management for Human Services

Foreign-Born and Total Population
Fairfax County, 1970-2006

Sources: U.S. Census Bureau and Fairfax County Department of Systems
Management for Human Services.

Fairfax County Foreign Born Residents...

- Foreign born residents accounted for 73% of the net increase in population between 1990 and 2000.
- In 2006, more than one out of every four County residents were foreign born.
- Among foreign born residents, no country of origin forms a predominant majority.
- The County's foreign born adults are highly educated, nearly 48% have a four-year college degree or more education (2006).
- A quarter of the County's households that speak a language other than English at home are linguistically isolated. This is 8% of all households (2006).

Among Fairfax County residents...

- Children are more racially and ethnically diverse.
  - 45% of persons under age 20 are racial or ethnic minorities compared to 38% of all persons.
- 38% of children have at least one parent who is foreign born.
  - Of these children with a foreign born parent, four out of five are US citizens.

Source: U.S. Census Bureau, 2000 Decennial Censuses, PUMS data.

Foreign Born Population by Region of Birth
2006

Source: U.S. Census Bureau, 2006 American Community Survey.

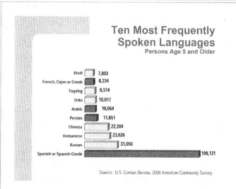

Ten Most Frequently Spoken Languages
Persons Age 5 and Older

Source: U.S. Census Bureau, 2006 American Community Survey.

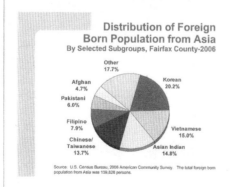

Distribution of Foreign Born Population from Asia
By Selected Subgroups, Fairfax County-2006

Source: U.S. Census Bureau, 2006 American Community Survey. The total foreign born population from Asia was 139,828 persons.

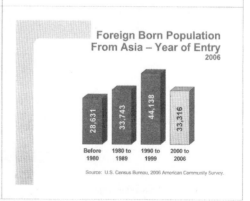

Foreign Born Population From Asia – Year of Entry
2006

Source: U.S. Census Bureau, 2006 American Community Survey.

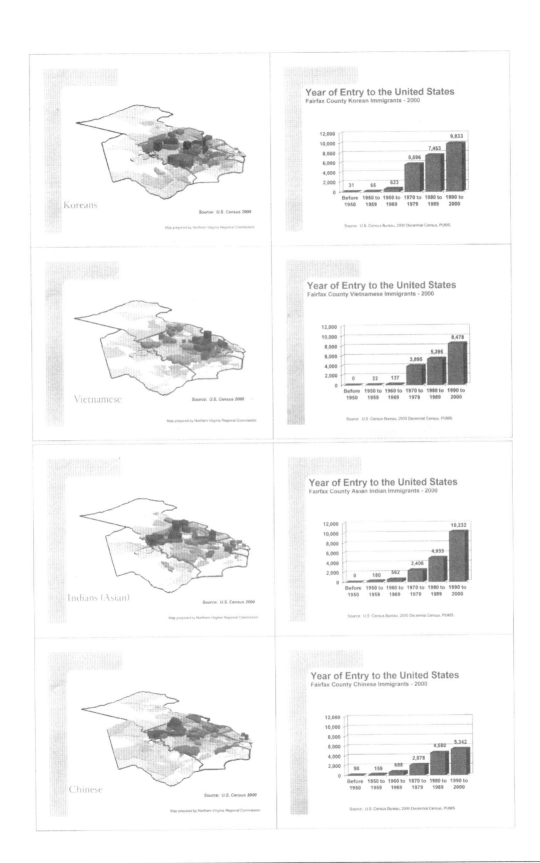

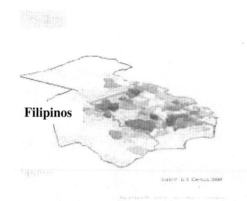

Filipinos

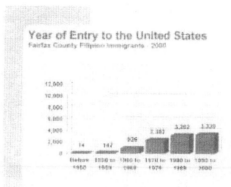

Year of Entry to the United States

more information..

Demographic and Economic Information
Homepage:
http://www.fairfaxcounty.gov/aboutfairfax

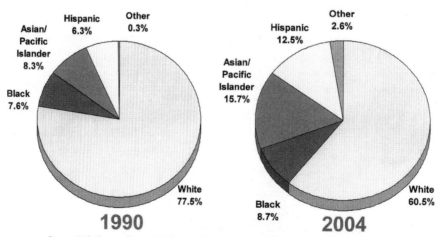

Fairfax County, Virginia
Racial/Ethnic Distribution
1990 and 2004

Source: U.S. Census Bureau, 1990 Decennial Censuses and 2004 American Community Survey.

Milestones of Fairfax County Asian American History Project from the year 2007
By Corazon Sandoval Foley
(Photos of FCAAHP milestone activities are courtesy of Cora Foley)

2007

May 28, 2007 – Memorial Day and 50th Anniversary Celebration for the Fairfax Memorial Park in Braddock Road where Braddock Supervisor Sharon Bulova and Corazon Sandoval Foley first met. Cora Foley requested support from Supervisor Bulova for a history project on the Asian American community in Fairfax County – a project that has been discussed in the Fairfax County History Commission since 1990, the first year when Asian Americans became the largest minority group in the county.

October 20, 2007 – Cora Foley organized a tabletop exhibit on the plans for the Fairfax County Asian American History Project and made a short presentation on the project at the annual conference of the Fairfax County History Commission.

2008

January 23, 2008 – Kick-off Meeting at Braddock Community Hall in Supervisor Bulova's Braddock District Office where some 20 volunteers met to discuss the project along with a presentation by Fairfax County Demographer Anne Cahill on the population trends in the Asian community. Terry Sam joined as the official photographer, along with team leaders Ted Gong and Soo Yee.

APAs in Fairfax County, Virginia gather for an informational session on the upcoming Fairfax County Asian American History Project.

March 19, 2008 – 2nd Meeting of the Fairfax County Asian American History Project in Braddock Hall when group leaders Hank Chao, Linda Yao, as well as the father-daughter team of Vy and Dzung Nguyen joined the project.

April 19, 2008 – The Fairfax County Asian American History Project Team participated in a briefing on Asian immigration history by Senior Historian Marian Smith of the Citizenship and Immigration Services of the US Department of Homeland Security. The team then lunched at Hank Chao's Chinatown Garden restaurant in a building that dates back to 1852 located in the area where DC's Chinatown started. Video tapings of team members for a documentary to promote FCAAHP were directed by Hank Chao.

April 28, 2008 – The Fairfax County Board of Supervisors (BoS) officially recognized the work of FCAAHP during the Fairfax County proclamation of May 2009 as Asian Pacific American Heritage Month. The BoS resolution included the following language: "Whereas a project began in January 2008 to focus on the experience of Asian Pacific Americans in Fairfax County will capture oral history interviews and develop community projects that may include articles, a video, a website, and publication of a book…"

May 14, 2008 – FCAAHP Potluck Dinner to celebrate Asian American Heritage Month in Kings Park Library. The FCAAHP website was demonstrated as well as the Fairfax County Vietnamese American website created by Vy Nguyen. Mary Lipsey presented oral history interview techniques while Hank Chao videotaped interviews with Sharon Bulova and other FCAAHP members and guests. The dinner was reported at the *Asian Fortune* edition of June 8, 2008. Cora Foley began posting youtube videos of FCAAHP interviews to encourage wider community participation in the project.

May 15, 2008 – Supervisor Sharon Bulova and Cora Foley attended a meeting of the Association of American University Women (AAUW) as part of the outreach to increase community support for the Asian American history project.

May 31, 2008 – The first of many Pohick Library meetings of FCAAHP for oral history interviews and discussions of Asian American history. The discussion was led by Veronica Salcedo, President of the Filipino American National Historical Society of Hampton Roads (FANHS-HR), on lessons learned from research and publication of the FANHS-HR book on Virginia's Filipino American soldiers entitled *"In Our Uncles' Words: We Fought For Freedom."* Salcedo also discussed the book on Filipino American Women entitled *"In Our Aunties' Words."* Hank Chao videotaped more oral history interviews that included participants from the Korean Central Senior Center. The leader of the Indian American team Jaya Kori joined FCAAHP at the meeting.

July 3, 2008 – FCAAHP Korean American team Soo Yee organized a meeting with Korean American high school students. Vy Nguyen demonstrated the

Vietnamese American history project website and explained how the project fit into her coursework at Flint High School. Videos of the meeting were posted in youtube.

July 13, 2008 – The *Washington Post* reporter Francine Uenuma joined Cora Foley in an oral history interview of the Nakamura family at the Ekoji Buddhist Temple in Burke, Virginia.

On the following day, Ekoji celebrated its 26th annual *Obon* festival in which Cora Foley participated and took videos that were uploaded in youtube FCAAHP files. The *Washington Post* published a front-page article on FCAAHP on August 14, 2008.

July 16, 2008 – FCAAHP meeting at Braddock Hall when Jaya Kori and Swati Damle joined as co-leaders of the Indian American team, as well as Masako Huibregtse as Japanese American team leader. Ted Gong showed a US government video welcoming new citizens. Terry Sam showed a PowerPoint presentation on his family's history. Supervisor Sharon Bulova announced the August 4th BoS recognition of Vy Nguyen for her FCAAHP work in developing the Vietnamese American website. The *Washington Post* reporter Francine Uenuma interviewed Sharon Bulova and participated in the meeting as part of her research on FCAAHP.

August 3, 2008 – Pohick Library FCAAHP meeting on historical research when Dale Hom, Chinese American official of the US Forest Service, discussed Chinese Historical Research in the West. It was the first time that FCAAHP displayed the *"Remembering 1882"* exhibit as part of the FCAAHP program. The exhibit theme: "Fighting for Civil Rights in the Shadow of the 1882 Chinese Exclusion Act."

August 4, 2008 – The Fairfax County Board of Supervisors had an official recognition of Vy Nguyen for her outstanding work in developing the FCAAHP Vietnamese American website. FCAAHP members had a reception immediately after the event when more oral history interviews were conducted and later uploaded in FCAAHP youtube files.

August 9, 2008 – FCAAHP members participated in the 5th annual Reston Asian Festival, the largest Asian festival in Northern Virginia sponsored by the Thai Tennis Association. Supervisor Sharon Bulova was the keynote speaker for the event.

August 14, 2008 – FCAAHP members visited the Chinese American Silver Light Seniors Association in Herndon Senior Center. They documented the activities of the group and conducted several oral history interviews.

August 15, 2008 – FCAAHP Korean American Team Leader Soo Yee organized a mentoring discussion with high school students by Fairfax Police Lieutenant Gun Lee and Fairfax Firefighter Hyun Lee that were documented as part of the history project.

October 12, 2008 – FCAAHP meeting on developing a video for the May 2009 Asian American Heritage Month programs that could include photos that have been taken during the many oral history interview sessions of Asian American county residents.

October 14, 2008 – Jaya Kori began design of the FCAAHP Indian American website.

October 17, 2008 – Cora Foley conducted oral history interviews at Burke Volunteer Fire Department \ with four Filipino American firefighters who were active in developing the Asian American Firefighters Association in the county.

October 18, 2008 – Cora Foley managed a tabletop exhibit at the Merrifield Festival on FCAAHP programs and conducted an oral history interview with Channel 10 official Maryam Shah on Fairfax Public Access (FPA) and the Asian American community.

October 20, 2008 – During the Fairfax County Board of Supervisors (BoS) meeting, then-Chairman Gerry Connolly for the first time officially recognized the month of October as Filipino American History Month in the county.

October 30, 2008 – FCAAHP meeting at Braddock Hall to discuss FCAAHP programs for May 2009 Asian Pacific American Heritage Month, including the first-ever naturalization ceremony in the Fairfax County Government Center. Another subject was developing an FCAAHP video using lessons from PBS programs on Asian Americans.

November 6, 2008 – FCAAHP members met with officials of the US Citizenship and Immigration

Services (USCIS) to discuss the FCAAHP-initiated first-ever naturalization ceremony at the Fairfax County Government Center for 75 new Americans of all races and ethnicities, as part of the leadership role of the county's largest minority group.

November 15, 2008 – Cora Foley made a presentation on FCAAHP findings at the annual History Conference sponsored by the Fairfax County History Commission.

December 2, 2008 – Cora Foley and Terry Sam visited the Korean Central Senior Center and conducted oral history interviews and documented the center's activities.

December 18, 2008 – FCAAHP Christmas party at Braddock Hall included discussions of plans for the May 2009 naturalization ceremony, including exhibit of photos and videos of FCAAHP history project.

2009

March 18, 2009 – FCAAHP working group meeting to plan details of the May 29, 2009 first-ever naturalization ceremony in the Fairfax County Government Center. The Fairfax County Public Library (FCPL) agreed to the FCAAHP request that the Pohick Regional Library display for two weeks in June 2009 the exhibit on "Remembering the 1882 Chinese Exclusion Act."

April 27, 2009 – The Fairfax County Board of Supervisors officially proclaimed the month of May 2009 as Asian Pacific American Heritage Month with Amy Trang of FCAAHP as official speaker. Many FCAAHP members participated and shared life stories that form part of the Asian American history project.

April 28, 2009 – FCAAHP meeting chaired by Chairman Sharon Bulova (she won in a special election on February 9, 2009 to succeed former Chairman Connolly who was elected Congressman in the 11th District). The meeting focused on final details for the May 29, 2009 naturalization ceremony for which Cox Communications agreed to be the corporate sponsor funding the reception following the ceremony.

May 13, 2009 – FCAAHP submitted a grant proposal for USCIS-sponsored $100k citizenship grant that was drafted by Cora Foley who also helped organize the Fairfax Asian American Citizenship Education (FAACE) Partnership with the Korean Central Senior Center, Chinese American Silver Light Seniors Association, and the Vietnamese American Voters Association.

May 21, 2009 – FCAAHP presentation on the status and findings of the history project at a luncheon sponsored by the Shepherd's Center at the St. Mary's Catholic Church with Chairman Bulova, Terry Sam and Cora Foley as speakers.

May 29, 2009 – FCAAHP made history with the first-ever naturalization ceremony in the Fairfax County Government Center co-sponsored by USCIS, Fairfax County, FCAAHP and Cox Communications. FCAAHP photos were shown in a looping video developed by Terry Sam. Cora Foley served as moderator for program that included presentation of colors by the Fairfax County Public Safety Honor Guard (with Asian American members); singing of the National Anthem by Tania Thornton (daughter of a Russian American naturalized on May 29th); welcome remarks by Cox Communications Vice President Kathy Falk; keynote speech by Chairman Sharon Bulova; remarks by Filipino American General (ret.) Antonio Taguba, 2007 Outstanding American By Choice; congratulatory remarks and Pledge of Allegiance by Congressman Gerry Connolly. Fairfax County Korean American Ted Kim, USCIS Field Director, presided over the formal naturalization ceremony that was followed by a reception at the Forum where citizenship poems were read by Yearn Hong Choi and Vijaya Ligade.

June 1, 2009 – The Fairfax County Board of Supervisors (BoS) recognized outstanding volunteers as Lord and Lady Fairfax awardees, including Corazon Sandoval Foley as Lady Fairfax (At Large) 2009, in part because of her leadership work with FCAAHP.

June 20, 2009 – Pohick Library meeting of FCAAHP with Dr. Franklin Odo, Director of Smithsonian Asian and Pacific American Programs, discussing Japanese American Life and Songs in Hawaii, along with poetry readings by Yearn Hong Choi and Vijaya Ligade. FCAAHP discussed development of a Literary Club for book and poetry readings. Ted Gong arranged for the two-week display of the "Remembering 1882 Chinese Exclusion Act" exhibit in Pohick Library.

June 22, 2009 – The Fairfax County Board of Supervisors (BoS) officially recognized the work

of the FCAAHP Task Force for the May 29, 2009 Naturalization Ceremony. The BoS also recognized the work of Terry Sam, FCAAHP official photographer.

June 27, 2009 – Pohick Library meeting of FCAAHP on Chinese American Life and Songs with Kathy Gong Greene (sister of Ted Gong) who sang several songs about the history of Chinese American life. Ted Gong discussed the 1882 Chinese Exclusion Act and US immigration history. FCAAHP members discussed developing the Literary Club, to be headed by Yearn Hong Choi, as well as initiating a Genealogical Club.

July 25, 2009 – FCAAHP Meeting at Virginia Room in Fairfax City Library to start the Genealogical Club headed by Roberta Chew with a briefing by senior librarian Suzanne Levy on library resources to assist the Asian American History Project.

September 10, 2009 – FCAAHP participated in the Fairfax County Census 2010 Complete Count Committee to help with outreach to the Fairfax County Asian Americans to participate in Census 2010.

May 2010 – Asian Pacific American Heritage Month with the publication of the FCAAHP book and the second FCAAHP-sponsored Naturalization ceremony in the Fairfax County Government Center planned for May 14, 2010.

More chapters in the FCAAHP Saga will be created and will be documented in future publications. The FCAAHP website will have updated information:
http://fairfaxasianamericans.community.officelive.com/default.aspx

2009 Update: Joseph Carabeo (in June 1988 photo) has grown to be an accomplished Filipino American Filmmaker in Virginia.

Photographed in June 1988, Elba Carabeo hugs her son Joeseph after it was announced he had checked out the millionth item at the Pohick Regional Library. Joeseph was six years old and a kindergarten student at Cherry Run Elementary. He has had a library card since he was four. Pohick Regional Library is the busiest branch in the Fairfax County system. Photograph by Paul Alers. Courtesy of the Burke Connection

Index: List of FCAAHP Participants

Participant	Group	Pages
Aggerwal, Neal	Indian American	219
Aguas, Pacita	Filipino American	54 - 55
Alam, Naila	Pakistani American	196
Arca, Cora	Filipino American	184
Arora, Vikas & Pooja	Indian American	130
Baban, Mark	Filipino American	189 – 190
Bacani, Albert & Nina	Filipino Americans	48 – 53, 155, 223
Balaram, Ravi Alexander	Indian/Filipino American	153
Berry, Jagdish & Shobha	Indian American	128
Bong-Wright, Jackie	Vietnamese American	113 – 119, 187, 223
Bradkey, Jonathan	Vietnamese American	124
Bui, Lam	Vietnamese American	121 – 122
Bui, Thu H.	Vietnamese American	178 – 180
Bui, Van-Nhi	Vietnamese American	123
Burnett, Kenneth	Indian/African American	145 – 148, 228
Carabeo, Joseph	Filipino American	241
Cerezo, Ana Riate	Filipino American	184
Chao, Hank	Chinese American	215, 222 – 223
Chen, Zhong Ying	Chinese American	199
Cheng, Francis & Theresa	Chinese American	153, 199
Chew, Roberta	Chinese American	204 – 206, 228
Choi, Chae Chung from Lois Brown	Korean American	87 – 89
Choi, Yearn Hong	Korean American	89, 98 – 104
Chu, Nhi Anh	Vietnamese American	107 – 108
Chu, Rose	Chinese American	186
Chung, Anthony	Vietnamese American	122 – 123
Damle, Subhash & Swati	Indian American	135– 137
DelaCuesta, Charles	Filipino American	54, 178
Dela Cuesta, Eppie	Filipino American	48
DeVera, Samuel & Patrick	Filipino American	189
Dietrich-Hall, Vellie	Filipino American	185
Du, Lan	Vietnamese American	106
Elmejjad-Yi, Jeung-Hwa	Korean American	94 – 95, 209 – 212
Elmejjad, Sonia	Korean/Arab American	143– 144
Foley, Corazon Sandoval	Filipino American	6 – 12, 168
Fong, Jackie and Jason	Chinese/Native American	141
Fugh, John L.	Chinese American	155
Gong, Linying	Chinese American	197– 198
Gong Ted & Russell	Chinese American	27 – 34
Gupta, Amar Anth	Indian American	129
Gupta, Sant	Indian American	219
Horio, Brant & Maya	Japanese American	73– 83
Hossain, Tania	Bangladeshi American	186
Huibregtse, Liz & Masako	Japanese American	194 – 195

6ussam, Abul	Bangladeshi American	181
Ichikawa, Grant	Japanese American	65 – 68
James, Sarita	Chinese American	25
Jung, Young-Hoon	Korean American	196
Kori, Jaya & Raj	Indian American	131 – 134
Krup, Sherina	Indian American	130
Kusano, John	Japanese American	207 – 208
Le, Brigitte	Vietnamese American	184
Le, Hung Ba	Vietnamese American	157
Lee, Ching-Jung	Chinese American	214
Lee, Gun	Korean American	191 – 192
Lee, Heisung	Korean American	167 – 168, 200, 217
Lee, Hyun	Korean American	190
Li, Veronica	Chinese American	227
Ligade, Vijaya	Indian American	133 – 134
Ly, Thuan	Vietnamese American	111
Marshall, Cecilia Suyat	Filipino American	56 – 59
Mathieson, Kathy	Chinese American	142
Matias, Isagani	Filipino American	189
Mehra, Urvashi	Indian American	128
Montano, Joe	Filipino American	186
Moon, Ilryong	Korean American	96 – 97, 170 – 171
Nakamoto, Gary	Japanese American	183 – 184
Nakamoto, Robert	Japanese American	84 – 86, 182 – 183
Nakamoto, Robert Jr.	Japanese American	155 – 156
Nakamura, Ken & Greg	Japanese American	73– 83
Nguyen, Andre	Vietnamese American	124
Nguyen, Hoainam	Vietnamese American	122
Nguyen, Lam	Vietnamese American	192 – 193
Nguyen, Man Minh	Vietnamese American	124 – 125
Nguyen, Peter	Vietnamese American	124
Nguyen, Thi Kim-Oanh	Vietnamese American	108 – 109
Nguyen, Vy & Dzung	Vietnamese American	120 – 121
Orlandella, Yukiko	Japanese American	64
Patel, Tushar	Indian American	127 – 128
Rajeswaran, Ramesh & Sucheta	Indian American	135 – 137
Ray, Wilna	Filipino American	55
Rishell, Jeanette	Filipino American	149 – 151
Sam, Carolyn	Japanese American	69 – 72
Sam, Terry	Chinese American	35 – 43
Saplan, Roger	Filipino American	213
Shah, Maryam	Afghan American	222
Sheikh, M. Siddique	Pakistani American	138 – 140
Singh, Baikunth	Indian American	127
Sun, Xianyi	Chinese American	199
Taguba, Antonio	Filipino American	153 – 155
Tai, Tin Yin	Chinese American	187 – 188

Tran, Nhon Phan	Vietnamese American	109 – 110
Trang, Amy	Vietnamese American	111
Ullagadi, Saroja	Indian American	129
Vo, Bao	Vietnamese American	123
Vu, Chi Lan	Vietnamese American	123
Wang, Yining Nathan	Chinese American	197 – 198
Williams, Ruth Baja	Filipino American	224 – 226
Wong, Sam & Ruth	Chinese American	23 – 25
Yao, Joe & Linda	Chinese American	25 – 26
Yee, Soo	Korean American	196
Yeh, Tony	Chinese American	185
Zee, Lily & Shaw	Chinese American	199

FCAAHP Bibliography:

Armor, John and Wright, Peter. Manzanar: *Photographs by Ansel Adams Commentary by John Hersey.* Vintage Books, 1989

Chang, Iris. *The Chinese in America: A Narrative History.* Viking, 2003.

Choi, Yearn Hong and Kim, Haeng Ja. *Surfacing Sadness: A Centennial of Korean-American Literature 1903 – 2003.* Dumont, New Jersey: Homa & Sekey Books, 2003.

Cordova, *Fred. Filipinos: Forgotten Asian Americans.* Kendall/Hunt Publishing Company, 1993.

Fairfax County 2007 Community Citizen Planning Committee. *Fairfax County Stories 1607 – 2007.* County of Fairfax, 2007.

Filipino American National Historical Society of Hampton Roads. *In Our Uncles' Words.* FANHS-HR, 2005.

Filipino American National Historical Society of Hampton Roads. *In Our Aunties' Words.* FANHS-HR, 2003.

Franconia Museum. *"Franconia Remembers."* Franconia Museum, 2003.

Hutton, Bud and Rooney, Andy. *Air Gunner.* Farrar & Rinehart, Inc. 1944.

Karnow, Stanley. *In Our Image: America's Empire in the Philippines.* Balantine Books, 1989.

Liu, Eric. *The Accidental Asian: Notes of a Native speaker.* Random House, 1998.

Mark, Diane Mei Lin and Chih, Ginger. *A Place Called Chinese America.* The Organization of Chinese Americans, Kendall Hunt Publishing Co. 1982

Martin, Ralph G. *Boy from Nebraska: The Story of Ben Kuroki.* Harper & Brothers Publishers 1946;

Matsumoto, Toru. *Beyond Prejudice: A Story of the Church and Japanese Americans.* Friendship Press 1946

McCrary, John R (Tex) and Scherman, David. *First of Many: A Journal of Action with the Men of the Eighth Air Force.* Simon & Schuster 1944

McWilliams, Carey. *Prejudice: Japanese Americans: Symbol of Racial Intolerance.* Little, Brown and Company 1944

Netherton, Nan and Ross. *Fairfax County: A Contemporary Portrait.* The Donning Company, 1992.

Stewart, Carroll "Cal". *Ben Kuroki: The Most Honorable Son.* Nebraska Printing 2004

Takaki, Ronald T. *Strangers from a Different Shore: A History of Asian American.* Little, Brown & Co.,1998.

Takaki. Ronald T. *A Different Mirror: a History of Multicultural America.* Little, Brown & Co., 1993, 2008

Wong, Sam. *Stories Not to be Forgotten.* 2007

Zia, Helen. Asian *American Dreams: The Emergence of an American People.* Farrar, Straus and Giroux, 2000.

Acknowledgments

The Fairfax County Asian American History Project would not have been as successful without the invaluable participation of the following project supporters:

- John Browne of Braddock's True Gold
- Linda Byrne of Providence Perspective Project
- Anne Cahill, Demographer of Fairfax County Government
- **COX Communications** – Janet Barnard, Kathryn Falk and Tania Hindert – sole corporate sponsor of the May 29, 2009 FCAAHP-initiated first-ever naturalization ceremony at Fairfax County Government Center for 75 new Americans.
- Christina Fullmer and Mark Thomas of Chairman Sharon Bulova's Office
- Jean Johnston of the Pohick Regional Library
- Ted Kim & Gloria Williams-Brevard of US Citizenship & Immigration Services
- Suzanne Levy of Virginia Room Library
- Mary Lipsey of Braddock's True Gold
- Katherine Smith of the Office of Equity Programs of Fairfax County Government
- Marian Smith, Senior Historian of the US Citizenship and Immigration Services

<u>**Pohick Regional Library,**</u> with the support of branch manager Jean Johnston, (shown in photo) has

become the center of many FCAAHP activities, including oral history interviews and display of the *"Remembering 1882"* exhibit.

Opened in 1987, Pohick Library is located at the intersection of Old Keene Mill and Sydenstricker on farmland owned for many years by the Jerman family. Woodrow R. Jerman (92 years old in 2009) inherited his grandfather's 182-acre farm that had been purchased in 1912 -- situated on both sides of Old Keene Mill in Burke with the home in which "Woodie" was born and was living in 2010. Developers of townhouses and shopping centers purchased the land after it became clear to the Jerman family that farming was no longer profitable in Fairfax County.

Pohick Library in left photo and the Jerman farm house. (Photos by Cora Foley)

SPONSORS of FCAAHP 2010 Book

The Fairfax County Asian American History Project (FCAAHP)
is grateful for the financial support from
community sponsors of the 2010 FCAAHP book.

JeungHwa Elmejjad-Yi

M. Siddique Sheikh

Base Technologies

Cox Communications

In addition, the following community donors also very graciously contributed to the printing in Fairfax County of copies of the book on the Fairfax County Asian American History Project for distribution free-of-charge to some high schools and libraries: Korean American Women's Chamber of Commerce, STAR TOWING, Bovex's Limousine Services, Dr. Vaqar Choudry, of Hagerstown Dental Center, Mr and Mrs. Reilly, of Fairfax, VA, and the Korean American Association of Northern Virginia.

celebrates our
diverse communities in

Fairfax County

and is a proud sponsor
of the

**Fairfax County Asian American
History Project**

www.cox.com

The Fairfax County
Asian American
History Project

Fairfax County Asian American History Project: Oral History Interviews, Research, Documenting, Recording, and the Fairfax County Naturalization Ceremony

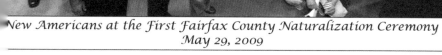

New Americans at the First Fairfax County Naturalization Ceremony May 29, 2009

Fairfax County Asian Americans: From Immigrants to Honored Americans

To Grant Ichikawa
With best wishes,

Fairfax County Asian Americans: Becoming American While Nurturing the Community and Asian Heritage and Culture

Fairfax County Asian American History Project Families

Korean Bell Garden
Design by Y. David Chung and the Hunt Laudi Studio

(Map labels: Cranes, Sun and Clouds, Sila Stone Well, Water Spring, Pine Trees, Mushroom, Korean Alphabet, Mountain, Rocks, Deer, Turtle, North)

Reflections on the meaning of the Korean Bell—Dreams of Peace
by Dr. Chang-Ho Ahn[1]

The Korean Bell Garden will be a cultural landmark that represents the heritage of Korean Americans living in the Washington DC metropolitan area, and will bring greater awareness of the richness of Korean culture to American citizens.

The Korean Bell that will be the centerpiece of the Bell Garden is majestic in its form, is engraved with intricate designs and patterns, and reverberates with a calm, soothing tone that is unique and creative, much like the traditional "Korean Bell". It is a bell that brings art and science together in perfect harmony, and will be a precious cultural landmark in Virginia, and the Washington DC metropolitan area.

Dr. Ahn is the Advisory Committee Chair of the Korean Bell Garden and is founder and CEO of Rexahn Pharmaceuticals, Inc. He is an internationally recognized drug development expert and a significant contributor for various social, political, business, and scientific causes. After co-founding the Society of Biomedical Research in 1990 he served as President during 2001-2004.

Right Photo: Sue Webb, Paul Gilbert (NVRPA), and JeungHwa Elmejjad-Yi, KACC Chairwoman,in Korea viewing the bell destined for Meadowlark.The trip was sponsored by the Korea Foundation in Oct 2009.

Ilryong Moon, NVRPA Executive Director Paul Gilbert, Fairfax Supervisor John Foust, KACC Chairperson JeungHwa Elmejjad-Yi, Fairfax Chairman Sharon Bulova, and Art Director David Chung

Meadowlark Botanical Gardens Park Planning

Korean Garden Site
건립 부지

Fairfax County Asian Americans: Korean Bell Garden Collaboration

Korean Bell Pavillion and Garden Signing Ceremony in April 2007

Fundraising Event for the Korean Bell Garden sponsored by the Korean Ambassador's wife, Mrs. Ah Young Han